A Message from Chris Elliott

This idea began as a calling from the Lord. As a current athletic trainer, and former athlete, I am by no means an author, nor have I ever dreamed of publishing a book. However, in 2020, I felt the Lord place this idea on my heart for a 365-day devotional for athletes. Initially, I felt like I was the wrong guy with the right idea. After several weeks of prayer, I decided to trust the Lord and embark on this journey. It was through these same prayers that I believed the Lord was directing me not to write the entirety of the devotional using my sole voice. Instead, the idea He was placing on my heart was to gather 364 other Christian athletes from different sports, levels, and backgrounds to also write an entry for this book, so that it might reach as broad of an audience as possible. After writing my entry, I reached out to a small handful of about 30 close friends and family members, who are also current and former athletes, to explain my heart for the project and recruit them to be a part of it. Not only did I ask them to write an entry, but I also asked them to refer additional Christian athletes they knew outside of my current circle. Those athletes agreed to join the project and refer me on to more athletes. Thus began a multiple year process of gathering phone numbers, sharing my heart for this project, and recruiting Christian athletes from all over the world to be a part of this devotional. What you are about to read is the collection of how Jesus Christ has impacted 365 current and retired, college and professional athletes through each of our sports. We are sharing with you what the Lord has taught us in our time as athletes and hope it encourages you to draw nearer to Him both in and out of your sport.

This is not *my* project, nor is it *my* book; rather, it is the Lord's. I believe I am just the person He used to get the ball rolling. It is as much mine as the other 364 athletes who joined in and helped bring this book to life.

From the start of this project, it was agreed upon that not a single athlete, including myself, will receive a penny from this book. We wanted to fully surrender this project to the Lord, including the money. 100% of the proceeds generated by this book is being donated to charity.

Thank you for picking this book up and embarking on this year-long journey with us. We pray it is a blessing to you, brings glory to Jesus, and encourages athletes all over the world to **LIVE** beyond the game, for the glory of God.

"In this you rejoice, though now for a little while, if necessary, you have been grieved by various trials, so that the tested genuineness of your faith—more precious than gold that perishes though it is tested by fire—may be found to result in praise and glory and honor at the revelation of Jesus Christ."
– 1 Peter 1:6-7 ESV

It's hard to rejoice in trials. My junior year of college my season was cut short by a ruptured disk and four broken bones. I remember the initial feeling of anger and depression looming over me wondering why God allowed this to happen. However, through these trials, God opened my eyes to how I had allowed basketball to consume every bit of my identity. It had become as much of a god to me as God Himself. I realized in that moment, when human nature turns a good thing into a god thing, it becomes a bad thing. I put all my faith and identity in my own production as a basketball player and ended up empty.

Trials are a necessary part of life because they reveal where we put our faith. Eventually our sport, the accolades, the records, and stats will all get taken away from us. The only thing that will remain constant is finding our identity and faith in Christ alone. I rejoice that through trials, God was able to reshape my focus and change my life.

When a good thing becomes a god thing, it becomes a bad thing. Take some time and ask God to show you if and how you have put your sport above Him.

Chris Elliott
Trevecca Nazarene University Men's Basketball
2012-2016

January 2

"For in Christ Jesus neither circumcision nor uncircumcision has any value. THE ONLY THING THAT COUNTS is faith expressing itself through love." – Galatians 5:6 NIV

As a high school and college athlete, I grew up unsure of my salvation. I was never 100% convinced I was doing enough, was good enough, or was spiritual enough to merit God saying, "OK, you're in!" The way I saw things, it was my job on this earth to do enough, be good enough, and be spiritual enough to get into heaven. (Oh, and also to make sure that others complied as well). If I did what pleased him, he loved me; if not, he didn't. Why? Because two thousand years of religious tradition says so. This thinking was only reinforced in sports by "playing time" which was performance-based. Heck, everything in my life seemed to be merit-based…grades were merit-based, as were relationships, job opportunities, and lifestyles.

But in the kingdom of God, there is a different economy. It is more about learning how 'to live loved' than earning God's favor. When the apostle Paul wrote this letter, he believed that by Jewish law, he had done enough, was good enough and was spiritual enough. And yet, all his merit counted for nothing until he understood and yielded in faith to Christ's finished work on the cross. When I understood the reality of this verse, in time, it changed my heart.

It may take me a lifetime to figure out what is truly meant by "expressing itself through love", but until I understand "THE ONLY THING THAT COUNTS" is faith in a free gift from a loving Father, I will never be 'enough'.

Mark Elliott
Vanderbilt University Basketball/Baseball
1976-1980

4

January 3

"Have this mind among yourselves, which is yours in Christ Jesus, who, though he was in the form of God, did not count equality with God a thing to be grasped, but emptied himself, by taking the form of a servant, being born in the likeness of men. And being found in human form, he humbled himself by becoming obedient to the point of death, even death on a cross."
- Philippians 2:5-8 ESV

My Senior season was set up to be my year - it was my second year as a captain, I was the only guard with significant starting experience, and I was a Senior (so I was entitled in my mind).

Four games into the season, Coach came to me and said they were starting a freshman guard and that I would come off the bench. I had a decision to make - turn inward and let everyone know I wasn't happy about it or humble myself and use this new circumstance for good. Thankfully, God gave me the wisdom to choose the latter and to cheer on and mentor that freshman guard who took my place (though it was really hard sometimes).

Jesus Christ set the ultimate example of this by letting go of his position, coming down to earth, accepting his status as a man and servant, and dying a humiliating death for us.

What status, position, or appearance are you holding onto or chasing that's preventing you from serving and loving others where you are right now and following God's calling for your life?

Steven Kaspar
Bucknell University Men's Basketball
2011-2015

5

January 4

"But he said to me, 'My grace is sufficient for you, for my power is made perfect in weakness.'"
- 2 Corinthians 12:9 ESV

The first track meet of my "walk-on" freshman season was looming. I would be racing against several SEC teams, and I was terrified to the point that I actually quit the team before the meet. I was overwhelmed with thoughts of failure and that I didn't belong with the competition. Fortunately, the Lord intervened, and I rejoined the team within 24 hours. A few weeks later, I found myself at the starting line with my heart pounding, adrenaline pumping, and thoughts racing. The 800m race is a blur, except for when the lyrics "I may be weak, but your Spirit's strong in me. My flesh may fail, but my God you never will" from an Elevation Worship song came clear to my mind as I rounded the last curve.

As a Christian athlete, I had to take my self-centered focus and change it to a God-centered focus. As someone who was afraid of failing in front of an audience, I had to choose to believe that God takes my weaknesses and uses them for His glory and that He wants me to seek His approval only. When we realize for whom we're competing and we're thankful for the ability to do so, our fears fade and there is a joy that is not contingent on the outcome.

Will you surrender to the Lord and allow Him to use you in the midst of your fears and weaknesses?

Anna Laura (Irvine) Kaspar
Samford University Women's Track
2011-2015

6

January 5

"Trust in the Lord with all of your heart and lean not on your own understanding; in all your ways submit to him, and he will make your paths straight."
-Proverbs 3:5-6

In sports it's easy to want to write your own story. We want our dreams and goals to work out exactly as we have it written in our head. We forget that God is the author, and that we are merely just a character in his book.

All my life, baseball was my big plan. I was going to be a shortstop in the MLB and no one could tell me otherwise. Not even the fact that I wasn't nearly good enough to accomplish that goal. I was humbled my junior year of college when I suffered a career ending injury for most; a UCL reconstruction in my right elbow. In that moment I realized that I was not in control; the Lord was. So I submitted to God's plan for me, and I put more focus in other areas of my life that I had been neglecting. I strengthened my Faith in the good Lord, I brought my GPA up from a 2.9 to a 4.0 in my last semester, and I learned what true work ethic was during my rehab.

In my last year of college, I made a position change from SS to a pitcher. This was definitely God's plan because I had never pitched before in my life, but I still ended up getting drafted. I believe it was God's way of showing me that He is the ultimate author to my story, and when you trust in Him, things will work out how they are actually supposed to.

Trust in our Author's story. Not what you think it should be.

Will Vest
Detroit Tigers
2017-Present

January 6

*"Let us run with perseverance the race marked out for us,
fixing our eyes on Jesus, the pioneer and perfecter of Faith."*
-Hebrews 12:1-2

Let's talk about rejection. People love hearing about a good success story, but let's get real. Rejection is extremely common and can feel excruciatingly lonely in today's culture. Each time we scroll on social media, we only see the highlight reel of everyone else's lives. Growing up, playing soccer for a D1 school was always my dream. My parents did everything they could so that I might be able obtain the dream they knew I always wanted. However, it turns out my dream of D1 college soccer was not my reality. I was CRUSHED, but I signed with a NAIA school that really wanted me. It wasn't my plan, but it turned out to be so much better. I was given the opportunity to play every minute of every game, have my education paid for, and meet friends that will last a lifetime!

Looking back on the rejection I experienced, I learned how to thank God for saying no to some of the prayers I so desperately wanted him to say yes to. Rejection hurts, but God always has a plan for our lives. He wants us to persevere through our hardships and our sufferings, because whenever we do, it is always worth it. God's plan is always worth it.

Dear Heavenly Father, thank you for always being my rock in the darkest times of my life. I pray that you would continue to give me the endurance to exude joy to those around me regardless of what my current circumstance is."

Allison Rice
Oklahoma City University Women's Soccer
2012-2016

January 7

"Therefore, put on the full armor of God, so that when the day of evil comes, you may be able to stand your ground, and after you have done everything, to stand."
-Ephesians 6:13

Through my entire athletic career, I look back on all the valuable life lessons I learned from coaches and teammates. One of the most important of these lessons was preparation. Coach Ken Niumatalolo preached to us on a daily basis "It is hard to win," because he understood what went into winning. He knew that games were not won on Saturday, but rather through proper preparation in the weight room, in film sessions, and on the practice field.

Although I was not the starter most of time in college, I prepared everyday like I was the starter because I wanted to be ready when my number was called. I wanted my coaches and teammates to be able to count on me when it was my time. As my faith matured, I realized that the only way I could be spiritually prepared to win the battle against temptations of the world was to strengthen my relationship with Jesus Christ through proper preparation. My preparation came through spending time in the Word, going to church, going to Bible study, and having quality conversations with believers and nonbelievers. Through this type of preparation, I was able to strengthen my relationship with the Lord and win the battles against the temptations of this world.

How is your preparation? Are you prepared to win the battle against temptation?

George Jamison
United States Naval Academy Football
2011-2015

9

January 8

"Whatever you do, work at it with all your heart, as working for the Lord not for human masters, since you know that you will receive an inheritance from the Lord as a reward. It is the Lord Christ you are serving." -Colossians 3:23-24

Who are you working for and serving? This was a question that convicted me early on in my college career. When you are playing a sport, especially at a high level, it can be very easy to get wrapped up in trying to impress coaches and teammates instead of playing for God. It quickly became exhausting for me to show up every day and think about all the eyes that were watching my every move. I found myself trying to impress the world, but when I didn't perform well, my mind was flooded with thoughts of shame, guilt, and despair.

Colossians 3:23-24 helped me to understand that God is the only one I should be working for. When this truth sank in to my mind, I found peace knowing that regardless of what the stat line said, God said "I love you and I am proud of you." God has allowed you to have your amazing talents and abilities in your sport so that you can have a platform that glorifies HIM. When you serve God in your sport, you will see burdens you've been carrying lifted off your shoulders, which means there is more room for peace and joy.

Challenge yourself today with the question I challenged myself with some years ago, who are you working for and serving? If the answer isn't God, pray for Him to be the answer starting today.

Shane Lantigua
Austin Peay State University Baseball
2013-2016

10

January 9

"Fight the good fight of faith. Take hold of the eternal life to which you were called when you made your confession in the presence of many witnesses." -1 Timothy 6:12

Fighting is engrained in the fabric of sports. During the offseason, we fight against fatigue to get stronger and in better shape, we fight to perform one more rep. In the middle of games/matches/races we fight against our minds telling us to give up or take the easy way out. We fight during these times so that in the end we are proud of the work we have put in. Whether we win or not, we are proud of the fight that allowed us to get to that point. The same can be said about our lives as Christians. Jesus does not promise an easy life as a follower of Him; He actually promises the exact opposite. There are times throughout the walk of faith when we have to fight against our flesh, culture, and other temptations. We do this so that one day we can glorify God with our actions, and also so we can look back and be proud of the life we have lived. Unlike in sports where you might fight hard and still lose, we have already won with Jesus. We might lose a battle here and there, but the war was won when Jesus was nailed to the cross.

At the end of the day, what kind of person do you want to be known as?

Tate Pierson
Belmont University Men's Basketball
2017-2022

11

January 10

"Trust in the Lord with all your heart, and do not lean on your own understanding. In all your ways acknowledge Him, and He will make straight your paths."
-Proverbs 3:5-6 ESV

Giving up control is one of the hardest things in life. As an athlete, we like to feel in control. We watch how we sleep, how hard and long we train, etc. However, we do not always have control of the outcomes of our competitions. The summer after my freshman year, I reported to camp in the best shape of my life and was ready to take on the world because I did everything I thought was right during the off season. Boy did that backfire. I remember an early season workout where I felt like my world was falling apart because there was nothing I could do physically to overcome the mental burnout and exhaustion that I was in.

I was too busy planning out each and every race to trust what God's plan for my season was. The best analogy for my season, and in the bigger picture, my life, was that I wrote down each and every plan for my future on a piece of paper, signed it and handed it to God. I realized that I was all wrong and needed to sign the bottom of a blank piece of paper, give it to God and say, "fill in the rest, I'm yours."

Take time to think about areas in your life where you need to give control to God.

Ben Moroney
Trevecca Nazarene University Men's XC/Track
2013-2017

January 11

"Blessed is the man who walks not in the counsel of the wicked, nor stands in the way of sinners, nor sits in the seat of scoffers; but his delight is in the law of the Lord, and on his law he meditates day and night. He is like a tree planted by streams of water that yields fruit in its season, and its leaf does not wither."
– Psalm 1: 1-3

College athletics allow for true, robust character development. I remember moments of competition (be that with other teams or with my own teammates): losing a starting spot, elation at victory, or devastation at defeat that revealed the less desirable depths of my character. How do we respond when we are stretched?

These verses of Psalm 1 remind me of my experience in athletics, namely the importance of rooting myself in the Word of the Lord. When we delight in Him and create time to see places of darkness or struggle in ourselves, we engage in the process of becoming a different kind of person. When we are planted by streams of water, pursuing an ongoing closeness with the Lord, we are able to yield fruit in season. The results may not come as quickly or noticeably as we would wish, but the Lord promises to shape us into resilient people who can handle the tumultuous winds of life as we walk with Him. Intentional time with the Lord gives us a steadiness, ensuring that we do not wither. When championships and accolades fade away, our character formed through such testing times remains.

How might you spend time delighting in the Lord and create space for Him to make you into a person of deep character?

Ellen Riggins
Samford University Women's Basketball
2013-2017

13

January 12

"Commit your way to the Lord; trust in him, and he will act."
-Psalm 37:5 ESV

Committed is a word that is often used to describe athletes. Committed to the game. Committed to their coaches. Committed to the team. I was unwavering in my dedication to volleyball. When I first tore my ACL as a junior in high school, I was committed to physical therapy because I was committed to the sport because I was committed to my will for my life. However, I was reminded that God's will for my life supersedes mine when I tore my ACL for the second time my freshman year of college. God revealed to me where my commitments ran thin.

There were warning signs. There was danger. Often I found myself helping the Lord accomplish something that I'd asked him to do. But the truth that God always has a purpose for the circumstances we don't understand was drowned in the noise. I was exhausted, overworked and unfulfilled. I knew I needed to commit to the Lord by living the Christian life in His strength, not my own. So I did exactly that; I surrendered all areas of my life to Christ. Now, I have the capacity to believe all that God has told me through His Word. Now, my will aligns with God's will for my life. Now, I can rely on the Lord to act on my behalf. My commitment to the Lord no longer falls short because His will is greater than mine.

For a second, reflect on your current commitments. Ask yourself if God's will is greater than yours. Pray that Psalm 37:5 would be true of your life as it relates to athletics.

Maiya Burns
Eckerd College Volleyball
2015-2016

14

January 13

"Such confidence we have through Christ before God. Not that we are competent in ourselves to claim anything for ourselves, but our competence comes from God."
– 2 Corinthians 3:4-5 NIV

In any sport, it is so easy to turn to your own accolades to lift you up and keep you moving forward. This works when we are doing really well and competing at our best, but what happens when we fall short of our expectations or other people's expectations of us? Too many times in my life I have fallen short of what I expected of myself, whether it was in practice, or a game, or even in the way I treated my teammates. It caused me to struggle with confidence when I was younger and I constantly told myself that I wasn't good enough.

The truth is, you are not good enough on your own. You are always going to let yourself down as well as those around you because we are imperfect beings. The only way you can reach any type of fulfilment is by finding your faith and keeping it at the forefront of your life, in and out of sports. Once you are able to accept that the successes and failures in your sport are not what truly matter, you will be able to understand the goodness of God's love and how truly unconditional it is. If you learn this, you will realize that your glory is really not yours alone, but glory that you can give to God for blessing you with the ability to play the sport you love.

In those moments where your own satisfaction or dissatisfaction start to overwhelm you, try to remember God's unconditional love for you, and in that, find peace.

Brooke Lenz
Abilene Christian University Women's Soccer
2016-2019

15

January 14

"You will seek me and find me, when you seek me with all your heart." -Jeremiah 29:13

We had just won the Southeastern Conference (SEC) Tournament Championship. It was the pinnacle of my career and something I had worked for my entire life. Eight days later it came to a screeching halt. After losing in the first round of the NCAA tournament, I laid on my hotel room floor and stared up at the ceiling. I wondered, "How could a feeling I've been chasing my entire life be gone so quickly?" It felt so empty.

Thankfully, in God's perfect timing, I had become a follower of Jesus about a year earlier. When I arrived at college, my life was flipped upside down by the gospel and understanding that Jesus saves us from *ourselves*. The only qualification He requires is that we admit our need. I chose to wholeheartedly surrender my life to Him and to walk with Him daily.

Prior to this, I had poured my whole life into the game of soccer. It gave me purpose and meaning and affirmation. What I learned from following Christ is that soccer cannot save me. When my relationship with Jesus became the deep, true source of my identity and purpose, I was able to put soccer in its proper place. That night, when I was laying on the hotel floor, I was upset and angry. However, I no longer needed soccer to make me feel like I was enough. I already knew I was, win or lose.

What things/people are you looking to for purpose, meaning, and affirmation? Have you surrendered *all* of your life to Jesus?

Kelsey Fenix
University of Kentucky Women's Soccer
2004-2007

16

January 15

"I will fight for you, you need only to be still." - Exodus 14:14

Playing soccer at Texas A&M had been my dream since I was a little girl and by the grace of God, He blessed me with the opportunity. I had high aspirations when stepping into college athletics, yet my freshman year, extenuating circumstances lead me to a place of darkness and depression, where I contemplated giving up soccer all together. Little did I know, God was doing a vast and redemptive work in my life, as He was preparing me to be a light for Christ through my story of Him rescuing me from the pit of destruction. He used me by providing a platform as a college athlete.

God often allows us to reach a place where we are stripped of all we thought would satisfy, whether it's success in our sport, a relationship, or fame and we are forced to decide…Is He Enough? God is a Faithful Father and He delights when our satisfaction is found solely in Him. Nothing else will satisfy our desire for more in this life, but Him. He always comes through and He will fight for you, because you are His child and were created by His loving, intentional hands for a unique purpose. Allow Him to use you through your sport and don't be discouraged when you meet trials of various kinds; God is always working for our good.

The platform God provides us with through our sport is a gift. How will you use your platform to be a light for God?

Haley Pounds
Texas A&M University Women's Soccer
2014-2017

17

January 16

"You will show me the path of life; in Your
presence is fullness of joy; at Your right hand are pleasures
forevermore." -Psalm 16:11 NKJV

Right after my senior year of college basketball, I began what would turn out to be the hardest waiting season of my life so far. I was waiting for a call to play professional basketball overseas. I was lost, frustrated and confused; why wasn't I receiving a call? It wasn't until I heard a sermon on joy that I realized what had been missing the whole time: seeking God's presence daily. So why is this significant?!

I've always considered myself a joyful person, but during this waiting season and long trial, I was anything but joyful. I was putting my joy in my earthly circumstances instead of putting my joy in my eternal Creator. I now understand that joy is a position of your heart and when your heart seeks God first, you have fullness of joy despite your circumstances.

When I finally let go of *MY* grip on *MY* plans for my life and asked God to show me His path for me and fill me with His joy, I received a call to move to Germany the next week. This is not a coincidence. So yes, your circumstances might not always be joyful, but when you seek God first and trust His plan for your life you will filled with joy despite your circumstances. My life motto now is Choose Joy, Chase Joy and Believe Joy. When you choose Jesus, you choose joy. When you chase Jesus, you chase joy. When you believe Jesus, you believe JOY.

Write down 5 things today that brought you Joy.

Kylee Ann Smith
Sturt Sabres / Lakeside Lightning Women's Basketball
2019-Present

18

"For by grace you have been saved through faith. And this is not your own doing; it is the gift of God, not a result of works, so that no one may boast." -Ephesians 4:8-9

As a college athlete, I remember these verses being so conflicting to me. As an athlete we have to work for every single thing that we get. I worked from the age of eight years old to be the best I could be at my sport. I worked for playing time, starting spots, scholarships, and more... but now, for salvation... my works didn't matter. In my mind, before I became a believer... I didn't understand how my "goodness" or my "works" weren't important.

If our works mattered, the cross wouldn't... and ultimately, I would choose the work of the cross over my ***best day,*** any day. I love that Paul clarifies that we have no one else to boast in but God and God alone. As an athlete, we know how easy it is to get big headed over our own accomplishments, but Paul makes it clear that when it comes to our salvation, there is no room to boast. I am so thankful that He doesn't depend on the things we can do for Him, yet He still gives us life, freedom, and joy.

If our works mattered, the cross wouldn't... and ultimately, I would choose the work of the cross over my best day, any day.

Katrina Bazzoli
Southwest MS CC / University of West Georgia Women's Basketball
2012-2016

January 18

"May the God of hope fill you with all joy and peace as you trust in him, so that you may overflow with hope by the power of the Holy Spirit." - Romans 15:13 NIV

What is the different between joy and happiness? Happiness is a feeling based on circumstances. Joy is an attitude that defies circumstances. There are so many ways in which we experience happiness as athletes. Hitting a big shot, making a game winning play, setting a record, or winning a championship just to name a few. While we all love to experience these moments of happiness, those feelings are temporary. What happens when we miss the shot, we lose the game, we don't get the starting position, we get hurt, or our athletic career ends? When there is no circumstance for happiness, are we still able to feel joy in those moments?

Too often as athletes we can mistakenly try to attach our joy to moments or the feelings we get from success or accomplishment. But when the lights go out, the crowd is gone, and the recognition we sought is no longer there, we can be left empty. Life will always give us moments of happiness well after athletics is gone. But where do you find your joy?

Are you living off circumstantial moments of happiness to try and bring the feeling of joy? Or are you searching after the overflowing joy that comes from the power of the Holy Spirit?

Matthew Elliott
Trevecca Nazarene University Men's Basketball
2006-2010

20

"I remain confident of this: I will see the goodness of the Lord in the Land of the living. Wait for the Lord; be strong and take heart and wait for the Lord." - Psalm 27: 13-14

The closer you hold something to you, the bigger it appears, it can even block your view of everything else. As you back it away, it falls into perspective as one piece of a larger image. God is painting a beautiful picture with your life through sports that you can miss if you don't put things into perspective. My sophomore year of college I had to sit out of every Spring tournament. Why had God brought me to this school just to sit out? My then-boyfriend, now-husband, was experiencing a very similar situation. He decided to transfer after that year. We look back now and can clearly see how God was painting our picture. If we had both been traveling every week, we would not have had the abundance of time to spend cultivating a relationship that survived two years of long distance. We have now been married for over a year and just welcomed our first child. God knew we needed to grow deep roots in our relationship that would withstand long distance. He was painting a beautiful picture for our life together, but we couldn't see it until later because our eyes were fixated on athletics. While sports are undoubtedly an important and valuable part of life, if you let them, they can block your view of the good and perfect picture that God is painting with your life. You don't want to miss it!

How might God be using your current circumstances or trials for a bigger purpose?

Emma Springer
Texas Tech University Women's Golf
2015-2017

21

January 20

"Whoever says "I know him" but does not keep his
commandments is a liar, and the truth is not in him, but
whoever keeps his word, in him truly the love of God is perfected."
-1 John 2:4-5 ESV

I remember being confronted by this scripture my junior year of college. I claimed to *"know God"* but I never really did *"keep his commandments"*. My life was dominated by my sin and my sport. I gave everything I had to baseball, and what was left I gave to just trying to be cool.

I venture to say that many of you athletes reading this have struggled with some of the things I struggled with- partying, idolizing sport, pride, lust, etc. As Christians, we should regularly ask ourselves "what is my life characterized by?" Romans 3:10-12 says *"none is righteous, no, not one"*. Our lives will never be perfect, but do we have a growing desire to *"keep his commandments"*?

For most of my college career I was just a *"liar"*. By the grace of God, this was revealed to me and God began changing me. I went from desiring to be the best player on the field and the "coolest" guy off the field, to having a growing desire to glorify God. As a result, baseball no longer ran my life, and I went from being overwhelmed by big moments to someone that my team counted on to produce.

If this scripture confronted you, I encourage you to spend time in God's word and plead with Him to change your heart. *He is faithful and will surely do it (1 Thessalonians 5:24).*

Mike Warren
University of Texas San Antonio Baseball
2010-2014

January 21

"Whatever you do, work at it with all your heart, as working for the Lord, not for men… it is the Lord Christ you are serving."
-Colossians 3:23,24b NIV

My heart still races when I hear a beep test starting or when I think about standing on the end line with coach about to say "go" for our tenth shuttle run. Thoughts like "I can't do this", "my body won't make this one", "I'm not fit enough" racing through my head. What I found in those moments of fitness testing, pushing our bodies to the limit, is that it can become a form of worship. Instead of letting my thoughts run wild, I started to turn my attention to the sacrifice of Jesus being on the cross. I would think about Him, after being beaten and flogged, carrying a cross for nearly 600 meters. How did He do that? Jesus very literally pushed His body farther than we can ever imagine.

We can change our perspective in those exhausted moments into thankful worship to a King who managed to carry a heavy cross while His body was broken. When I shifted my attention towards Him, I thought the least I can do is run another sprint as hard as I possibly can. After all, we are serving Him in every little thing we do. Even that tenth shuttle run.

The next time you are exhausted in the field of play, see if you can shift your attention to Christ. The cross will fuel you in a new way.

Morgan Springer
Georgia Southern University Women's Soccer
2009-2013

23

January 22

"Count it all joy, my brothers, when you meet trials of various kinds, for you know that the testing of your faith produces steadfastness. And let steadfastness have its full effect, that you may be perfect and complete lacking nothing."
      -James 1:2-4 ESV

Trials come to make you better, not bitter! This wasn't easy for me to learn. At the start of my sophomore season of football, I found out that my mother had been diagnosed with breast cancer. She passed away two months later. At that time, joy was the last thing I was considering. I missed 2 weeks of the season, and I was never able to find a spot in the rotation. My mom had always been the person I called on to help me plan and achieve my goals. My plans of having a breakout season had disappeared, and I had become stuck trying to determine my future without the help of my mom.

Thankfully, I found help in someone who could help me much greater than my mom ever could, and his name is Jesus. In my trial, I felt like I had lost two things around which my life had revolved, my mother and football. In those losses, however, I gained a personal relationship with Jesus, and that outweighs any loss I could ever experience in this life. The LORD revealed to me that I had been TRYING with my plans, but instead I needed to put my TRUST in His. That is when I found my joy!

As a competitor, TRYING hard is something that almost comes naturally, but now I challenge you to TRUST God just as much.

Jacolby Whitaker
Stephen F. Austin State University Football
2014-2017

24

"God, my shepherd! I don't need a thing. You have bedded me down in lush meadows, you find me quiet pools to drink from. True to your word, you let me catch my breath and send me in the right direction. Even when the way goes through Death Valley, I'm not afraid when you walk at my side. Your trusty shepherd's crook makes me feel secure. You serve me a six-course dinner right in front of my enemies. You revive my drooping head; my cup brims with blessing. Your beauty and love chase after me every day of my life. I'm back home in the house of God for the rest of my life."
Psalm 23:1-6 The Message

One of the biggest things I learned in college was the need for rest. Rest and recovery are so necessary for your well-being as a person and your mental health as an athlete. During off days, my time of rest was my Jesus time. This verse helped me feel grounded and at peace during my busy weeks and hard days. Reminding myself that I could always rest by His still waters and know that He is always chasing after me to make me feel loved and secure, were my moments of reprieve for those stressful instances. You wouldn't keep playing on an injury or not take time to recover after a hard game, so take time to find your rest, and go to Him when you're weary from your grind.

What are some of the ways that you find rest during your week? Try to take some time today, or this week, to pray and remind yourself that He will always lead you to quiet waters when you need it.

Lauren "LT" Thompson
Belmont University Women's Basketball
2013-2017

January 24

"Then Job arose and tore his robe and shaved his head and
fell on the ground and worshiped... The LORD gave, and the LORD
has taken away; blessed be the name of the LORD."
— Job 1: 20-21 ESV

My first four years of college soccer were filled with constant setbacks and trials. With an injury resulting in a redshirt season, struggling to get playing time, and facing prejudice for my faith, I met each struggle with groaning and frustration.

I was so consumed with my own misfortunes and failures that I neglected to see the work God was doing in my life to refine and strengthen my faith. I focused on how God was failing to use my soccer career for MY good, instead of seeing that He was using my soccer career for HIS good.

If I could go back, I would try to respond to my trials like Job. Job lost everything including his family, and his first response was to fall on the ground and worship! His act of thanking God is the perfect picture of faith and trusting the Lord with his life amid uncertainty.

After experiencing these struggles, God has taught me that regardless of what I am going through, God is good. He will see me through my trials and use my story to glorify His kingdom. Now when the Lord gives and when the Lord takes away, I try to respond by blessing the name of the Lord in worship and thanksgiving.

Reflect and write down three trials in your life that God ultimately used for good. If you encounter a trial today, challenge yourself to respond in worship and thanksgiving.

Emily Kaestner
University of Oregon / Campbell University Women's Soccer
2016-2021

January 25

"Not only so, but we also glory in our sufferings, because we know that suffering produces perseverance; perseverance, character; and character, hope. And hope does not put us to shame, because God's love has been poured out into our hearts through the Holy Spirit, who has been given to us."
-Romans 5:3-5

I dislocated my shoulder a little less than halfway through senior year of college which ultimately ended my career right then. During the time I was out, my team was winning and being very successful without me on the court. I found it to be very difficult to try and be happy for my team when it felt like I wasn't contributing at all to the success.

God really showed me through that time, with this verse, that there is indeed growth in suffering and reminded me that He understood my pain and frustration. Sometimes the hardest part is feeling alone in the pain and sadness. Knowing that my God had experienced the same feelings before helped me be an encouragement to my team and strengthened my relationship with Him even more.

When trials come your way, instead of questioning God and asking "why did this have to happen", thank Him for it, because it will only draw you closer to Him.

Connor Sears
Covenant College Men's Basketball
2013-2017

January 26

"If the world hates you, keep in mind that it hated me first. If you belonged to the world, it would love you as its own. As it is, you do not belong to the world, but I have chosen you out of the world. That is why the world hates you." John 15:18-19 NIV

Sometimes what is popular isn't always right. My freshman year of college was a challenging time both physically and spiritually. I grew up playing on sports teams where the majority of my teammates shared my faith in Christ, but when I reached college level, everything changed. For the first time in my life, I found myself being made fun for my belief in Christ. It was hard to wrap my head around because I had attended a Christian school until that point and had never been called out for my faith. Making friends was tough at first because I was the "church goer" or the "religious" guy on the team. It was through these trials with my teammates that I realized I was right where God wanted me to be.

Being different from everyone was a good thing. It was through that difference that God used me to be a light to others that didn't have anyone else pointing them to Jesus. After all, Jesus doesn't love us because we are popular, He loves us because we are His.

Has your faith been tested and made you feel unpopular? I challenge you to relentlessly pursue and invest your time in those people because you never know who is watching and could be led to Christ because of it.

Will Jamison
University of Mississippi Baseball
2012-2014

"Now unto him that is able to do exceeding abundantly above all we can ask or think, according to the power that worketh in us."
-Ephesians 3:20

Growing up in New Orleans, Louisiana during a time when it was the murder capital of the world wasn't easy. Every day was about survival. Sometimes that meant defending myself in a fist fight. Other days that meant making the tough decision to walk away when facing peer pressure to do things that were illegal. My mother was a single parent, working two jobs and going to school. Things were hard, to say the least.

Although hardship was my physical reality, my foundation was built on God's word due to my family's faithful commitment to church and prayer. I knew more Bible than I knew lyrics. During tough times I would lean on this Scripture as not only a sign of surrender to God, but also to remind myself that God has already given me the power to overcome whatever obstacle was present. The right-now-ness of this Scripture is what I love the most. It's immediate access to the power of God, and guess what…When we surrender to Him, He's able to more than we can "ask or think." Sometimes we need a reminder that He's God. As great as man can be, we all have our limits. But with God, all things are possible, even the things we don't even know to think about.

The next time you find yourself doubting yourself, speak this Scripture over your own life, be reminded of the power of God and realize that the power is already inside of you.

Shan Foster
2008 Dallas Mavericks, 2nd Round Draft 51st Pick
5 Year Pro Career

January 28

"Am I now trying to win the approval of human beings, or of God? Or am I trying to please people? If I were still trying to please people, I would not be a servant of Christ."
-Galatians 1:10 NIV

In College, I won a lot of awards for both soccer and academics. I reached the pinnacle of my athletic career in man's eyes, but it still left me empty and searching for more. I was so focused on being the best and was always looking around to see who saw what "great things" I was doing. God showed me how little all of that meant when I graduated and entered into the real world. I had just finished my first year of teaching in a Title 1 high school and was reflecting on how hard the year had been. It hit me like a brick wall, it was Jesus who got me through the year. Never once did those awards that I thought were so important to win help me in any way.

While God gives us the incredible gift to play sports, it is so important to remember who we are in Him and Him alone. Sports will end one day and they do not define us. There is a God-sized void in our lives and we can nurture that through sports, but never try and replace God with any award or accomplishment. Sports are purely a platform to spread the word and what a powerful thing to possess! Jesus is so faithful to us and trust me when I say He is the only person who deserves our attention and gets all the glory.

Where in your life or sport are worldly awards/idols distracting you from Jesus?

Abbie Alosi Moroney
Trevecca Nazarene University Women's Soccer
2013-2017

30

January 29

"Do not be deceived, my beloved brothers. Every good gift and every perfect gift is from above, coming down from the Father of lights with whom there is no variation or shadow due to change."
-James 1:16-17 ESV

Do we realize that what we see as "perfect" is often not in alignment with what Christ sees as perfect for us? We are living in a world where there are so many reasons for us to complain. Complaints about lifestyle, material things, envy, and so much more, but do we realize how much of this is about perspective? Perspective can create a grateful heart, or a prideful heart.

We can all sit and consider how bad we have it, but I assure you that is coming from a comparison to someone else, often being fed by someone else too ("Deceivers"). Instead, look at Jesus Christ. He lived a sinless life and yet He died a horrific death so that we could receive the most perfect gift of all. While it was happening, the disciples did not look at this scene of Jesus on the cross as a perfect gift for them, rather a great tragedy, which it was. Yet, they came to see the true reason behind it, and just how magnificent and eternal it really was. When we focus on Jesus and trust in the good news that He is, a grateful attitude will be the result no matter the circumstance. Realize that each moment is an *opportunity* not to think of ourselves, but to accept the perfect gift in our lives that God promises, whether it feels that way or not. Trust God and gratitude overflows.

No matter the current challenges, minutes played, family issues, etc., can you put your focus on what brings immense gratitude?

Easton Bazzoli
Cedarville University Men's Basketball
2013-2017

31

January 30

"Have nothing to do with irreverent, silly myths. Rather train yourself for godliness; for while bodily training is of some value, godliness is of value in every way, as it holds promise for the present life and also for the life to come."
– 1 Timothy 4:8 ESV

Being an athlete means pushing your body to reach its maximum potential. While this is a great way to steward the gifts given by God, it is not the most important thing in this life. Starting my freshman year of college, I sinfully placed a hyper focus on my appearance. I frequently compared myself to my teammates on how skinny I was, how much muscle I had, and how my overall body looked. From the wickedness of my heart flowed out sinful habits of restricting my diet and obsessing over caloric intake and output. But what the Lord has patiently taught me over the years is that while bodily training is of some value, godliness has value in every way. Rather than worshiping my appearance for selfish ambition and vain glory, I am enabled by God to be all-consumed with the joy of knowing and becoming like my Lord and Savior Jesus Christ.

Godliness is precious because it points to the saving work of Christ on our behalf. It shines a light in the darkness. It enables people to see your good works and give glory to the Father. Put to death the sins of the flesh and live for the glory of God alone today.

How are you training in godliness? Ask God to reveal an area of growth and seek accountability for it within your church.

Ashley Stamps
Abilene Christian University Women's Soccer
2018-2021

January 31

"Humble yourselves, therefore, under God's mighty hand that he may lift you up in due time."
-1 Peter 5:6

It's often said that God's never late. His timing is perfect and has purpose beyond what we can see. Unfortunately, it's usually easier to say that than it is to truly believe it for ourselves. Personally, I spent the first year of my college football career in anonymity as a scout team wide receiver who felt unseen and irrelevant. Coaches barely knew my name and my hard work seemed to go unnoticed. Just one year before, I was captain of a state championship team with aspirations of making an impact on a college team. Little did I know that God was humbling me and shaping me to seek His audience first. Things didn't get better my freshman year, but I started a prayer group on the team and was determined to share the love and light of Jesus with those around me – regardless of whether I ever played in a game. I realized my impact on the lives of those around me was eternally more important than what I ever did on the field. In His providence, God allowed me to be a significant contributor on our team the following year. Playing further elevated my platform to share the joy I found as a Son of God and encourage others to find their worth apart from their performance. God used the trials of my freshman year for my growth and His glory. And while I didn't understand his purposes at the time, His timing was perfect.

Take time to consider where you need to trust God's timing in your life.

David McIntosh
University of North Carolina Football
1999-2002

33

February 1

"But you are a chosen race, a royal priesthood, a holy nation, a people for his possession, so that you may proclaim the praises of the one who called you out of darkness into his marvelous light."
-1 Peter 2:9 CSB

I grew up loving the game of basketball and I always dreamed of going to the WNBA. Basketball was the head of my life while Christ was behind all of the worldly things I loved. When I signed a scholarship to play basketball at Mississippi College, I had no idea that God was about to change my life for the good. My first year, I decided to party and care very little for my academics and by the end of my Junior year, I was walking into academic probation. My second year, I was forced to sit out from the sport I put all of my hope in. During my academic probation year, I got involved with the Fellowship of Christian Athletes. At this time, I did not fully understand what my purpose was, I just knew I was a basketball player. I prayed and accepted Christ to be my Lord and Savior and God gave me the verse 1 Peter 2:9. It was not long before I realized that I was using the platform that Christ had given me for all the wrong reasons and I learned that I had been walking in darkness for years. I loved sports but now I was growing to love the Gospel. My Bible was no longer just a book, but it became my personal love letter from God and my way of advancing his Kingdom here in human history.

Focus on the one thing (God) and the one thing will take care of everything else.

Ashley Minor
Mississippi College Women's Basketball
2014-2017

February 2

"And we know that in all things God works for the good of those who love him, who have been called according to his purpose."
-Romans 8:28 NIV

My sophomore year of college was plagued with words such as "rusty," "behind," and "below- average". These words were foreign to me, so as you could expect, I was struggling- mentally, emotionally, and spiritually. A few games into the season, I sustained a season-ending injury. What happened after that changed my life. God needed to remove that part of my life to remind my why He blessed me with it in the first place. In all of our imperfections, short comings, and failures- we are *still* enough. He reminded me that there is so much more to life than putting the ball in the back of the net- there is relationship to be cultivated, growth to be cherished, perseverance to carry on, and strength that can only come from the One who gave us the ability in the first place.

Reframing our mindset from setback to opportunity is a game changer. During that challenging season of life, I faithfully and confidently identified the truth behind being created *on* purpose and *for* a purpose. Amongst the ever-changing seasons of life, we can always count on our constant and loving Father to safely guide us according to His good and perfect plans.

When God has different plans than you originally intended for your life, take a moment to think about all the opportunities He will provide for you moving forward according to His will.

McKenzie Dixon
Austin Peay State University Women's Soccer
2015-2019

February 3

"Go up to the hills and bring wood and build the house, that I may take pleasure in it and that I may be glorified, says the Lord. You looked for much, and behold, it came to little. And when you brought it home, I blew it away. Why? declares the Lord of hosts. Because of my house that lies in ruins, while each of you busies himself with his own house." – Haggai 1:8-9 ESV

Oh how easy it is to put our little and finite kingdom filled with selfish desires above the kingdom of our heavenly Father. The more we choose to busy ourselves with building our own house, the less we glorify Him, the less we seek His presence, and the less we create space for the Lord to dwell within our temple. Especially as athletes, the nature of our flesh is to struggle mightily for personal gain, accolades, playing time, and to be seen. All of these "gains" come at the neglect of glorifying the Lord's house. How gracious of our God to evaporate this "gain" and blow away the selfish house that we attempt to build on our own, so that we may instead work to build up His all-satisfying, life-giving, grace-infused house. Without the powerful, saving grace of Jesus bought for us by His blood on the cross, we will choose to build our self-serving kingdom over and over again. Praise God for His constant, redemptive work in us through His Son, so that today we may choose to recalibrate our work in a way that will bring Him the most glory and honor.

God doesn't call us to build our kingdom, but His. Ask God to make known the way that you should go today, through the guidance of the Holy Spirit, so that you may glorify His kingdom.

Annalise Kit
Clemson University Volleyball
2017-2021

36

February 4

"And whatsoever ye do, do it heartily, as to the Lord and not unto men," - Colossians 3:23 KJV

Growing up as a coach's kid, I always wanted to please my dad. But after a great high school career playing for him, I was crushed I hadn't reached that dream. Even during my college career from LSU to Rice, I always wanted to make him proud and please him. But this was actually a performance treadmill, trying to perform to please others was a never-ending treadmill that never satisfied. I later realized that no matter if I won or loss, my dad actually was very pleased and loved me, similar to my Godly father. This taught me trying to please and perform for him was actually just me running a treadmill for me. Later in my college hoops journey I completely committed my life to Christ; realizing that ultimately using my gift to honor my Father in heaven was the real championship. The words in Col 3:23 became real to me in a game I played versus the Chinese Jr. National Team. It was a sold-out arena and we were playing on a tour in East Asia. Our coach told our team before the game that he loved us, have fun, play free, and play for our Father in Heaven. A pregame speech telling me to play free of the burden of performance. I remember smiling and feeling free and confident to play! This was a new freedom in Christ. Playing for an audience of one, playing for my Father in heaven, and playing with Christ.

Who are you performing for? Are you playing in freedom or on a performance treadmill?

Omar Mance
Louisiana State University / Rice University Men's Basketball
1998-2003

37

February 5

"If I glorify myself, my glory means nothing. My father, whom you claim as your God, glorifies me." -John 8:54 NIV

As athletes, we are naturally competitive because we are driven to win. Competitive against rivals, our own teammates and even ourselves. That competitive nature can be a great driving force and is what often times leads to victory. It's good until we start using it to glorify ourselves instead of God. God gifted me with the ability to play volleyball and a very competitive spirit. In college especially, I used that gift to glorify myself.

Each week and each season, I strived to win personal conference and division awards. If I won those awards, my sense of accomplishment only lasted until there was another award to chase after. If I didn't get the award, I felt failure.

The "glory" I thought I brought to myself meant nothing. I lost sight of God and why God had given me those gifts—to glorify Him. I had been using my God-given gifts to lift up and glorify myself and was left empty, instead of glorifying the One who had blessed me with those gifts. I've learned now, after graduating, how God is the only one who can redeem and glorify me, and how I could have used my gifts to glorify God instead.

If you're still playing sports, be honest with yourself—are you striving to glorify yourself, or to glorify God? If you've graduated beyond sports, are there areas in your life that you are using to glorify yourself instead of God? How can you move to glorify God instead?

Anna Burton
Newman University Women's Volleyball
2014-2017

"For by His grace you have been saved, through faith — and this is not from yourselves, it is the gift of God — not by works, so that no one can boast." - Ephesians 2:8-9

As an athlete, it has always been about performance, production, approval. The coaches, the fans, even family and friends cheer you on when you do something good, and then don't cheer very much when you mess up. For me it has always been about performing well to earn the starting spot or striving to get signed to an NFL team and make the roster. In sports you have to earn it. LeBron James often says "nothing is given, everything is earned."

The Gospel could not be more different, and this is a challenge for us. Our entire lives have been about performing and earning it. This is not the case when it comes to Jesus. The Gospel is this — by Grace we have been saved. It was and is the cross that saves us. It is not up to us to earn it — you can't earn what has already been done for you. Why is this so hard to grasp? Why do we constantly find ourselves trying to earn God's approval?

If we could earn our salvation, the cross wouldn't mean anything. Instead of striving to earn something that has already been gifted to you, receive it with a sense of humility and awe. His Grace is sufficient and the cross is enough — it always will be. He loves you as you are. This is the beauty of the Gospel.

In what areas in your life are you trying to earn God's approval? How will you live your life in response to this Gospel freedom?

Caleb Scott
Vanderbilt University Football
2014-2017

February 7

"Everyone then who hears these words of mine and does them will be like a wise man who built his house on the rock. And the rain fell, and the floods came, and the winds blew and beat on that house, but it did not fall, because it had been founded on the rock. And everyone who hears these words of mine and does not do them will be like a foolish man who built his house on the sand. And the rain fell, and the floods came, and the winds blew and beat against that house, and it fell, and great was the fall of it." -Matthew 7:24-27 ESV

Looking back at my career I often wonder how I did not see it coming. Life was great, baseball was great, and I had a great support group to cheer me along the way. Dedicated, focused, maybe even possessed is the way I went about my athletic career. I wanted to be successful and a winner. Long story short, I am the foolish man who built his house on a large pile of sand.

The storm came in the form of an elbow injury and some bad luck on the succeeding surgeries. My identity was in baseball and when it was over, I was broken. I swore to myself that I would be fine when it was all over, but I wasn't. It did not matter what I told myself, I had built my foundation on chasing my worldly desires. I depended on myself and let pride get in the way of me building my foundation in Christ. The best thing about God though is that He never gives up on us and my story is not over.

We cannot control every outcome, even though as athletes we try to. Let's continue to solidify our foundation in Christ and play the game of life for His glory, not our own.

Cory Luebke
San Diego Padres/Pittsburgh Pirates/Chicago White Sox
2007-2017

40

February 8

"But those who hope in the LORD will renew their strength.
They will soar on wings like eagles; they will run and not grow weary,
they will walk and not be faint."
- Isaiah 40:31 NIV

No human is immune to facing trials throughout his or her life. God often uses these experiences as a tool to draw us nearer to Him. When I was a junior at Austin Peay State University, I was supposed to get drafted in the 2015 MLB First-Year Players Draft. I prepared my whole life for that day and honestly invested too much of my value in becoming a professional baseball player. One can imagine my disappointment after my name was not called during those long three days of the draft. I was mad, sad, embarrassed, and confused all at the same time. Although this trial was not the end of the world, it was the most important thing to me at the time.

In a moment of vulnerability, I went to my room, opened up my Bible to a random page, and began to read. I happened to land on Isaiah 40:31. The passage opened my eyes and heart to God's truth. I needed to put my hope and trust in the Lord instead of my athletic ability. It was that simple. A heavy weight immediately lifted off of my chest. I was able to play the sport I loved with no pressure because I put my life and worth in God's hands. Every aspect of my life continued to improve because my focus shifted to give everything to the Lord and rely on Him to guide me to do His will.

I challenge you to put your full hope and trust in God and watch His plans surpass anything you could have dreamt up for yourself.

Jared Carkuff
Toronto Blue Jays / San Diego Padres Organizations
2016 - 2019

February 9

"The thief comes only to steal and kill and destroy; I have come that they may have life, and have it to the full."
- John 10: 10 NIV

Do you remember the greatest game or race of your life? Odds are that day comes quick to memory for you. What about for others? Maybe your parents could recall the year or season when you had *your* game/ race, but the details or stats aren't as clear as they are in your memory. What about your teammates or friends? They might not remember at all.... Now, think about the time when you showed up for your teammate(s)- at a parent's funeral, season-ending injury, broken relationship, or even the conversations when they wonder if God even cares about them. I bet your teammate remembers those moments with perfect clarity. Why is that?

Jesus is talking to his friends about life, probably the same way you do with your teammates, when He tells His friends what *life to the full* looks like. Jesus described this life to the full as meaningful relationships with Him and others. *The thief* (Satan) tries to steal true life from us by making it all about us. At the end of your life, no one will remember the greatest game you ever had. However, they will remember the defining moments of your relationship where you showed up for them in a meaningful way.

What do you want people to remember about you? Are you living life to the full or living for yourself? Jesus offers life to the full through Him... that is the only thing that will last.

Bailey Bell
Union University Men's Cross Country & Track
2012-2016

42

February 10

"For the wages of sin is death, but the gift of God is eternal life in Christ Jesus our Lord."
– *Romans 6:23 NIV*

As an athlete, you and I both know that gameday is only a fraction (a small one, at that) in the totality of sports. Exponentially more time is invested in other aspects of sports such as practice, weight training, and recovery to name a few. One of my personal favorites from when I played sports was watching film. This concept that my actions on film would result in praise or criticism depending on the outcome of the play made sense in my mind.

However, when I started exploring what I believed in spiritually, this formula of *performance = result* started to break down. When I die, do I sit down for a final film session with God to see if I did enough to get into Heaven? I know I probably have some "good plays" on my life film, but what about all those bad ones?

Thankfully, Scripture gives us the answer in Romans 6:23. In fact, it tells us that what we deserve for our "bad plays" in life is death (or a loss of relationship with God). But God, in His mercy, has offered all of us a gift, one that cannot be earned. Eternal life with Him is found through the person of Christ, and thankfully not in our life's culmination of what we put on film.

Spend time meditating on God's mercy. If you have accepted the gift in Romans 6:23, praise God today that He has made that known to you. If you haven't, consider if you would like to accept that gift today – one which can never be taken away.

Connor Huffman
The University of Texas Football
2014-2017

February 11

"Let us not become weary in doing good, for at the proper time we will reap a harvest if we do not give up."
-Galatians 6:9 NIV

It's easy to keep pushing ourselves when we see results. We've all heard the saying, "the way you practice is the way you'll play", so we were taught to push ourselves hard behind the scenes so that we can reap the benefits on game day. As athletes, we can't expect to perform our best if we aren't putting in the work during practice. This is exactly what our walks with Christ are like. You get out of it what you put into it. We can't expect our relationship with Christ to grow, if we aren't consistently putting our trust and faith into Him. We put so much effort into our sport every day, but do we put that same effort into our relationship with Christ?

I know I've caught myself giving more to the game than to my Creator, but the moments I decided to put Christ first, were the moments I felt more joy than soccer could ever bring me. One day you'll lace up your cleats for the last time. Our time on the field will come to an end, but God's love for us is never ending. We may not see the results of our devotion to Christ as fast as we may see them on the turf, but we will reap a harvest so much greater. At the end of the day, we must decide what's more important: a momentary feeling of success on the field or the eternal joy of reuniting with Christ?

Take time to reflect and ask God to reveal areas in your life that you are putting more effort into than you are in your relationship with Christ.

Kobi McNutt
University of Louisiana Women's Soccer
2017-2020

44

February 12

"Do nothing out of selfish ambition or conceit, but in humility count others more significant than yourselves. Let each of you look not only to his own interests, but also to the interests of others. Have this mind among yourselves, which is yours in Christ Jesus, who, though he was in the form of God, did not count equality with God a thing to be grasped, but emptied himself, by taking the form of a servant, being born in the likeness of men. And being found in human form, he humbled himself by becoming obedient to the point of death, even death on a cross." – Philippians 2:3-8 ESV

Watching from the sideline can be difficult. Supporting your team and those playing above you on the depth chart can be challenging, but it is so worth it.

As one who did not receive some of the opportunities I wanted to have and missed opportunities that were given to me by my own errors, I was often consumed with myself and did not consider my teammates or my coaches as more significant than myself. On the contrary, there were many times I put myself and my own desires before my teammates and coaches.

After I finished playing and I had more time to reflect on my experience as an athlete, I realized that the only things from sports that have eternal value are relationships. The relationships built with others on a team are such a gift. Building relationships and sharing Christ with teammates is what makes all of those early morning workouts, film sessions, and long practices so worth it.

Take some time to think of ways that you can serve and encourage your teammates and coaches.

Josh Covey
University of Texas Football
2015-2018

45

February 13

"Let another praise you, and not your own mouth; someone else and not your own lips." – Proverbs 27:2 NIV

Baseball is a 'game of failure' evidenced by the fact that the highest-achieving players do not succeed (when hitting) the majority of the time. I learned early on that a key to success was learning to handle these failures. As a result, I focused on having a positive mental attitude. This did make a difference, and as my confidence grew, it played an increasing role in my successes. However, I noticed that what started out with good intentions evolved into something that was potentially harmful; and that was arrogance or conceit.

One man's confidence is another man's arrogance. This became an important distinction that I tried to balance. I became hyper-focused on winning with good sportsmanship. I learned how to remain confident in my abilities and hard work, but to let others do the talking. Jesus and how He lived His life gave us the ultimate example of 'humbling oneself'.

Athletes, especially successful athletes, are confident in their abilities and what they will contribute to their team's success. Keep that fine line between confidence and arrogance in mind; when speaking publicly, as your ability to influence is on full display. Others are free to praise, just not your own lips.

Ray Suplee
University of Georgia Baseball - 1990-1992
New York Yankees, Baltimore Orioles, Tampa Bay Rays - 1992-1997

"Not only so, but we also glory in our sufferings, because we know that suffering produces perseverance; perseverance, character; and character, hope. And hope does not put us to shame, because God's love has been poured out into our hearts through the Holy Spirit, who has been given to us."
-Romans 5:3-5 NIV

Although I've worked my whole life to become a college athlete, it's been the hardest thing I've ever done. It's difficult to work as hard as you can and it still not be enough. It's hard to persevere when you feel like circumstances are unfair. It's hard to keep going after being told countless times that you'll never make it. I have learned through countless trials that God uses our hardest times to reveal our need to rely on Him. Suffering well allows us to look more like Jesus. No matter if I strike out, hit a home run, or never see the field, I am significant because God says I am. I am made in the Image of the Creator of the Universe. I am fearfully and wonderfully made.

I am so much more than my sport. I can compete and live freely because I know that I am fully accepted and loved by God, despite my performance. God has a purpose and plan for me, right where I am. Even if I don't ever see the result of it on this side of Heaven, God is working through me in my pain for my good and His glory. I can have joy in the midst of my suffering because I have hope that my future is secure, regardless of my circumstances.

Suffering well allows you to look more like Jesus. Ask God for courage and strength to sustain you as you view your suffering from an eternal perspective.

Shelby Suplee
University of Georgia Softball
2018-2021

February 15

Jesus said to her, "Everyone who drinks of this water will be thirsty again, but whoever drinks of the water that I will give him will never be thirsty again. The water that I will give him will become in him a spring of water welling up to eternal life."
– John 4:13-14 ESV

When Jesus encounters the woman at the well, He knows and understands her heart. He looks through her physical thirst and sees that she needs something that will quench the thirst of her spirit.

This world offers us many different flavors of water. Growing up, sports were often what I looked to as my well of fulfillment and satisfaction. However, just like any idol this world offers, sports will often leave you feeling empty, no matter your level of success. Something that is meant to be enjoyable can quickly become the thief of your joy. This is a result of a flawed perspective of sports and the role they play in our lives as believers.

Instead of viewing your sport as an end itself, I encourage you to view competing as a way to worship the one true God. Instead of seeing athletics as "who you are", I encourage you to know that your identity in Christ does not change based on the results of a game. This shift in perspective can only come through a personal relationship with Jesus. He is the only one that can teach you the gratitude and humility it takes to play sports the right way.

Never allow sports to become an idol. Always look to Jesus for your identity and your satisfaction.

Walker Jones
University of Alabama Football
2013-2016

"Rejoice always, pray continually, give thanks in all circumstances; for this is God's will for you in Christ Jesus."
— 1 Thessalonians 5:16-18 NIV

In losses, or times that seem unfortunate, it can be easy to overlook valuable lessons God intended for us. After redshirting my freshman year, the next two seasons we found ourselves going 2-10 in back-to-back seasons. We worked extremely hard as a team, but the wins just weren't adding up. Too often I found myself asking God why us? How can one team work so hard, experience so many trials and very little success? We combined for a 4-20 record during those two seasons and I was so laser focused on what I felt wasn't happening, that I neglected to notice my own opportunities within my relationship with Christ.

As Christian athletes, experiencing trials is one thing, but deepening our relationship with Christ and glorifying Him not only during the wins, but especially during the losses, I believe is a pivotal lesson God teaches us in life. With a renewed focus, the hard work continued. I continued to give thanks in the hard circumstances, and was voted team captain my senior year. Our team experienced great success that year by tying the school record for most wins in a season (9-4) in school history. Again, I gave thanks.

Wins in life are great, however, rejoicing in the Lord and glorifying Him should be intensified during trials and tribulations we experience in life. Ask God to reveal areas of your life where you are neglecting to pursue and glorify Him.

Johnell Thomas
Vanderbilt University Football
2008-2012

February 17

"This is the day the Lord has made; let us rejoice and be glad in it." - Psalms 118:24

I was fortunate enough to play baseball at the collegiate level at the University of Alabama and then at the professional level for several years. I was able to fulfill a lifelong dream by playing at the highest level and face the best hitters in the world. It was truly a dream come true, and I'm very thankful that the Lord blessed me with that opportunity.

As a relief pitcher, I came to understand that each day, each game, each pitch matters a great deal. The only thing I could ever impact (not control) was the next pitch. I couldn't do anything about what happened yesterday, and I wasn't guaranteed tomorrow. I learned that I had the best chance of success if I focused on the next pitch, and nothing more. This verse helped me narrow my focus on the singular task at hand, and that made all the difference.

If you focus your energy, attention, and faith on what is right in front of you... it allows you to free yourself from the failures of yesterday and the pitfalls that tomorrow may bring. This day, this opportunity, this pitch... that's what the Lord has given you, so make the most of it.

Taylor Tankersley
Florida Marlins
2004-2010

50

February 18

"Delight yourself in the LORD, and he will give you the
desires of your heart. Commit your way to the LORD; trust in him,
and he will act." -Psalm 37:4-5 ESV

Placing my trust in an invisible God is something I constantly struggle with. It is difficult for me to give up what is tangible for something I cannot touch or see. After an All-American sophomore season at TCU, I felt God telling me it was time for a change. Texas A&M University was where He led me. The next year would bring much discomfort as I tried to adjust to a new school with new friends all while being ineligible to play. "Why?" I wondered. By MY standard, life had been going according to plan. He would soon provide an answer.

God would use this time of change to draw near to me. Baseball took a backseat to Godly friends and a strong church community. I found out what it truly looked like to delight in The Lord. I was praying, reading my Bible, and craving a stronger relationship with Him. Looking back, trusting in God eventually led to delighting in Him. When I began to delight in The Lord he began to act and give me the desires of my heart. Lifelong friends, my lovely wife, success on the field, and a love for an amazing University was where my desires were, even if I didn't know it, and He met me there.

What are the desires of your heart? Are you letting The Lord
work in your life? He requires us to give up control to truly see
Him act.

Boomer White
Texas Christian University / Texas A&M University
2013-2016

51

February 19

*"Therefore, if anyone is in Christ, the new creation has come:
The old has gone, the new is here!" -2 Corinthians 5:17 NIV*

Where do you find your identity? For a large part of my life, I found mine at 60 feet and 6 inches. How I felt, how I treated others, and how I lived my life all revolved around my passion for the sport I fell in love with at 5 years old. I soon realized the problem in putting my identity in baseball was that my confidence and joy in life fluctuated with my ability to perform and perform well on the field. But Christ quickly shattered this lie when He revealed to me that my true identity was not found in baseball but found in Him and Him alone.

What does it mean to find your identity in Christ? It means placing your confidence for life and eternity in Him and nothing else. It means being formed into the image of the Lord and wanting others to see Jesus when they look at you more than you want them to see your athletic abilities. It means regardless of your circumstances you find joy in knowing you are a child of the Most High. As a Christian athlete, it is important to remember that you are not defined by your performance on the field, but how you live your life off the field.

Take some time to pray that the foundation of your identity would come from your relationship with Christ. If you truly put your faith in Him as your Lord and Savior, your identity is secure in Him - both on and off the field.

Matthew Sims
University of Texas at San Antonio/Atlanta Braves
2010-2014

52

"There is a time for everything, and a season for every activity under the heavens: a time to be born and a time to die, a time to plant and a time to uproot, a time to kill and a time to heal, a time to tear down and a time to build, a time to weep and a time to laugh, a time to mourn and a time to dance... a time to love and a time to hate, a time for war and a time for peace. – Ecclesiastes 3:1-8 NIV

I remember at times during my college life as an athlete looking forward to whatever was next. The next game, the next semester, the next season, the next break, or even the next chapter of my life. The reasons could have been many of things; wanting to play better, wanting to get to the season where I was on the court more, wanting more free time, and the list could go on. There is always a "next thing" that sounds better or more fulfilling.

However, God has a season for everything that He wants us to endure, learn from, or enjoy. There is nothing wrong with striving to be better for what is next. However, be grateful for the NOW! This is where you are and enjoy the grind of practice, the time with teammates, and coaches. Most importantly, be present with God now and your relationship with Him.

Push yourself through the challenges that you face, learn from your failures and successes that you are facing, and enjoy being an athlete and all the rewards and lessons that come from that. The season you are in right now is the season God wants you in.

PAUSE: Enjoy where you are currently at. Enjoy the season of life you are in now and make the most of it.

Reece Chamberlain
Belmont University Men's Basketball
2010-2015

February 21

"His delight is not in the strength of the horse, nor his
pleasure in the legs of a man, but the Lord takes pleasure in those who
fear him, in those who hope in his steadfast love." -Psalm 147:10-11

Have you ever tried to get someone else's validation through your performance? I know I have. I felt as if the support I got from others was a physical representation of how pleased God was with me. This way of thinking brought me comfort when I succeeded, but when poor performances came, the strain of trying to measure up to the approval of man and God became my downfall. How the world responded to my performances determined how I saw myself, and I figured that God was disappointed when I wasn't winning. But, my friend, God's approval is not something that we contend for through competition, rather it is living through our faith in Jesus Christ that we can please the very heart of God.

I love how these verses from Psalm 147 include what we as athletes tend to struggle with - using our physical accolades to warrant approval. This verse says that we aren't called to perform, we are called to participate. We are encouraged to join in relationship with Jesus. My friend, if you want the weight of performing for approval removed from your shoulders, know that it is through relationship with God that you bring Him delight. Regardless of your performance, He loves you. He is pleased to call you His own.

Pray and thank God that you are free from the weight of performing for His love. Write this down so you remember it.

Gabriel Willis
Liberty University Men's Track and Field
2020-2024

"You, my brothers and sisters, were called to be free. But do not use your freedom to indulge the flesh; rather, serve one another humbly in love." -Galatians 5:13

We need to redefine success. If you are anything like me, your definition of success has been skewed in many ways. You may have been taught growing up that success is graduating high school, getting into college, being an All-American, receiving sports recognition, and making money. Sound familiar...?

God designed us to be great. In the very beginning He said to rule over the Earth. However, somewhere along the way we have distorted the interpretation of ruling the Earth for our benefit instead of for God's glory. We have forgotten that worldly and kingdom success are very different. So, what is your definition of success?

Kingdom success is this: (1) Listening to God every day. (2) Trusting and believing that what He has for your life is better than what you can do on your own. (3) Doing what He tells you to do.

My prayer is that your definition of success will slowly change to becoming more like Jesus every minute you compete; and when you see the fruits of your hard work pay off, your immediate thought will then be marked with a "Thank you God". That is a sign of true success.

Brothers and sisters, your teammates are looking at YOU to step up and lead your team spiritually. What if your teammates and coaches were able to experience the true character of Jesus by you simply serving humbly in love?

Marissa Guimbarda
Clemson Softball
2019-2022

February 23

*"You will seek me and find me when you seek me with all your
heart." — Jeremiah 29:13 NIV*

For a long time, the only thing that had all of my heart was the
game of baseball. Everything I did and everywhere I went revolved
around this game. And only when it was stripped out of my hands
because of a devastating nerve injury did I finally come to realize that
my heart wanted more. I remember being so angry at God because of
this injury. I went out to the field one night when the lights were off
and I sat in centerfield. Infuriated, I called out, "Where are you, God?
How could you let this happen?" I had given my whole heart to
baseball yet, there I was, broken and shattered.

It wasn't until the next day that a friend of mine showed me
this verse. "You will seek me and find when you seek me with all
your heart." That's when it hit me. As I sat on that grass last night
asking God where He was, He had been there all along. He had never
left. I was blind to the work He was doing in my life because my heart
was distracted. It wasn't fully His. And He doesn't want just half of
our heart. He wants all of it.

Sports are good things. Baseball is a good thing; a gift from
God himself. But, when we put more hope in the gift rather than the
Giver, our hearts are surely to be broken. Do you want to see God? Do
you want to watch Him go to work in your life? Go all in with Him.

**What things in this world are getting more of your heart's
attention than God?**

Reid A. Petty
University of Texas at Arlington Baseball
2015-2019

56

Do not be anxious about anything, but in everything by prayer and supplication with thanksgiving let your requests be made known to God. And the peace of God, which surpasses all understanding, will guard your hearts and your minds in Christ Jesus.
– Philippians 4:6-7 ESV

Humble yourselves, therefore, under the mighty hand of God so that at the proper time he may exalt you, casting all your anxieties on him, because he cares for you.
– 1 Peter 5:6-7 ESV

God's desire is that you would not fear. In fact, He is so adamant that He mentions in His word some 366 times not to fear, worry, or be anxious! As an athlete, it can be easy to struggle with this command though. After all, we have a lot to be anxious about, right? Managing course work, friendships, and trying to be a great teammate can be stressful.

The demands of being a great student athlete are often overwhelming, but God offers us a solution. He tells us to be honest with Him about our struggles and instructs us to be thankful in the midst of them. In response, He promises us peace beyond our understanding. Praise God that He never leaves us in our weakness!

Be honest with God about what you fear and start practicing thanksgiving today. Tell Him 3 things you are thankful for.

Trevor Carr
University of Texas Football
2016-2018

February 25

"And whatever you do, in word or deed, do everything in the name of the Lord Jesus, giving thanks to God the Father through him." - Colossians 3:17

I wish I could say that my life reflected this verse throughout my college career...sadly, it did not. I lived life for myself...elevating my needs and desires above all else. I knew about Jesus, but I certainly didn't live my life in accordance to His word and I did not give Him his rightful place on the throne. I had put myself on the throne instead. This certainly worked for a while...having a busy social life and a successful tennis career was a temporary substitute for true joy and peace which can never be found in temporal things. It was only after I graduated and started working that I began to see my need for something deeper. I was invited to a Bible Study and as I began to study God's deep and infallible Word, my life began to change. I began to understand for the first time that the Bible was not just a collection of stories but a deep and rich narrative about the life, work, and sacrifice of Jesus Christ. I understood this story has incredible meaning for my life as well and I was never the same. To understand that the God of the Universe loved me and wanted a relationship with me made me eager to take myself off the throne so that He could take His rightful place there.

If you do have a personal relationship with Christ, have you given Him his rightful place on the throne?

Cynthia Knowles
Texas Christian University Women's Tennis
1978-1982

58

February 26

"So we do not lose heart... For this light momentary affliction is preparing for us an eternal weight of glory beyond all comparison, as we look not to the things that are seen but to the things that are unseen. For the things that are seen are transient but the things that are unseen are eternal."
-2 Corinthians 4:16-18 ESV

As athletes, we are not strangers to the on-field hardship and trials that our sport brings. Everyone has dealt with injury, difficult losing seasons, or not starting when we felt we should. Many of us have learned how to lean on God while navigating those difficulties. But what happens when life brings severe difficulties off the field?

Many of you have already had experiences like this, and some of you will in the future. For me it was a serious bout with anxiety and mental health. For you it may be something different.

Whatever trials come your way, God is always bigger. I constantly reminded myself that my struggle was only a "light momentary affliction" in comparison to the eternal Joy that only God provides through his Son, Jesus Christ.

It may be harder to process and deal with these hardships when you have workouts, class, study hall and then practice filling your schedule every day. In the darkness, we must always remember that our current hardship pales in comparison to the love, protection and glory that God has for us.

Remember that God is good and that today's hardships will hardly compare to the future eternal Joy that He provides.

Cleveland McCarty
Colorado University Men's Lacrosse
2016-2021

59

February 27

"My help comes from the LORD, who made heaven and earth. He will not allow your foot to be moved; He who keeps you will not slumber. Behold, He who keeps Israel shall neither slumber nor sleep." -Psalm 121: 2-4 NKJV

October 5, 2014, is a day I will never forget. I was playing with the Tennessee Titans in a Sunday afternoon game against the Cleveland Browns. I got injured on a play and was helped off the field to the locker room, where I learned that I had ruptured my right Achilles tendon. As I sat in the training room, I heard a voice say, "Your career is over." I began to sob. I had played football for so long. It wasn't the only thing I knew, but it was a place where I greatly excelled. I kept asking God "Why?"

It wasn't until after surgery and completing rehab that I realized God wanted my full attention; that He wanted my identity to be in Him and not in being an NFL football player. That wasn't something I immediately wanted to embrace. But after many tears, prayers and conversations, I have finally come to terms with how my career ended (though it's not like God needed my approval). In accepting what happened and moving forward, I am now able to spend time with my family; watching my children grow and being the husband God called me to be.

God's plan for your life is perfect whether we see it at the time or not. Allow Him to show you where your true purpose is.

Bernard Pollard
Kansas City Chiefs / Houston Texans /
Baltimore Ravens / Tennessee Titans
2006-2014
Super Bowl XLVII Champion

February 28

"So, whether you eat or drink, or whatever you do, do all to the glory of God." -1 Corinthians 10:31 ESV

From a young age, we start comparing ourselves to others. In the world of sports, it becomes almost an obsession. Collegiate athletics is the ultimate peak of comparison. Comparisons crowd our minds and suck the confidence and value out of us. That's what happened to me halfway through my collegiate career. I had let the world of sports define who I was and, to be honest, it was a dark place. The only place I had left to turn was to Jesus and it was the greatest comeback story ever! It is in those moments that the Lord draws near to us more than ever.

We have this innate feeling in each of us to desire something greater than ourselves. The Lord put a "hole" in us that only He has the capability of filling. As athletes, we try to fill that hole with success. Championships, playing time, accolades, etc. The hard truth is that none of those will ever satisfy your soul. The love of the One who created you is the only thing in this lifetime that will bring you peace. When you shift your thinking from ME to HIM, it is truly life changing. There is nothing better than experiencing the love of Jesus Christ. So, hold tight to His promises. Hold fast to what He says about you that is true. And never forget that Jesus Christ is the only thing that will ever satisfy your soul.

Ask the Lord to reveal to you what you are trying to fill that "hole" with. Ask Him to cleanse you of putting other things before Him.

Emily Barnett
Samford University Softball
2017-2021

61

March 1

"He must increase, but I must decrease." – John 3:30 RSV

Being a student-athlete in college, no matter what sport, comes as no surprise a complete challenge, and there's no doubt on my team I faced that challenge daily. Whether it was straining to earn playing time, the respect of coaches, or whatever it was in that season, it is easy to get caught up in focusing solely on ourselves.

The most freeing thing for me in my time as a student-athlete came when I finally realized that it was not about me. It was more than the team I was on, my University, and anything imaginable. Understanding that, as a follower of Christ, my allegiance was to Him, first and foremost. As we see in the Gospel of John, John the Baptist epitomizes this reality perfectly. People from all around look to him as the center piece, but John the Baptist recognized that he was called to be the window to Christ. Daily, we have the choice to be a mirror and reflect our self-centered motivations, or we can choose to be windows to the Heart of Christ in the world. Mirrors to self-righteousness weaken God's message; windows empower His message.

John the Baptist illustrates that just like our athletic skills, this Heart for Christ is not an overnight effort, but instead it is the result of months and years of devotion to the One who gave it all. Everything John the Baptist did pointed to Christ; can you say the same thing about yourself today?

Make a decision today to be a window to Christ's Heart.

James Sherman
Texas State University Football
2014-2018

March 2

"Not only that, but we rejoice in our sufferings, knowing that suffering produces endurance and endurance produces character, and character produces hope, and hope does not put us to shame, because God's love has been poured into our hearts through the Holy Spirit who has been given to us.
– Romans 5:3-5 ESV

Playing college volleyball: That was always the dream. But when it finally became a reality, the "honeymoon phase" of it all quickly faded away. I stretched myself so thin between my sport, academics, friends and family, and just life in general that I found myself so miserable. I knew playing professionally was not an option for me so then why was I voluntarily putting myself through all this work? I began to question what God was doing and why He allowed me to suffer like this.

It wasn't until recently that I looked back at that girl I was three years ago and the person I am today. The Lord used all of those trials to mold me just how He wanted me. The late nights, early mornings, sore muscles, blood, sweat and tears weren't for nothing. He gave me a firm foundation to build the rest of my life on. He wrote that chapter of my life better than I ever could and for that, I am eternally grateful.

Trust this chapter of your life because you know the Author. He has you exactly where He wants you.

Ashtynne Alberts
Clemson University Women's Volleyball
2018-2020

63

March 3

"Let not the wise man boast in his wisdom, let not the mighty man boast in his might, let not the rich man boast in his riches, but let him who boasts boast in this, that he understands and knows me, that I am the Lord who practices steadfast love, justice, and righteousness in the earth. For in these things I delight, declares the Lord."
- Jeremiah 9:23-24

Ultimately, our lives hinge on the ability to make right choices and decisions. By God's grace, I made the most important decision a person can ever make. I invited Jesus Christ to be the Lord of my life and made a commitment to follow Him. It hasn't been easy. In fact, He challenges us that the Christian journey is filled with things like suffering, disappointment, and, at times, even persecution. However, His promise is trustworthy…. That He will not leave us to face this life alone. There is hope, redemption, and joy in a life with Christ.

My personal journey has been one of ups and downs. I've tasted both the sweetness of being a professional athlete, and the bitterness of growing up with trauma and tribulation. God has been ever-present in both places. He has taught me that my identity neither lies in successes nor failures, but in the fact that I am a child of the living God! There is so much peace in surrendering to a God who cares about every detail of my life.

What are you defined by? Is it some sport statistic or athletic achievement, or is it the way you love God and others?

R.A. Dickey
15yr MLB Veteran
2001-2017
2012 Cy Young Winner

March 4

"Rejoice in the Lord always; again I will say, rejoice."
-Philippians 4:4 ESV

Circumstances in this world shift constantly. I could always count on every season and offseason having highs, lows, and the mundane, daily routine. For me, nothing was better than practice with my teammates on a beautiful fall day or competing under the lights in front of a home crowd. Few things were harder than daily early-morning offseason workouts or battling for playing time. There is a lot of encouragement in Scripture I sought in those moments, and Paul's letter to the Philippians is one of my favorites. I have always been struck by the number of times Paul encourages his readers to rejoice. By challenging his readers to rejoice in the Lord always, Paul is claiming that, in the Lord, there is *always* a reason to rejoice.

One of the most freeing seasons in my time as a collegiate athlete was when the Lord prompted me to situate my circumstances within the larger picture of His redemptive work. With this perspective, I was able to live, train, and play with joy as my circumstances dwindled in the presence of who God is and what He has done. Jesus Christ has made me His own and in that I can always rejoice—no matter the circumstance. As a follower of Christ with the incredible opportunity to be an athlete, practice rejoicing in the Lord always. The more you make that *choice*, the more you will draw closer to the One in whom we can always rejoice.

Jesus Christ has made you His own, and in this you can always rejoice. How can you *choose* to rejoice in the Lord every day?

Virginia Poe
Furman University Women's Soccer
2015-2018

March 5

"I have told you all this so that you may have peace in me. Here on earth you will have many trials and sorrows. But take heart, because I have overcome the world." -John 16:33 NLT

The difference between successful athletes and unsuccessful athletes is the space between both ears. The game is 90% mental. That space dictates your talent, and brothers and sisters that is an enormous mountain to overcome on our own. During my first season of college softball, I was in my head about everything. Overthinking the game I love, becoming terrified to put my cleats on and walk up to the plate because I was so afraid of failure. Dry of confidence, God led me to John 16:33.

In this life, we WILL have trials and sorrows; mountains that we cannot move. But when Jesus tells us to "take heart", He's telling us to have courage, confidence, and trust that He has conquered it all. Our Lord is within us, changing our fears into faith, so why be in your head at all?

Rather than say, "God, look how big my mountain is", we confidentially revert to "Mountain, look how big my God is!" So, get out of your head, take heart that Christ Jesus is within you, He goes before you, He has been where you are, and He has overcome it all. He knows that space between both ears, and He has given you all the confidence and strength you require to be successful in your sport.

I challenge you today to let Jesus into your mind. What mental mountain can He overcome for you?

Amanda Fleming
Furman University Softball
2017-2021

66

March 6

"Therefore I take pleasure in infirmities, in reproaches, in needs, in persecutions, in distresses, for Christ's sake. For when I am weak, then I am strong." - 2 Corinthians 12:10 NKJV

Taking pleasure in hardship like the Lord commands is something I strive for every day. I had just begun my soccer career at the age of four, and already knew that I was in love with the game when I started showing signs of a serious illness. At age five, the doctors diagnosed me with graves disease (hyperthyroidism). This autoimmune condition put my faith to the test, not only in my day-to-day life, but also tested me in my sport. The symptoms of migraines, bloody noses, vomiting, increased heart rate, and more, made it difficult to perform at my highest level all of the time.

Why would God do this to me? How could He allow me to suffer like this? I often let the mountain of my pain allow me to doubt God's goodness. But how wrong was I! Through my illness, I was able to see God's hand of control in every aspect of my life, especially my sport and love for soccer. Christ uses us at our weakest, because it is in those times when our faith is put to the test. But it was when I was at my lowest, weakest points that God's presence was with me more than ever.

Spend a moment to reflect and to thank our Lord for the trials you have endured or are enduring presently. God promises you His presence and will use them for good.

Maggie Lacey
University of Oregon Women's Soccer
2019-2023

67

March 7

"And Asa cried to the Lord his God, 'O Lord, there is none like you to help, between the mighty and the weak. Help us, O Lord our God, for we rely on you, and in your name we have come against this multitude.'"- 2 Chronicles 14:11 ESV

It is easy to praise God in our best moments, but many times we fail to do so during our trials. Although the Lord gave King Asa victory and peace for over thirty years, Asa still struggled to trust in God. When King Baasha of Israel attacked the Kingdom of Judah, Asa chose to trust in himself by devising his own plan rather than trusting in God to overcome his challenge, which led to defeat.

During my time at Austin Peay, I trusted that God was in full control of my career and would bring success my way. My sophomore and junior seasons, I tore my MCL and had a hernia causing me to miss the majority of these seasons. During this time, I became obsessed with making myself stronger so that I could avoid injuries. I no longer prayed over my health or my career, because I thought that I could handle it myself. The first game of the following season I completely tore my ACL, ending my season. This opened my eyes back to trusting in God and he allowed me to fully recover and have the best season of my career for my senior season. I learned a valuable lesson that it is foolish to lean on my own understanding. Adversity will always strike, but we must remember that God strengthens those who are fully committed to Him.

How often have we praised God in our best moments, but tried to do everything on our own in our lowest moments?

Shaun Whittinghill
Austin Peay State University Football
2015-2019

68

March 8

"Everyone then who hears these words of mine and does them will be like a wise man who built his house on the rock. And the rain fell, and the floods came, and the winds blew and beat on that house, but it did not fall, because it had been founded on the rock. And everyone who hears these words of mine and does not do them will be like a foolish man who built his house on the sand. And the rain fell, and the floods came, and the winds blew and beat against that house, and it fell, and great was the fall of it." - Matthew 7:24-27 ESV

My career was not smooth sailing. I had a tough injury during my recruiting years in high school. During my junior season in college we won just 3 games. My second season professionally my team was nearly relegated. I spent time on the bench during another season. The list goes on!

We can be tempted to think that walking with the Lord means only good things will happen to us. Then when we come face to face with difficulties in our sport, we can get crippled with the question, "Why me?"

This parable reminds us of the truth. In both stories the circumstances do not change: the rain falls, the floods come, and the wind blows. All of us will face struggles in our career, but as believers, we have a foundation that will keep us strong and unwavering. Not only that, God has a habit of using storms to strengthen our faith and for His good.

What is your foundation? What storms have you seen the Lord bring you through already?

Jennifer Ludemann
University of North Carolina Wilmington Women's Soccer
2009-2012

69

March 9

"Come to me, all you who are weary and burdened, and I will give you rest. Take my yoke upon you and learn from me, for I am gentle and humble in heart, and you will find rest for your souls. For my yoke is easy and my burden is light." - Matthew 11:28-30 NIV

As athletes, we know that it takes a lot of hard work to be good at our craft. We know that it requires countless hours of training and preparation just for one game. In soccer, most professional teams train 450min (5 days x 90min) to every one, 90min game!

Some days, it is a grind and it feels like we are trudging through the mud. It can feel like we are striving aimlessly in order to perform. It can feel like, no matter how hard we work, we will never be good enough for the standard.

In these times, Jesus offers reprieve. In the same way that He offered rest to the towns of Galilee in Matthew's Gospel, He offers rest to us. He doesn't give us a step-by-step guide to restore us when we are tired, He simply offers Himself. Jesus is the solution. Period. What source are we going to when we are weary?

We do not need to wrestle and toil in order to find peace. Jesus is the Prince of Peace. He is our Wonderful Counselor. He is our Rock and our Salvation. In sport or in life, when we are feeling burdened, we know that we need only to turn to our Savior for rest.

Jesus is the solution. Period. What source are we going to when we are weary?

Samantha Hope
University of North Carolina Charlotte Women's Soccer
2007-2011

"Henceforth I call you not servants; for the servant knoweth not what his lord doeth: but I have called you friends; for all the things that I have heard of my father I have made known unto you. Ye have not chosen me, but I have chosen you, and ordained you that ye should go forth and bring forth fruit, and that your fruit should remain: that whatsoever ye shall ask of the Father in my name, he may give it you." -John 15:15-16 KJV

Jesus chooses us as friends here. He specifically calls us out and reminds us that He chooses us. Jesus, the King, calls us His friend. That is difficult to comprehend. The Lord used this verse to make Himself known to me. I played overseas in Sweden for two years after college and for the first time in my life, I was not around fellow believers. I had taken my community for granted without knowing it. When I was finally alone in my faith, I realized how special my community was. I am so thankful for team environments that illustrated the meaning of friendships in such a powerful way. The battles, the early practices, the adversity, and the shared goals link teammates together so quickly and powerfully. In this verse, Jesus not only chooses a sinner like me to be His friend, but also reveals the importance of community. Ultimately, when the final whistle blows the only thing that remains is the relationships that were built. No one cares about the stats.

Jesus chose you as a friend. Have you accepted His desire for relationship?
You know all of your best friend's stories. Do you know His?

Carrie Maxwell
University of North Carolina Charlotte Women's Soccer
2009-2013

71

March 11

"Have I not commanded you? Be strong and courageous. Do not be afraid; do not be discouraged, for the Lord your God will be with you wherever you go." -Joshua 1:9 NIV

When I accepted Christ my sophomore year of college, I wasn't really sure what that was supposed to look like. I had always relied on myself for answers to my own life, and now I was being called to submit to God's plan for my life. I was struggling in my sport, which led to my grades falling, and my decision making to become irresponsible. It wasn't until I finally hit rock bottom that I realized that a change was needed. I decided to finally go all in and submit to God, as I had promised so many times before. I read my Bible and prayed daily. Not for the results that I desired, but for a heart of faith and obedience. I wish I could say that I was not filled with fear taking this step in my relationship with God, but I knew that someone had to give, and it wouldn't be Him.

With time, I became a better teammate, friend, and brother in Christ to everyone around me. Doors were opened for me that I couldn't have imagined for myself, and although I love the memories from my playing career, the impact I'm blessed to have on others today as a coach is what I'm most proud of. I put away my pride and fear of what was to come, and trusted God's plan over my life. I've done nothing but try and remain faithfully obedient to Him, and He has continued to bless me through the calm and the storm.

Get real with God and pray that He would reveal the areas in your life that are preventing you from going all in with Him.

Adam McGuire
Texas Lutheran University Football
2011-2015

72

March 12

"Yet the Lord longs to be gracious to you; therefore, he will rise up to show you compassion. For the Lord is a God of justice. Blessed are all who wait for him!" -Isaiah 30:18 NIV

Injury is a subject focused on often when it comes to athletes and their faith, but it can be the most important. I came across this verse while praying after a broken foot took away my senior year of high school basketball. I had been working hard to earn a scholarship and felt God had taken away the path He had laid before me. But God's plans are far greater than our own. We say we know this and understand it, yet it is hard to practice. Once I came across this verse, I told Him I would let His will be done. I let go of the anger and frustration I was holding in my heart against Him and just worshiped Him.

Three months later, I decided to practice my faith in Him. I had a doctor's appointment for an x-ray taken three days prior. I felt as though God spoke to me, telling me it was time to bring my shoes with me as I had practice right after. The doctor told me the bone had healed. I looked at my parents, told them about the shoes, and there gained my lifelong testimony that I've carried throughout my collegiate and professional career. God had a plan to give me a way to share His word with the rest of the world through the sport I loved.

Take time to sit quietly and tell the Lord you will practice patience and wait on His plans for you.

Zachary Hankins
Ferris State University/Xavier University Men's Basketball
2014-2019

March 13

"My sheep hear my voice and I know them, and they follow me." -John 10:27 NIV

The Creator of the Universe, who made the stars align and the sun rise every day, wants to speak to you. Let that sink in. The Lord wants to have conversations with you, in the morning, throughout the day, after practice. As an athlete, you have a lot on your plate, but just like talking to your teammate or best friend, talking to Jesus can be that conversation in which you talk then listen, talk then listen. The Lord has so much to say to us and in a world full of voices vying for our attention, it takes consistency and focus to tune the world out and hear His still, small voice.

As an athlete and coach, I know the struggles and joys that athletes face. There are so many ups and downs through wins, losses, injuries, healing and more. Sometimes you feel alone and feel like you have no one to turn to or you don't know your next step to take. Talk to the Lord. He is always there and will guide you to take your next steps throughout your life, giving you wisdom and peace. Spending time with Jesus will help us tune out the confusion that we so often face in our lives as we try to make decisions, and in turn, He will bring direction and peace. The Lord is so patient and loving and wants to have conversations with you throughout your day. Get to know Him and He will open doors and bring you peace, joy and beautiful surprises to your life!

Lord, I want to hear Your voice. Speak to me, Father. What do you want to tell me today?

Becky Audi Easton
University of Connecticut / Clemson Volleyball
1992-1993

March 14

"In his grace, God has given us different gifts for doing certain things well. So if God has given you the ability to prophesy, speak out with as much faith as God has given you. If your gift is serving others, serve them well. If you are a teacher, teach well."
- Romans 12: 6-7 NLT

All throughout life, we hear about what different people are good at and what they are not. Whether it be sports, academics, music, or whatever the case may be, many people would refer to these "talents" as their "spiritual gifts". Growing up I had always heard that playing sports was a spiritual gift that God had blessed me with. But the struggle that I've had for my entire career was trying to figure out a way for me to give thanks to The Lord for blessing me with these talents. Of course, prayer and telling the Lord thank you over and over is a way of giving thanks, but I was searching for something more.

What I found out through Scripture, was that with the gifts that God gives us, we give thanks by using our gifts to their fullest potential. I learned that fulfilling our spiritual gifts did not mean performing "well" on the field or court stats-wise, but it means that we perform to the best of our ability and give glory to The Lord with our performance whether it be good or bad.

When you step off the field or court, no matter the outcome of your performance, give thanks to The Lord for your ability/opportunity to play your sport and give Him glory.

Jeremiah Boyd
Arizona Diamondbacks Organization
2023-Present

March 15

"Jesus answered, 'You don't understand now what I'm doing, but it will be clear enough to you later.'" - John 13:7 MSG

My freshman year of college I had to redshirt because there was a problem with my academic records. I was told that if I wanted to play Division I, I will only have three seasons. That freshman year wasn't easy, because even though I was part of the team, I was not allowed to travel, sit on the bench, or play with the team. I was only allowed to practice. Things got better my sophomore and junior year where I got to enjoy two seasons. My senior year came, and I had a season-ending injury (broke my fibula). I was devastated and I did not understand why that would happen to me. Why would I only be able to play two of the four seasons? I started praying a lot and started understanding that God is good and faithful, and His plans are greater than what we can imagine. I relied on Jesus like never before and trusted His plans. From that moment amazing things happened to me. I was granted a medical redshirt and was given another year of soccer. I found the perfect school to start my master's and play soccer, in the same city where my now fiancée lives. At that time, I was supposed to play only one more season, however, since no situation is too big for God, I ended up having two more seasons to play at my new school. God is so faithful.

I challenge you to draw closer and trust God even more during difficult times.

Pamela Peñaloza Pardo
East Tennessee State University Women's Soccer
2015-2021

"This is the confidence we have in approaching God: that if we ask anything according to His will, He hears us."
- 1 John 5:14 NIV

It's easy to believe that God isn't listening to our prayers when our prayers seemingly go unanswered. Early in college, I faced multiple injuries that left me disheartened and unable to play. I was consistent in my prayers, praying for healing and strength to get back on the court. However, I continued to hit road blocks in my rehab, pushing my return to play date further away. I was frustrated with God. I was faithful in my prayers and putting in the work to heal, but my physical wounds weren't healing. Eventually, my mindset and my prayers changed. Instead of praying for physical healing to put me back in a space that I once was, I prayed for emotional healing to help me be the best servant in the space I was currently in.

I was so resentful that my selfish prayers weren't being answered, I forgot that my purpose is to further the Kingdom of God. By not answering my self-serving prayers, God reminded me of that purpose. Instead of listening to the words of my prayers, He listened to my heart and gave me what He knew I needed most. Once I was healed emotionally and spiritually, the physical healing came as well.

Take time to reflect on your prayers. Are you praying with selfish intent? Or are you praying in a way that will further your relationships and the Kingdom?

Allye Beth Deaton
Texas Christian University Volleyball
2017-2019

March 17

"Consider it pure joy, my brothers and sisters, whenever you face trials of many kinds, because you know that the testing of your faith produces perseverance. Let perseverance finish its work so that you may be mature and complete, not lacking anything." -James 1:2-4

When I played my first college match at the University of Missouri, I felt a high of adrenaline that could not be matched. I was on top of the world, and full of personal pride. After transferring to Clemson, I was quickly humbled. Through team strife and two major knee surgeries, it was easy to feel demoralized. I quickly learned how painful it could be to make a sport your idol. For 3 years, I prayed and prayed for change and for deliverance from my problems, but it did not end up that simple. Through the struggles I faced, I gained endurance that I would have never understood in the moments that I cried out for help. I didn't understand it until my senior year of college, where I was able to lead with resilience and God-given endurance. I think that when we are enduring something, we forget the God-given joy that we can have in those situations when we draw near to Him. Situations that the enemy attempts break our faith with, can be turned into divine encounters when we lay our struggles at the foot of the cross. This life is hard, and with a world that idolizes perfection, we must take heart and know that our Savior has already conquered the world. The same God of the universe wants to use your situation to produce a God given endurance that *no one* can take away.

How can your trials produce endurance in your life? How can you use this endurance to serve others around you?

Tate Schroeder
Clemson University Women's Tennis
2016-2021

78

March 18

"For where you have envy and selfish ambition, there you find disorder and every evil practice." – James 3:16

My heart pounds heavily in response to my nerves as I watch my best friend take her final high jump attempt. I breathe deep as she begins her approach, gaining speed while getting closer to the bar. With the world moving in slow motion and the environment silently anticipating, she jumps, clearing the bar. The crowd cheers with happiness for her accomplishment, while my feelings quickly change from heart pounding nerves to heart crushing defeat and utter bitterness knowing that my best friend just broke my high jump record.

During my high school years, I was infected by the poisons of jealousy. This poison pierced the roots of my emotion, my *why*, and my relationships. I became encompassed by the desires of wanting what others had, particularly what my best friend had, that I lost sight of what I was given. I felt betrayed, that God loved her more, and that nothing I had was good enough. I grew to hate track because of it. It was years before I realized I was breaking God's heart by focusing on the things I didn't have, and it wasn't until I shifted my perspective to the things God blessed me with, that I found peace. God created **you** as He desires **you** for a special purpose. You know what's cool? God is jealous too. He seeks **you**. Our God is jealous for our heart; in return, we should only be jealous for His.

When I feel overwhelming jealousy, I list everything God has blessed me with. I challenge you to do the same.

Emma Arblaster
Liberty University Women's Track and Field
2018-2022

March 19

"Then the Lord asked Moses, "Who makes a person's mouth?
Who decides whether people speak or do not speak, hear or do not
hear, see or do not see? Is it not I, the Lord? Now go! I will be with
you as you speak, and I will instruct you in what to say!"
          -Exodus 4:11-12 NIV

For much of my career as an athlete, I had always been told I
wasn't big enough to play college football. It was always my dream to
play for Clemson University under Coach Swinney. However, much
like Moses before he led the Israelites out of Egypt, I began to believe
the lie that I wasn't big enough or talented enough to do what God
was calling me to. Over time, it became clear to me that the Lord
gives us exactly what we need in order to succeed where He wants us
to succeed. I began to transform my way of thinking. Later that year,
Coach Swinney gave me an offer as a preferred walk-on. Since then, I
have been moved from a walk-on to a full scholarship athlete.
In life, we will have many opportunities to listen to many different
voices around us. If I would have listened to man's voice, I would
have never believed in myself or that I was "enough" to chase my
dream. When I started listening to who God said that I was, that I am
more than enough and worth dying for, then I began to believe that
there was nothing that I couldn't do. What we choose to listen to will
determine our activity and productivity in life.

Begin listening to who the Author and Maker of your life says that
you are, and make sure that your habits are aligned with turning
your dream into a reality.

                                          Will Brown
                              Clemson University Football
                                          2017-2021

"But seek first the kingdom of God and His righteousness, and all these things shall be added to you." - Matthew 6:33 NKJV

Have you ever felt like your priorities were out of whack? Like something is off, and you can feel it. My sophomore year of college I was sitting in my room, wondering why I was so miserable. I had spent most days crying, frustrated with myself, with softball and life. It felt like an endless cycle of practice, school, practice, and no matter what I did, I couldn't figure out how to change it. Exhausted and tired of feeling this way, I finally stopped and asked the Lord for help. In His kindness He pointed me to this verse, and showed me how I had been so focused on school and softball, I had forgotten about Him.

As an athlete, it's easy to feel overwhelmed and consumed by your daily schedule. To constantly be focused on everything going on around you and put God on the backburner. But putting God first allows Him to take care of everything else. Once I began to seek God first in my life again, everything else fell into place. I was no longer miserable or stressed about school or softball, in fact I was doing better in both. God in His goodness, knows everything that we need, and when we seek Him first, we allow Him to take care of the rest.

Take a moment and ask the Lord what you're seeking first in your life currently. If it's not the Lord, ask Him to show you ways you can put Him first again.

Allison Kotlar
University of Dallas Softball
2013-2017

March 21

"Whatever you do in word or deed, do everything in the name of the Lord Jesus, giving thanks through Him to God the Father."
-Colossians 3:17 NASB

As a high school football player attempting to follow Christ, I did not understand how Christianity impacted me as a football player. I wasn't actively trying to look like the world, but I wasn't seeking how I could follow God as a Christian athlete.

As my college football career began, The Lord taught me about surrendering all aspects of my life. I learned about how my sole identity was founded in Christ - and from this arose me as a football player. As I began attempting to practice obedience in these areas, Jesus showed me that it wasn't just legalistic external conformity He is after, but there is actually far more joy to be had when we do things God's way. Jesus is intimately concerned with the posture of our heart and wants to give you far more joy!

We can worship Jesus by encouraging teammates during a lift (Hebrews 10:24). We can consistently do the little things right (Luke 16:10). We can have supernatural joy because The Lord is our strength (Nehemiah 8:10)! We can represent Jesus by engaging mentally during film sessions (Matthew 22:37). Every moment we have is an opportunity to worship the Lord (Romans 12:1) and find abundant joy in Jesus (John 10:10).

Your identity as a Christian should define all aspects of your life. Take a moment and identify activities when your focus is not on Christ. Pray for a heart that will be centered on Jesus during these activities and for wisdom on how to apply that focus.

Tim Yoder
University of Texas Football
2015-2018

March 22

"For we walk by faith, not by sight." - 2 Corinthians 5:7 ESV

Life may present itself with a lot of challenges and obstacles that one may not have expected to happen. Tough times may emerge in life that may leave one asking God the question, 'Why me?' But sometimes we may be viewing other people's life and assume that others are faring well and having a perfect life. We may tempted to compare ourselves to others thinking that they have a better life compared to ours.

My senior season was cut short by a broken fibula and multiple torn ankle ligaments. Just when everything was going great, I was playing the best football of my career, and right when I was preparing to leave for the NFL. The direction of my career was uncertain, and the direction of my life was uncertain because football more or less was my life. Filled with every emotion from anger and frustration to depression. I took a step back, and reminded myself, *For we walk by faith, not by sight.* (2 Corinthians 5:7).

Walking by faith means living a life focusing on the things not seen by our human eyes but focusing on the promises of God in our lives. Therefore, instead of complaining or being anxious, we should just trust God having this confidence that He is faithful to deliver us from any situation we are in. This conviction has helped shape my life from there on out.

Take a step back, and try not to look at everything from a physical perspective. Try and think/find your inner conviction in the word, allowing you to grow and become stronger day by day.

Cody Thompson
Seattle Seahawks
2019-Present

83

"For it is by grace you have been saved, through faith – and this is not from yourselves, it is the gift of God – not by works, so that no one can boast. For we are God's handiwork, created in Christ Jesus to do good works, which God prepared for us to do."
– Ephesians 2: 8-10 NIV

For athletes, the sport we play can easily become our identity. The passion and continuous drive to succeed and advance one's career as far as we can, can consume us. For most of my career and/or life I was the "baseball guy". All my focus and determination was set to become the best ball player that I could be, with one goal in mind-become a Major League Baseball player. In 2014, my dream was achieved by being drafted and as I started this new journey, the gratification that I thought I would receive once getting there was underwhelming. I always felt that once I achieved this goal, I could then start to use it to be a better Christian.

As the verse explains God doesn't care about our worldly "works" or "boasts" from sports because ultimately He blessed us with His grace long ago. Jesus knew the satisfaction I desired would never be fulfilled by the amount of work, achievement or success here on Earth. Only by God's gift, His grace, will our inner desire be filled. I felt comfort knowing that my identity was no longer in sports but in being a son of God so carefully prepared by Him.

Reflect on this verse, are you seeking worldly desires for satisfaction? Give thanks to God for His grace.

Seth Harrison
San Francisco Giants
2014-2016

March 24

"Therefore I remind you to stir up the gift of God which is in you through the laying on of my hands. For God has not given us a spirit of fear, but of power and of love and of a sound mind."
– 2 Timothy 1:6-7 NKJV

There are going to be times in life where your faith will be tested. Sometimes we feel like winners, sometimes we feel like failures. When things get tough, remember all of the people God has placed in your life that have poured into you, mentored you, loved you, cared for you, and have put their arms around you.

There is a gift that God has placed in each of us. It's easy to get discouraged after using our gifts and not getting the outcomes we are looking for. Stirring up the gift means to kindle afresh, to fan a flame, to start from a fresh beginning. Jesus Christ died, yet was raised by the Spirit of God that dwells in us today.

Stir up the gift of God that is in you, because <u>your family</u> needs your gift. Stir up the gift of God that is in you, because <u>your team</u> needs your gift. Stir up the gift of God that is in you, because <u>the world</u> needs your gift.

Austin Medley
Villanova University Football
2010-2014

85

March 25

"Cast all your anxiety on him because he cares for you."
-1 Peter 5:7 NIV

One thing I've always longed for, both in and out of the gym, is to be loved and accepted. For years I placed all of my self-worth on whether or not a coach or a judge was satisfied with my performance. I thought that there was no way I could love and accept myself if others didn't love and accept me first, and how could anyone love and accept me if I wasn't performing to my potential as an athlete? More often than not, the love we receive from others is conditional. Any coach or teammate is going to love you if you're contributing points to the team. Anybody can deal with you when you're happy and confident and everything is going perfectly in your life.

The question is: who cares just as much about you when you are struggling as they do when you are succeeding? I don't just mean giving you the standard "everything will be okay" speech. Who in your life truly cares enough to actually listen with no judgement when you are struggling? The answer is God. I have learned that it doesn't matter how seemingly small your problems seem to others. If they matter to you, they matter. God doesn't care whether I score a perfect 10 or if I'm cheering on my team from the sidelines; He cares about my happiness and well-being.

God doesn't just love you when you're at the top of your game, He truly *cares* about you as a person. I challenge you to take just a couple of minutes today to fully open your heart to God and witness the freedom and healing He can bring to you.

Marissa Oakley
University of Georgia Gymnastics
2018-2021

86

"May God be gracious to us and bless us and make his face shine on us—so that your ways may be known on earth, your salvation among all nations." -Psalm 67:1-2

As a student athlete I was so self-centered. I had grown up in church, but I certainly didn't have a relationship with Christ. Occasionally I would pray asking Jesus for some sort of fortune in sports. "Give me playing time this year," was my prayer in college football. I thought I could manipulate God into giving me what I wanted. My vision for my life was too small.

A lot of Christians see Psalm 67 and stop at verse 1. God wants something so much bigger for our lives. If you have accepted God's free gift of salvation through Christ, He not only wants to bless you, He wants to use you. Verse 2 starts, "so that....". The Psalmist prays that God would bless Israel *so that* God would be known in all the earth. He wants to bless you *so that* He would be made famous through your life to a broken world. He wants to be gracious to you *so that* your faith would be irresistible to people. God wants to give you purpose.

God has given me a purpose bigger than I could have ever imagined. I have lived in East Asia now for two years and have had the opportunity to see God's heart for a lost people that does not know Him. That is our *"so that."*

God wants to invite you into His story of redeeming the whole world to Himself. What does that look like with your sport/team?

Carl Stephens
Texas Christian University Football
2012-2013

March 27

"Restore to me the joy of your salvation, and uphold me with a willing spirit." - Psalm 51:12 ESV

I used to have the idea that believing in Jesus and growing closer to him was a linear process. All I had to do was obey God and do things that made Him happy. If I did that, I thought that I would always feel joyful in my relationship with Jesus, that I would never make the same mistake twice, that I would grow closer to Jesus every single day without fail.

A few years and a lot of failure showed me that this couldn't be further from the truth. There are going to be days when you are walking closely with Jesus, feeling his presence, and wanting what God wants, finding your joy in him. Other days, there's nothing there– you're going to fail and fall into sin, and reading the Bible will feel like eating cardboard. This is not abnormal–it's real life, and it's discouraging. But knowing God is not a clean, linear process. I lose joy in my salvation more than I'd like to admit. But God does not leave it all up to me. He gives me strength to follow Him. He restores my joy in Him. He reminds me of what He did through Christ to save me from my sin. He gives real, tangible, life-changing joy on tough days and good days. We can rest in the fact that crying out to God for restoration is not a sign of weakness, but an essential part of following Him.

God doesn't expect you to sustain yourself, because He wants you to find joy and endurance in Him.

Mitchell B. Tyler
Yale University Football
2020-2023

March 28

"In view of all this, make every effort to respond to God's promises. Supplement your faith with a generous provision of moral excellence, and moral excellence with knowledge, and knowledge with self-control, and self-control with patient endurance, and patient endurance with godliness, and godliness with brotherly affection, and brotherly affection with love for everyone. The more you grow like this, the more productive and useful you will be in your knowledge of our Lord Jesus Christ." - 2 Peter 1:5-8 NLT

There are several qualities often found in the most productive athletes within a particular sport: strength, speed, skill, etc. Unless you're born with certain genetic gifts and abilities, a lot of time and effort are required in order to develop these qualities.

I learned the same to be true in my relationship with God. The qualities mentioned in 2 Peter 1 aren't acquired through our own strength, talents, or earthly success. Rather, they're a result of our *response* to God's promise of eternal life through our Lord, Jesus Christ – His life, death, and resurrection.

"Moral excellence", "patience", and "godliness" are all qualities only God can provide. Like strength and skill, they must be developed over time as we walk with Him daily (through prayer, scripture, fellowshipping with other believers, and sharing our faith). God has called you for a great purpose in His Kingdom (His team). Remember, He's not looking for your perfection, but for your humble *response.*

Which of the qualities in 2 Peter 1 stand out to you the most?

Khalil Lee, PhD
Troy University Football
2008-2009

89

March 29

"My son, despise not the chastening of the Lord; neither be weary of his correction: For whom the Lord loves He corrects, just as a father the son in whom he delights." -Proverbs 3:11-12 KJV

The Greek word for "weary" translated here can mean grieved. As a collegiate athlete, I played football for the University of Wisconsin. Throughout my collegiate career, I received five surgeries and two infections, one that almost even killed me. It was challenging to clothe, feed, and even walk myself. Those were some of the most humbling times no doubt. Yet, it was here where God exposed me the most to Himself.

Over time, I learned that God was refining me; purifying me by the tribulations of life. I heard about the character of God, but it was here where I experienced Him. I learned that He was burning the weeds in my heart that weren't conducive to the seed of Jesus Christ planted in my heart. It postured me to depend on Him intimately in ways I had never known. He revealed to me sin I had masked and nurtured. Previously, I had known Him as just God, but since, I have come to know and experience Him as a loving Father due to His grace and mercies.

When you're grieved from life's tribulations, choose to reflect on God's character through His word. Ask yourself how God, as a Father, is revealing more of Himself to you.

D'Cota Dixon
University of Wisconsin Football
2014-2018

March 30

"Do not conform to the pattern of this world, but be transformed by the renewing of your mind. Then you will be able to test and approve what God's will is – His good, pleasing, and perfect will." -Romans 12:2 NIV

When I started my freshman year, I placed all of my focus on acclimating myself to a new environment and being accepted onto a new team. Excellence was being demanded from all areas and I worked hard to please the people surrounding me. While these people undoubtedly had my best interest in mind, I fell short of making sure that I was pleasing the One whose opinion was most important.

I spent all of my time and energy working towards making good grades and earning a playing position my freshman year. Early into the season, my coaches decided to redshirt me. While at the time it seemed like a tragedy, I now know that God was giving me exactly what I needed – undivided time to spend focused on my relationship with Him. It was through this process and many nights of prayer that I came to realize that I was answering to the wrong people. God is jealous for our attention and He cares enough about each of us to pull us back towards Him when we continually fall into a routine of pleasing the world. He has allowed me to find peace and rest in Him because He is unchanging and His plan for each of us is always good.

Do you trust that God is jealous of your attention? Where in your life have you been working to please people other than God?

Jaeger S. Bull
Rice University Football
2017-2022

91

March 31

"Therefore, everyone who hears these words of mine and puts them into practice is like a wise man who built his house on the rock. The rain came down, the steams rose and the winds blew and beat against that house; yet it did not fall, because it had its foundation on the rock. But everyone who hears these words of mine and does not put them into practice is like a foolish man who built his house on sand. The rain came down, the steams rose, and the winds blew and beat against that house, and it fell with a great crash."
- Matthew 7:24-27

In the parable of the wise and foolish builders, Jesus starts by addressing "everyone." Jesus then gives us a commandment to put his "words" into practice in our own lives. This is a **commandment,** and not a suggestion or request from the Lord. We live in a world where society and the enemy sell us the lie that we have the ability to develop our own fleshly truths or the ability to create our own moral compass. This parable shows us that building our lives on our fleshly truths and not building on the truths told to us by the Lord is a path to destruction. This parable is simple, convicting, and comforting all at the same time. Build on the rock in all circumstances and you will make it through this life. You may be beaten and battered by the storm, but you will still stand in the end. My prayer is that you would ask the Lord to circumcise your heart and search you for areas of your life that might be built on sand and instead build it on the Rock.

What areas of your life have you substituted the commandments of The Lord with your own fleshly truths?

Kyle Klotz
Belmont University Baseball
2015-2019

April 1

"Oh, the depth of the riches and wisdom and knowledge of God! How unsearchable are his judgments and how inscrutable his ways!" - Romans 11:33 ESV

This scene is one of the most painful in the game of golf. Any competitive golfer knows the feeling. The downward spiral makes even spectators uneasy. The summer after my final year of collegiate golf—and my last competitive golf tournament to date—I was leading the Virginia State Amateur Championship going into the last five holes. Then, the dreadful snap hook into the trees compounded by a double sandy error and three putt took me out of contention in a matter of minutes. And yet, it was one of my most liberating golf moments.

For most of my competitive career, my emotions and the overwhelming urge to quit mid-round controlled me. But those final holes God blessed me with a composure rooted in the unwavering hope found in Jesus Christ that I had never experienced before. I walked off the 18th green to a company of younger players that thanked me for modeling how to lose graciously, and we promptly joined in the celebration of my former roommate's win that catapulted her into her professional career. In the words of John Piper, "God is always doing 10,000 things in your life, and you may be aware of three of them." We have hope in this promise that God's purposes will not be thwarted.

Meditate on these truths then encourage someone else today that we serve a God of infinite wisdom, sovereignty, and love.

Whitney Herr
Virginia Tech's Women's Golf
2015-2018

93

April 2

"Do not grieve, for the joy of the Lord is your strength."
- Nehemiah 8:10 NIV

Think back to your first recreational team. Why did you sign up? Why did your parents drive you to practice every Wednesday night? My first YMCA team was called the Volleychicks, and nine-year-old me signed up because I thought volleyball would be fun.

Fast forward nine years, I am playing collegiate volleyball. I was winning individual conference awards, yet I felt completely empty inside. It felt as if I was simply going through the motions. Volleyball had no more meaning to me, it was simply what I did, how I paid for school, something that brought me pain— emotionally, mentally, and physically. I had lost touch of my why.

I thought back to the famous words my father would tell me whenever I came home from the gym crying, "whenever it isn't fun anymore, it's time to give it up." This made me start praying to enjoy and cherish my time as a student-athlete. I realized we are never promised tomorrow, so my goal for each day and each practice was to have fun and play for God's glory.

Joy is one of the fruits of the spirit. It is within us when we accept Christ as our Savior. The thing about joy is it can be found in everything you do for the Lord. I am three years removed from my sport, and still strive to find this same joy in my day-to-day life. It is so fulfilling and truly a gift from God.

Think about three things that bring you joy. Are you still seeking joy in your sport? If not, how can you get your joy back?

Ashleigh Martin
Texas Christian University Volleyball
2015-2017

94

"But you are a chosen people, a royal priesthood, a holy nation, God's special possession, that you may declare the praises of him who called you out of darkness into his wonderful light."
- *1 Peter 2:9*

"Anna, you've *made* it." I have heard that phrase quite often. According to worldly standards, they are right. I've competed at a Junior Olympic gymnastics level, won numerous state titles, trained under an Olympic coach, double-majored as a Division I, Ivy League athlete, and won four team championships in three years. I should feel on top of the world, right? So, why didn't I?

My collegiate gymnastics career was nothing I thought it would be. I was always coming back from an injury or surgery. I didn't hold individual records and I wasn't racking up event gold medals. My accomplishments never felt 'enough' for my team.

However, I have joyful news for the athlete that feels the pressure to prove: No championship, grade, award, or diploma will ever compare to the freedom, joy, and identity found in Jesus Christ. I've *made* it, not because I competed in college gymnastics, but because my value is solely dependent on who God is and who He says I am. It's not in the dark lies of the world. Though we are competing **in** a world that leaves us unsatisfied; remember we compete **for** a God that has overcome that *same* world. He has, and will continue to, overcome every feeling of not 'enough' we might have.

Write down how you are feeling today. Where are you feeling unfulfilled? How can you allow God to change your mindset?

Anna Jennings
Yale University Gymnastics
2016-2020

April 4

"Rise up; this matter is in your hands. We will support you, so take courage and do it." - Ezra 10:4

I came into college ready to continue my swimming career. I was excited to improve and be a part of an incredible team. Severe injuries came into play upon my arrival, and I have since endured two spinal fusions along with 20 other spinal procedures to keep me as a functional 22-year-old. Countless people told me to quit but I refused. I came here for a purpose and although I had been sidetracked, I rejected the idea of quitting. I just had to find another way to achieve my goals. Through all of this I have found the Lord. My college career was nothing like I planned, but it forced me to take courage, to trust God and most importantly, and to love myself without swimming.

My message to anyone reading this is: take courage and rise above. Break away from this identity you are so consumed with. You are not ONLY an athlete. That person inside you itching to break out is way more powerful than you could ever imagine.

Love others passionately, love yourself, but most importantly love the Lord with all you have. He is your everlasting Father, who has made you to love others and use your platform for His glory. I urge you to love what you do, but never forget who you are.

All the courage we need is already inside of us. We just need to get quiet, stop the fearful, doubting voices, reach down inside ourselves to bring up the courage Jesus has provided through His victories and deposited in us through the Holy Spirit!

Sydney Olsen
Texas Christian University Women's Swimming
2017-2021

April 5

"For we walk by faith, not by sight". - Galatians 5:7

Discipline, time management, hard work, and intense preparation are a few crucial traits needed to survive the rigors of playing basketball in the Ivy League. As an athlete, I always strive to be prepared for all potential scenarios, intensely training my body and mind to execute the game plan well. However, rather than listening to the Lord's plan, I stubbornly move forward with my seemingly perfect ways, even when it clashes with God's divine agenda. Feelings of confusion, hurt, or failure result because my strategy isn't working!

Despite playing four seasons, my college basketball career was certainly not as expected. In addition to coaching changes, I also suffered two major, freak injuries during both my freshman and junior seasons. Along with multiple x-rays, MRIs, nerve tests, and CT scans, I saw several doctors and trainers to diagnose my physical issues. The two injuries left me in constant physical pain, and with feelings of anger, depression, loneliness, and uncertainty of my purpose.

After college, I realized that God had been using my academic pursuits as an outlet to vent emotions and frustrations from basketball. Without knowing it, He was preparing me for something other than a career in sports. Since undergrad, I have earned an M.B.A. and am currently beginning the final year of a doctorate. This was definitely not part of my original agenda, but His plan is perfect and our story is not yet complete.

Trust. His. Plan. Even when we don't understand what is happening, we must firmly believe that God is in control.

Daniel Edwards
Princeton University Men's Basketball
2010-2015

April 6

"God paid a high price for you, so don't be enslaved by the world." -1 Corinthians 7:23 NLT

The simplest way to assess the value of something is to look at the price that was paid for it. As athletes, we tell ourselves that we become more valuable when we perform better and less valuable when we perform worse. We let the term "starter" become a price tag for our lives. During my soccer career, I was constantly evaluating myself. "Did I make enough saves to stand out?" "Was my footwork quicker than hers?" My value was a constant fluctuation tailored to my last performance.

After feeling unsatisfied both on the bench watching my team play and as a starter achieving success, I realized my life needed something more. During my junior year of college, I learned that Jesus came to the earth and performed perfectly. He was tempted to sin and fall short, but He never did. He walked to the cross knowing what He would endure, but He determined that my life was worth it.

Now that my hope is in Jesus, my value is not determined by what I do; it is determined by what Jesus has already done. The price tag on my life no longer changes because Jesus does not change. He bought my life by paying the price of His own and that truth lets me live with the freedom of knowing I am valuable and loved because my Creator has shown me so.

Make a list of ways you might be allowing something or someone other than Jesus define your worth. Pray that God would help you be reminded of how valuable you are in Christ.

Kaitlin Maxwell
Missouri State University Women's Soccer
2016-2021

April 7

"You are the light of the world. A town built on a hill cannot be hidden. Neither do people light a lamp and put it under a bowl. Instead they put it on its stand, and it gives light to everyone in the house. In the same way, let your light shine before others, that they may see your good deeds and glorify your Father in heaven."
-Matthew 5:14-16

The world we live in today glorifies the ability to blend in. But blending in and being a follower of Christ are in direct opposition. Jesus calls His disciples to be a light in a dark world and challenges them to stand out among others because it brings glory to God.

However, if we are honest with ourselves, standing up and shining for Christ can be hard, especially in environments like a college campus. The temptation to live like everyone else and give into the flesh surrounds us all the time and sometimes it is easier to put our light under a bowl. It is in these moments of spiritual warfare that it is important to remember our calling as followers of Christ. We are called to shine, which means prioritizing the word of God, not the culture of this world. Our goal to advance the kingdom must take precedent over everything else, even sports, status, and fleshly desires.

Take some time to reflect and ask yourself if you have been a light for Christ or blending in with the world. Wake up each day and pray for the strength and courage to shine for the God that saves.

Josh Adkins
New Mexico State / University of Texas San Antonio Football
2017-2022

April 8

"But as for you, be strong and do not give up, for your work will be rewarded." – 2 Chronicles 15:7 NIV

As an athlete, injuries are not uncommon. I had many that impacted my ability to compete. Doctors and coaches were not just telling me that it was okay to quit, but many people were even encouraging me to. But I had one coach who told me that injuries were speed bumps, not roadblocks. He encouraged me to keep going to the end. When I finished my senior year, I was competing at my highest level.

Through my struggles with injuries, I learned a lot about not giving up. God used those four years to show me that when struggles come, persevering to the end is worth it. Not just in athletics, but in the bigger pictures of serving Him. Life is not always easy. Jesus tells us that trials will come. There will be times when you want to give up. But as followers of Christ, we know that in the middle of those challenging times God promises to be with us. When we look to Him to be our strength, we see those trials not as roadblocks, but speed bumps. They may slow us down, but they won't stop us. I learned that when things get hard, remembering that He is faithful gives me strength. So, lean on Him for strength and keep going. Keep chasing after Jesus. In the end, it is worth it. Jesus is worth it.

Reflect over some challenges you are facing currently. Take some time to talk to God about them and ask Him for strength to keep going.

Alyssa Trembly
MidAmerica Nazarene University Women's Track and Field
2015-2019

April 9

"…though I myself have reasons for such confidence. If someone else thinks they have reasons to put confidence in the flesh, I have more." - Philippians 3:4

Through my early years playing volleyball at the University of North Texas, I struggled to have confidence in my performance. Every single step I took (literally) played a role in my execution on the court. If one small step was not perfect, it looked bad to my coaches and upperclassman. Being perfect and being a starter is what I placed my value in. It got extremely tiring. My mental game dragged me down and I forgot how to play the sport I loved. I always fell short of perfection and beat myself up for it. I lost my confidence. My self-value depleted greatly, and I found myself disappointed about who I was. It wasn't until I dove deeper into my faith that I began to discover where my true confidence lies.

I was selfish to believe that my volleyball performance deserved all my self-value. Learning to place my value and confidence in the Lord wasn't easy, but it was much better. Confidence in Jesus Christ never failed me. Confidence in my game always did. Memorizing this verse helped me fight this battle and win it. Confidence in anything worldly is going to eventually fail you. When I found my true confidence, my performance found a way to exceed greatly.

Are you placing your confidence in something worldly? If so, what is it? Pray for the strength to place your value and confidence in Jesus Christ first.

Miranda Youmans
University of North Texas Volleyball
2017-2021

April 10

"The rain came down, the streams rose, and the winds blew and beat against the house; yet it did not fall, because it had its foundation on the rock." - Matthew 7:25 NIV

As an athlete, I was always told I needed to "buy in." I needed to buy into training, the team culture, nutrition, rehab, academics, and literally anything else you can think of. I trained harder than anyone, I watched film till 3 AM, I ate as healthy as I could. I was bought in. Nobody had to question it; they knew. It wasn't long before my identity was so wrapped up in being an athlete that a bad game or a rough day at practice would leave me devastated. My self-worth was dependent on how I performed on the court and what my stats were.

In Matthew 7, Jesus shares about a wise man who built his house on rock and a foolish one who built his house on sand. I was the foolish man. I had built my identity on being an athlete, and when the storms came, my house fell with a great crash every time. Using athletics as the cornerstone of my life left me constantly broken and defeated.

I had to rebuild my house. I needed to buy into my faith and relationship with Jesus just like I had with being an athlete. A foundation built on the Lord can withstand even the strongest of storms. Buying into Jesus has brought me so much joy and peace, something that stats and accolades never could.

What foundation is your house built on? What are you the most bought into in your life?

Katy Keenan
Texas Tech University Volleyball
2015-2018

April 11

"And let us consider how to stir up one another to love and good works, not neglecting to meet together, as is the habit of some, but encouraging one another, and all the more as you see the Day drawing near." Hebrews 10:24-25

When I was playing college baseball at TCU, I had no idea the importance of deeply rooted, Biblical community. I had grown up the "good Christian" kid who was surrounded by natural community in a small town, and I did not have to be intentional to create it. It was just all around me via sports, school and camp.

Then I went to college. And I proceeded to isolate myself from other people. No one knew the real me because I would not really let anyone in. Over time, this and several other unhealthy things, led to depression and loneliness.

Fast forward to the end of college, through a series of significant hardships and acute pain, I found myself at rock bottom and completely disconnected from people. The pain of my loneliness forced me to deal with who I believed God to really be.

It was there I finally met the real Jesus. I fully surrendered my life to Jesus.

Soon thereafter, God showed me the power and provision of his original design of Biblical community. I got in a group of men to share struggles with, confess sin regularly and encourage me on a regular basis. The process was hard as I had a lot to get into the light. But slowly, over time, I began to experience freedom in my life.

Are you in need of life giving, Biblical community?

Austin Adams
Texas Christian University Baseball
2004-2007

103

April 12

"A man without self-control is like a city broken into and left without walls." – Proverbs 25:28 ESV

Self-control and self-discipline require sacrifice and can take years to develop. As a student athlete at The University of Oklahoma, I worked to strengthen my physical and mental discipline. I learned that in order to become a better athlete and to glorify God, I needed to hold myself accountable beyond the weight room and track. I realized that I needed to practice self-control in my relationships, in my eating habits, and in my free time. I often found myself exhausted and unmotivated when I didn't set the right boundaries. Once I practiced healthier habits, I started building better relationships, getting better grades, and performing better on the track.

As followers of Christ, we are called to offer our bodies as a living sacrifice. Without self-control through sacrifice, the life of an athlete loses structure and leaves itself vulnerable. Practicing self-control is a great way to glorify God.

Take time to reflect on what boundaries you might need to strengthen or build in order to better yourself and most importantly glorify God.

Brooks Glanton
The University of Oklahoma Track & Field
2018-2020

April 13

"For the moment all discipline seems painful rather than pleasant, but later it yields the peaceful fruit of righteousness to those who have been trained by it."
– Hebrews 12:11 ESV

There is an undeniable resemblance between spiritual discipline and athletic discipline, though they take different forms. Ultimately, our goal is to continue improving and becoming better athletes or better followers of Jesus.

We can identify a couple of distinct parallels between the steps taken to build our spiritual discipline and those taken in commitment to our sport. For example, going to practice is like attending a group Bible study and attending a private lesson is like meeting with a mentor. But then we must consider, which activities are we better at making time for? Today, there is so much pressure on athletes to be the best they can be, but not enough focus on young adults becoming the best disciples they can be.

I encourage you think about your commitment to your athletic discipline, and then to your faith. How do they compare? We are called to be followers of Jesus, but we cannot do that properly without first cultivating a relationship with Him and His people. I encourage you to seek the peaceful fruit of righteousness by creating lasting habits and lasting relationships that guide you towards the love of Jesus.

How strong is your spiritual discipline? What steps can you take this week to pursue Jesus more in your everyday life?

Megan Porter
Texas State University Women's Volleyball
2016-2019

105

April 14

"But whatever were gains to me I now consider loss for the sake of Christ. What is more, I consider everything a loss because of the surpassing worth of knowing Christ Jesus my Lord, for whose sake I have lost all things. I consider them garbage, that I may gain Christ." -Philippians 3:7-8

My first few years of college I felt like I had it all. I was playing Division 1 soccer, I was accepted into the nursing program, and I had a great social life partying on the weekends. What more could I want or need? It was not until I met Jesus that I truly saw what I was missing. That whole time I was believing a lie. I thought I had found the key to happiness and the purpose to my life. Jesus blew up my world. A relationship with Him was like nothing I had ever experienced before. I remember reading Philippians 3:7-8 for the first time and thinking, wow, that is the truth. Everything the world offers is garbage in comparison to pursuing a relationship with Jesus. No amount of success, achievements, or experience can amount to what Jesus is offering us.

Like James 4:14 says, our lives are like a mist. Our careers as athletes no matter how far you go, are a mist. Our achievements and successes are a mist. Everything in life is temporary, lasting only a small amount of time. But Jesus is not. A relationship with God is for eternity.

Take some time and think about where you are trying to find your joy, purpose, and fulfillment. Is it in temporary things of the world? Or is it in Jesus, the one who is offering an eternity with Him?

Caroline Janike
University of Missouri Kansas City Women's Soccer
2015-2020

April 15

"Do not lay up for yourselves treasures on earth, where moth and rust destroy and where thieves break in and steal, but lay up for yourselves treasures in heaven, where neither moth nor rust destroys and where thieves do not break in and steal."
– Matthew 6:19-20 ESV

Anyone that plays a sport knows there is a great joy that comes with it. As athletes for Christ, we know our talents have been given to us by Him, to honor Him. We glorify Him, we give Him thanks, we love Him, but we often make it an idol in our lives very quick. I got the privilege to have a multi-homerun game this year and as a hitter, it makes you feel like you are on top of the world. It makes you feel like you don't have any worries because everything is going so right with what you do. Not that enjoying these things is wrong in anyway, but they have the tendency to make you complacent and forget about what really matters most, that is making disciples and building for a Kingdom that does not fade, like our personal achievements will.

We begin to think our stats and numbers mean more when in reality they mean absolutely nothing in the greater scheme of life. Jesus tells us in Matthew the importance of building for a Kingdom over building wealth for yourself. We as athletes, in the same way, must prioritize and value building for his Kingdom over our own personal goals.

In what way are you putting your craft over the Lord? Is it even in competition with Him? If it is, take a second to pray and love Him more than your work.

Sean Klein
Presbyterian College Baseball
2018-2022

107

April 16

"Consider it pure joy, my brothers and sisters, whenever you face trials of many kinds, because you know that the testing of your faith produces perseverance. Let perseverance finish its work so that you may be mature and complete, not lacking anything."
- James 1: 2-4 ESV

Thinking back, I put running at the center of almost every decision I made in life for a long time until recently. It was not until I got injured that I felt God really tugging at my heart to question my behaviors. In college I developed chronic foot pain that left me questioning why God was putting me through this. Why was He taking away the sport that I put everything into? I lost hope that I would ever be able to compete again. I realized that God was testing me. He was giving me this hardship to see if I truly put Him first in my life. I became confident in Christ and realized I would continue to feel empty if He was not the center of my life. My mindset shifted to one toward Him, not myself. Even in times when we feel hopeless, we must draw near to God because every part of our life is His plan. The dark times we face only bring us closer to him and transform us into more Christ-like people with a purpose to serve Him.

You will face trials of all sorts. Do not let the devil take hold of you during those times, instead allow them to strengthen your walk with Christ.

Riley Coggin
Clemson University Cross Country and Track
2018-2021

April 17

"Carry out each other's burdens, and in this way you will fulfill the law of Christ." - Galatians 6:2 NIV

As athletes, we're programmed to seek validation for our performance from others. Outside of athletics, we can carry over this mindset as we try to please our friends. As part of the Church, we carry over this mindset as we strive to serve others for the sake of Christ.

But if you're like me, sometimes you transform this good intention into a detrimental action. There's a fine line between people-pleasing and actually serving others. Trying to please everyone leaves you feeling empty when you aren't constantly receiving affirmation. The enemy works to make you think that you're pursuing the Lord's commission to love others well when in reality you're serving your own desires for achievement out of insecurity.

On the other hand, carrying the burdens of others means you're lifting off the distractions of the world so that others can finally see Light. Serving with the Spirit of Truth is fulfilling to the soul, and you're left feeling energized rather than running on empty.

Be intentional with your thoughts, words, and actions. Each moment of the day is an opportunity to point others to the Cross. Are you at practice to appease your coaches—to feel worthy by their standards? Or do you utilize the talents God blessed you with to show the world that only Jesus defines your worth?

What does serving your team look like? How can you repurpose each rep at practice to glorify Jesus?

Montana Watts
Southern Methodist University Women's Volleyball
2016-2020

109

April 18

"I can do all things through Christ who strengthens me."
-Philippians 4:13 KJV

As a college and professional player, I often found myself asking Christ, why me? What is your plan for me? Fast forward 30 years and I was called to coach a High School baseball team at a small private high school. Teaching boys baseball and life as a Christian athlete at times has been perplexing.

Several years ago, I asked my team if they were familiar with the verse Philippians 4:13. Most had it memorized. I asked them if they believed it was true? They quickly answered, "Yes." So, if that is the case, can my smallest player hit 20 homeruns this year. Again, they answered, "Yes."

I believe this single verse is more misunderstood and does more damage to our faith and Christian witness than any other I have experienced. I asked the boys to all research the history of the verse and report back. Paul authored the verse at difficult time in his life. In the original text, though, we find Paul saying, "I can **endure** all things," not I can **do** all things, as it is translated today.

Christ will give us the strength to endure suffering and persecution when we testify to the world that He is Lord. Imagine how the pitcher feels when he surrenders a homerun. Does He not love the pitcher equally? Does a parent love one child more than the other?

Next time you experience success on the field of competition, be thankful and respectful toward your opponent, knowing Christ loves you both.

Mike Kripner
Cincinnati Reds
1978-1982

April 19

"For God was in Christ, reconciling the world to himself, no longer counting people's sins against them. And he gave us this wonderful message of reconciliation. So we are Christ's ambassadors; God is making his appeal through us. We speak for Christ when we plead, "Come back to God!""
-2 Corinthians 5:19-20 NLT

Just as LeBron James is a brand ambassador for Nike, and Stephen Curry is a brand ambassador for Under Armour, when we accept Jesus as our Savior, we become brand ambassadors for the Kingdom of God. This is why we cannot look like the world. When we spread the life changing Good News which is The Gospel to others, those around us should be able to clearly see through our lifestyles that we are in Christ and not prisoners to the ways and the patterns of this world. Every morning before you go about your day remind yourself that as a follower of Christ you are a brand ambassador for the Kingdom of God, and let this heavenly sponsorship guide every decision that you make. Stay encouraged, Believer, continuing to seek the Lord through who He has revealed Himself to be in His word and letting Him continue to shape and mold you by renewing your mind.

"Prove by the way you live that you have repented of your sins and turned to God." – Matthew 3:8 NLT

Madison Cone
University of Wisconsin Football
2017-2021

April 20

"Therefore I tell you, do not be anxious about your life"
-Matthew 6:25

I vividly remember my first division 1 basketball game like it was yesterday. There I was running onto the court at an away game against Purdue University with thousands of people in the stands. Despite just having been saved, I was constantly an anxious wreck, and as I was running onto the court I remember shaking with anxiety about my performance. As we lined up for layup lines, I clearly remember a comforting message from Jesus, "You have the Creator of the Universe with you, why are you full of fear?" This hit me like a pile of bricks and helped put my heart at ease.

Let's take a moment to remember how Jesus was treated on the day of His crucifixion. He was mocked by many because of his claims to be Lord and King of the Jews. Look at Jesus' words about anxiety again for a moment, "Do not be anxious about your life," those are words spoken by Jesus himself! I would argue every time we are filled with anxiety and worry, we actually are mocking Him as Lord. Jesus told us time and time again not to worry about our lives, and when we worry, we basically say to Him, "Yeah yeah, I know you said not to worry, but this right now is bigger than You, so I have the right to worry." My challenge to you is to view anxiety and worry in this light, to realize that it is actually mocking Jesus and His commands as our loving Lord and Savior.

Prayerfully ask God to reveal that He is in complete control and deeply loves you.

Landon Taliaferro
Fairfield University Basketball
2018-2020

April 21

"Seek me, and live." – Amos 5:5 ESV

Often, I have to be reminded it's that simple. The verse starts with one focus (God!), and then God doesn't say "seek me… and break the school record" or "seek me… and hyper-analyze what to eat/how to warm up/what pre-race superstition to apply." He just calls us to *live*, because living itself is the biggest gift when it's with Him. As a college freshman, I was overwhelmingly seeking my own recognition. All I wanted to do was contribute, to earn my place, to show the upperclassmen and myself that I was worth it on their world-class standards. The summer after my first year, I didn't know if I could continue. Worn down by workouts, feeling out-of-place on my team, and doubtful of my own ability to run, I remember my life changed upon hearing the lyrics, "I'm no longer a slave to fear. I am a child of God." God did something miraculous in my heart. When my focus shifted away from myself to Him & loving my teammates, I showed up to practice and just *lived*. And over time, that freedom-centered consistency turned into endurance and faster races and opportunities I never could have expected in track.

My most challenging races, feedback from coaches, and cycles of self-doubt occurred when my heart, if I'm being honest, was nowhere near seeking God first. He is the only one whose approval matters, and He's already given it to us. Now it's time to walk in His grace and compete, race, and *live* freely.

What is your heart seeking right now before God? How do you see that impacting you in your sport & your life?

Gabby Crank
University of Texas Women's Track & Field
2015-2019

113

April 22

"Know that the Lord is God. It is he who made us, and we are his; we are his people, the sheep of his pasture."
– Psalms 100:3 NIV

As athletes, we tend to place a great emphasis on what we can control. We work tirelessly to become masters of work ethic, routine, and the ability to project poise in turbulent situations. During my playing career, I regularly focused on what I could not control as opposed to the comfort and provision of the Lord. Injuries, loss of loved ones, and racial discrimination plagued my high school and collegiate basketball career. Both on and off the court issues would keep me up at night, trying to find a solution that I could implement to "fix" what was happening. Prayerfully reflecting on the trials I faced allowed me to realize that while we are called to work, no amount of earthly acts could possibly vault me into a position of power that is exclusively reserved for our Lord and Savior. My life is not my own and the quest for full and complete control is a fool's errand, one destined to bring nothing but perpetual emptiness.

Our sports have a tendency to make us feel like the world is all about us. At some point that ball stops bouncing or the phone stops ringing, but the provision and love of Christ is eternal. Find your identity in Christ alone and know we are His, in both good times and bad. I rest comfortably in the fact that through all things, I am His.

Only the living true God is self-existent, self-sufficient, and in control. Take a moment to bask in the knowledge the Lord is our Shepherd, our Good Shepherd, leading us in His ways.

Myles Johnson
Dallas Baptist University Men's Basketball
2012-2017

April 23

"So Peter got out of the boat and walked on the water and came to Jesus. But when he saw the wind, he was afraid, and beginning to sink he cried out, "Lord save me."
-Matthew 14: 29-30 ESV

As an athlete, it's easy to look around us and focus on our current circumstances. In fact, as a human being in a fallen world, we are prone to it. As I look back on my college tennis career, I see the pattern of that very thing: the tendency to be consumed by worldly circumstances. Those circumstances were very real, of course, but just like Peter, when I took my eyes off Jesus to focus on the wind and the waves, I would start to sink.

But Jesus is better than the how and why of our current circumstances. He is better than our wins and losses. He is better than our status on the team. He is better than the praise and accolades from others. He is even better than the years you've spent practicing and competing. And when we're floundering in the wind and the waves and we cry out like Peter to say, "Lord, save me," He is faithful to reach down and take hold of us.

God has called you look to Himself, rather than whatever court or field you're on at the moment. Ask Him to reveal the things of this world that threaten to steal your focus from Him.

Kelly Sommer
Middle Tennessee State / Auburn University Women's Tennis
2005-2008

115

April 24

*"Do not be anxious about anything, but in everything by prayer
and supplication with thanksgiving let your requests be made known
to God. And the peace of God, which surpasses all understanding, will
guard your hearts and your minds in Christ Jesus."*
– Philippians 4:6-7 ESV

Balancing life, school, and sports is not easy and having an
anxious mind through it all can sometimes take the joy out of
everyday life. I realized this one weekend during my Senior year when
my mom came to visit me for a home football game. I had so much
going on that next week with school and cheer that I allowed my
anxiety from my upcoming next week to ruin the time I had with my
mom. After she left to go home, it hit me. Instead of casting my
worries upon God, I allowed my anxious mind to consume me and my
happiness.

It's okay to be stressed from time to time but allowing stress
to interfere with your daily life only takes away from the joys of life.
Life is a constant grind. Lean on God when you are feeling
overwhelmed. Take your trials and tribulations to Him because He
will give you peace! He knows the plans He has for you, so trust in
Him and find joy in the tasks set before you.

**When you find yourself to be overwhelmed or stressed, set aside
all distractions and take time to talk to God. Tell Him what
worries you! He's listening and knows exactly how to comfort you.**

Brooklyn Hollon
Clemson University Co-Ed Cheer
2017-2021

April 25

"Dear friends, although I was very eager to write to you about the salvation we share, I felt compelled to write and urge you to contend for the faith that was once entrusted to God's holy people."
Jude 1:3 NIV

I was involved in many different organizations in college. I found it hard to "fit in" with each group, especially when I was surrounded by unbelievers. Jude is telling the believers of the church that they are to "contend for the faith," because of the false teachers/unbelievers entering their community. What does it mean to "contend for the faith"? Well, the word contend, from the Greek word *agónizomai,* means to struggle. We know that suffering will never go away until He returns, however, we can rejoice knowing that persecution is used to advance the Church. Now, the "faith" Jude is referring to is not the knowledge that God is real, but in fact, it refers to Christian doctrine as a whole. This could include the apostles' teaching, Jesus' teaching and the doctrine given by God himself.

Therefore, contending for the faith means that you are suffering for the Christian doctrine so that we can multiply the citizens of Heaven. Suffering for the faith does not have to be a profound act every day. Most days it could look like showing up to practice early, setting up the gym, picking up trash, and selflessly putting my teammates before myself. Make yourself uncomfortable today, for the sake of the Gospel.

How can you challenge yourself to become uncomfortable and "contend" for the faith today?

Kelley Skinner
University of Texas at Dallas Women's Basketball
2017-2021

117

April 26

"For am I now trying to win the favor of people or God? Or am I striving to please people? If I were still trying to please people, I would not be a slave of Christ." -Galatians 1:10 HCB

A huge majority of people love to have a little bit of affirmation every once in a while, at least I do. It makes us feel good for the time being. However, it can begin to have adverse effects if approval from people above you (coach, boss, parents, etc.) doesn't always happen how you want it to. Being that hindsight is 20/20, I sure wish I would have known about this verse back when I was playing in college. As a freshman, I came in thinking I had something to prove, especially to my coaches but, to no surprise, that became toxic to the point where everything I did off the field changed who I was when I left. It wasn't until my junior year that God helped me realize my priorities were out-of-whack. I had idolized approval from everyone accept the One that truly matters, God.

Confirmation from others is naturally a part of what we all desire. The problem is when we make our focus words from other people instead of God's word and what He thinks about us. Putting your faith in things that are not permanent is a setup for failure. Praise God that He helped me realize that He will never stop pursuing me no matter how I performed. His words gave me life and purpose.

Deciding to prioritize Gods approval above everything else is one of the most important decisions you could make. But first, follow Him.

Wesley Purcell
Austin Peay State University Baseball
2012-2016

118

April 27

"One day as Jesus was walking along the shore of the Sea of Galilee, he saw two brothers—Simon, also called Peter, and Andrew—throwing a net into the water, for they fished for a living. Jesus called out to them, "Come, follow me, and I will show you how to fish for people!" And they left their nets at once and followed him." -Matthew 4:18-20

We are called to follow Christ regardless of the cost. In this passage, we see Peter and Andrew turn from casting their nets to catch fish to instead catch people. We see a heart shift here. They go from focusing on their craft to immediately leaving their nets and saying yes to Jesus' invitation without hesitation.

Everyone wants to cut down nets, win championships, and hang a banner. I was no exception to this. My entire goal was to cut down nets, but little did I know, I would be called to drop my net instead and follow Christ. So often we get wrapped up in the pressures of our sport, we forget why we play. We fall into worshiping the gift, instead of the Giver. In shifting from cutting the net versus dropping the net, we go from a success-driven to a spirit-led mindset which creates space for freedom and enjoyment of the gift. These verses remind us who our priority should be: Christ. When our priority is Christ, naturally we will love His people and want to share the good news we have experienced.

What is one way you can shift your priority to Christ and go out of your way to love one of your teammates this week?

Sydney Goodson
Texas Tech University / Kansas State University Women's Basketball
2017-2021

April 28

"Whatever you do, work heartily, as for the Lord and not for men, knowing that from the Lord you will receive the inheritance as your reward. You are serving the Lord Christ"
-Colossians 3:23-24 ESV

Working hard is a huge part of being an athlete, and likely you have gotten to where you are in your athletic career because of your hard work. But even when we feel like we're doing the best we can athletically, it can still leave us feeling discontent in one way or another. My freshman year of college I was so focused on working hard, but for the wrong type of reward. I wanted recognition for my name, my abilities, and my hard work. No matter how many goals I achieved, no reward seemed to be enough. I had to learn that God had created me for a much different purpose than performing well on the field for personal gain.

God gave us abilities athletically to use as a platform to work hard for Him. Not playing for myself, but playing for the One who created us and equips us to perform the way we do. My job is to serve the Lord Christ, and it is a privilege to use my sport to do this! I get to compete freely, without the expectations to please the world. Use what God has given you for His purpose. It has a reward that will last forever, far beyond our athletic career.

You have God-given talents. Think about the platform you have and how you can serve Christ with what He has given you.

Rylan Childers
University of Missouri KC / University of Kansas Women's Soccer
2018-2022

April 29

"We remember before our God and Father your work produced by faith, your labor prompted by love, and your endurance inspired by hope in our Lord Jesus Christ. You became imitators of us and of the Lord, for you welcomed the message in the midst of severe suffering with the joy given by the Holy Spirit. And so you became a model to all the believers in Macedonia and Achaia. The Lord's message rang out from you not only in Macedonia and Achaia—your faith in God has become known everywhere. Therefore we do not need to say anything about it."
− 1 Thessalonians 1:3,6-8 NIV

Endurance definition (n): "the fact or power of enduring an unpleasant or difficult process or situation without giving way." As athletes we know this word well. We've had to endure hard practices, losses, and all that athletics includes. I see this as a similar parallel to our relationship with Jesus. Enduring the hardships of standing out when it's uncomfortable, trusting God with the unknowns, and choosing Him every day. Our sport is an important part of our lives, yet our relationship with Christ is what endures forever. The most fulfilling times of my college career have been seeing others impacted by Jesus. The way we show endurance in trials can impact our own and others' faith, allow us to experience God's joy and hope, and can create opportunities to share the Gospel.

How we endure trials can grow our own relationship with God and impact others. Ask God to show you ways to impact those in and outside of your sport.

Grace Ball
University of Missouri Kansas City Women's Tennis
2017-2022

121

April 30

*"When Jesus received the sour wine, he said, "It is finished,"
and he bowed his head and gave up his spirit." – John 19:30 ESV*

*"And do not be grieved, for the joy of the Lord is your
strength." -Nehemiah 8:10 ESV*

A common misconception has developed around Christianity
that once we are in Christ our lives will become easier. However,
Jesus Himself tells us in the Bible, "In the world you will have
tribulation." (John 16:33). The Son himself is warning us that we will
have trouble in this world, we will experience pain, hurt, and suffering
regardless of whether or not we are in Christ. Lucky for those in
Christ we have a hope that transcends all understanding. Jesus saying
"Tetelestai" or "It is finished" means that we already have victory in
Him. When He gave up His Spirit, He transcended into hell to
conquer the grave of sin and death once and for all. Because of Him
those things no longer have a hold on us if we truly believe it. We are
challenged not to be grieved by our current circumstances, but rather
to find strength and joy because the implications of His sacrifice. No
matter what battle we are in the midst of, we can have assurance that
the war has already been won by our Father. We know the end result,
so CHOOSE JOY in every circumstance! Live in the hope He
provides.

**CHOOSE JOY when you experience suffering and persecution
from this world today and every day.**

Garret Jansen
University of Iowa Football
2015-2019

May 1

"But the Lord said to Samuel, "Do not look on his appearance or on the height of his stature, because I have rejected him. For the Lord sees not as man sees: man looks on the outward appearance, but the Lord looks on the heart." -1 Samuel 16:7 ESV

My body had been on display since the age of 5 when I started competitive dance. For as long as I can remember, I hated what I looked like. Every part of me was never good enough and I couldn't do anything to fix it. I don't remember the first time I felt horrible about myself, but I do remember how bad it hurt. This became a never-ending cycle that spiraled out of control. I was at the end of myself. I had no choice but to fully surrender it all to the Lord.

This is a place I believe a lot of people have been in but do not necessarily like to admit… and I get it! It's so hard to take the hands off the steering wheel of our lives and trust that the Lord will fully take care of whatever we are struggling with. Following Christ does not exempt us from thoughts of body shame, but it does equip us with truths that will help us combat those terrible thoughts. God loves us because we are His children, made in His image. Beauty is fleeting but God's love for us is eternal and that is something we can cling to. Let's vow to fight our insecurities with the truth that prevails over all.

Write down three truths from Scripture that you can combat any negative thoughts you have about yourself with. Keep that notecard in a spot where you can read it out-loud every day.

Taylor DeLong
University of Minnesota Dance Team
2014-2018

May 2

"Humble yourselves, therefore, under the mighty hand of God so that at the proper time he may exalt you, casting all your anxieties on him, because he cares for you."
- 1 Peter 5:6-7 ESV

Athletes so often hold all the weight of the game on their shoulders. So much so that the pressure can be overwhelming and turn to severe anxiety. These verses personally helped me get through a time where I was overwhelmed with the weight of the game so I could finally enjoy the sport I loved!

To get through this time as an athlete, I spoke to God about my anxieties as much as possible. I came to realize that the game I loved was just that, a game. What truly fulfilled me in life was my relationship with God. When we realize that our pressures in life are so small in the eyes of God, we also see that His solutions and His presence are so big. In humbling myself under God, I was soon able to let go of all the anxieties these pressures held over me. I spoke to God about these stressors, and everything became so much clearer, including my relationship with Him.

When the weight of our game begins to get to us, what we need to do as athletes is call on God and return to our roots as His children. Pray to him about these anxieties of our game so we can get back to focusing on our passion for the game and our love for Christ.

I challenge you to write down what anxieties you have and pray about them. Take time to speak to God and open your heart to Him.

Emily Kraft
Mars Hill University Women's Track and Field
2019-2022

May 3

"Whatever you do, work at it with all your heart, as working for the Lord, not for human masters." (Colossians 3:23 NIV)

Playing football in college has taught me so many lessons, but it has really shown me the importance of having my identity rooted in Jesus Christ. I like to think of identity through the lens of labels. Our world loves to put labels on people. As a college athlete, the labels people have placed on me at times have seemed like a huge deal. For example, coaches label their players as starters or backups. Teammates or fans may label players based on their performance in a game. Even a single play can cause people to label athletes in a positive or negative manner. At times, these labels have made me feel like I was riding a rollercoaster of highs and lows.

My faith in Jesus has helped me to realize that I will always feel let down if I choose to listen to the way others define and label me. Through the ups and downs that I have experienced through college athletics, God has shown me the importance of living my life according to the way that He labels me. In the Bible, God defines us as His children. He says we are loved, and we are made in His image. He also calls us redeemed and forgiven. Choosing to live by these powerful, true, and eternal labels has helped to set me free from the ups and downs of college athletics. My identity is secure in Jesus, regardless of any outcome on a football field.

What would it look like for me to fully live according to the way that God defines me?

Hamp Sisson
Furman University Football
2018-2022

125

May 4

"Come to me, all of you who are weary and burdened, and I will give you rest." -Matthew 11:28 CSB

Speed. It is an element to every form of athletics. The words "you're too slow" are simply unacceptable in an athlete's mind. I was always trying to raise my game being the fastest, strongest, and best I could be. But what happens when you're speeding through life and realize you have lost the joy that comes with it? I was racing through life trying to be the best athlete, friend, and student; trying to get everything done, when one day I realized I didn't even have time to enjoy all I was doing. Next thing I knew, my athletic career was over due to a neck injury, and I didn't even know how to live at a non-accelerated pace. But through the trials, I realized God had been calling me to slow down and enjoy all the gifts He had given me, both from athletics and outside of it. I was so caught up in getting it all done, I forgot that God wants His children to rejoice in all we do, because He is the one who *gave* us the ability to do it.

When we come to Him with all our burdens, only He can relieve them. When we come to Him with joy and thanksgiving, He rejoices. But if we don't slow down long enough to take the time to rest with Him and thank Him, then we are defying the biggest blessing we have – a Father who is eager to love, help, and give rest.

Set a daily goal of spending at least 10 minutes alone with God.

Jordan Kiley
Sam Houston State Volleyball
2017-2019

126

May 5

"If one part suffers, every part suffers with it; if one part is honored, every part rejoices with it."
-1 Corinthians 12:26 NIV

Going to college across the United States was the scariest thing I've ever done to this day. Leaving everything familiar behind, not knowing if I was truly being called. But I found myself reading about the mighty warriors in the Bible. Gideon was the biggest underdog fighting thousands of troops with only a couple hundred in his army. He told God he had the wrong guy. But where Gideon was weak, God's power was revealed. He listened to God's calling even though it didn't feel right to him and was scared but knew that he was called. In the midst of the whirlwind of committing to play volleyball at GCU the Holy Spirit was leading me to this team. There is PURPOSE for you on your team and sometimes you may never even see the fruit, but it's there. Being on a team is like being part of the Church. Just like everything is centered around the success of the team, absolutely everything you do in your life should be done for the Kingdom and the glory of our Heavenly Father. How you treat your teammates, your mentality, your peace, your HOPE. Our goal should be to make the Gospel known. The Lord might lead you into something scary like what He did with Gideon and that might be the place you are called to build the Kingdom. Now the question is, will you go?

If you don't play a single point your entire collegiate career, will you still count it as a win?

Grayson Browning
Grand Canyon University Men's Volleyball
2018-2023

May 6

"For God has not given us a spirit of fear, but of power and of love and of a sound mind." - 2 Timothy 1:7 NKJV

It may be surprising to hear that most people aren't as fearful of failure as much as they are of success. Through the ups and downs of being athletes, we strive for perfection by practicing and persevering through trials. But sometimes even when we know we have practiced and fully prepared, we fail to perform without fear. As children of the Father, we can take hold of the promise of His word and perform without fear when we are in the heat of the battle. Nerves are only a natural reaction to a person who cares deeply about what they are doing. We remain fearless by remembering that our 'spirit is of power and love and sound mind.' While we will inevitably feel anxious when called upon to use those skills, it's in those moments that God is truly able to reveal to us and those around us His promise that we are created to perform with power, love, and sound mind. Through this God is able to perform great things for His glory no matter our success or failures.

Whatever your failures or successes are to this point you can choose to take hold of His promise right now knowing that He is enough. With Christ we have already won- so go play and live like it today.

Are you living and playing resting on the fact that you are made with a spirit of power, love, and sound mind or have you been fearful to succeed?

Jacob Davis
Florida State University Men's Golf
2004-2006

May 7

"No, dear brothers and sisters, I have not achieved it, but I focus on this one thing: Forgetting the past and looking forward to what lies ahead, I press on to reach the end of the race and receive the heavenly prize for which God, through Christ Jesus, is calling us."
-Philippians 3:13-14

Think of a time in your sports career where you made a mistake. Maybe you missed a wide open lay-up, or a ground ball went in between your legs, or in my case, dropping a catch in a crucial moment in a game. Whatever those mistakes were, I know for me, whenever I made one, I would dwell on it and replay it over and over again in my mind which led to me defining myself by those mistakes.

In the verse above, Paul is talking about how he doesn't focus on the past, but he is pressing on to receive the prize that God is calling him to. I remember going into my senior year of college football when I discovered this verse and it started to shift my thinking and allowed me to play in freedom, not defining myself by how good or bad I performed, but defining myself by who God says I am. Did making mistakes still stink after I learned this truth? Of course, but the one thing that made a difference for me, was knowing that I am not defined by those mistakes and just like Paul, I can press on and continue to perform and play in freedom.

Athlete, how can remembering this truth allow you to perform in freedom?

Reggie Green
University of Pittsburgh / Robert Morris University Football
2013-2018

129

May 8

"...I consider everything a loss compared to the surpassing greatness of knowing Christ Jesus my Lord, for whose sake I have lost all things. I consider them rubbish, that I may gain Christ and be found in Him, not having a righteousness of my own, but that which is through faith in Christ..." - Philippians 3:8-9 NIV

Late in my baseball career, I realized the importance of prioritizing my goals and focusing on those that were most important. Although success on the field was a good goal, it was not what was most important to me, and anytime it became my focus, I paid the price.

Focusing on success magnified my failures, and I would become crippled by fear, doubt, and negativity. I couldn't perform when success was most important, but when I got my priorities back in line, my performance would improve drastically.

Outside of baseball, I have the same struggle. I often put the pursuit of less important things in front of what should be most important, my relationship with Christ. When I don't put my relationship with Jesus first, everything suffers.

In Philippians 3, Paul says, that no matter what he may accomplish in his life, it is all worthless compared to knowing Christ and being found in Him. That is the true definition of success and is in line with what Jesus says in John 15:5, "...If a man remains in me, and I in him, he will bear much fruit; apart from me you can do nothing."

Lord, may we be found in You.

Trey Hearne
St. Louis Cardinal's Organization
2005-2010

May 9

"Consider it pure joy, my brothers and sisters, whenever you face trials of many kinds, because you know that the testing of your faith produces perseverance."
- James 1:2-3 NIV

As athletes, we face trials every day. My career was plagued with injuries, ones that were usually prolonged because they took a while to figure out. The spring of my freshman year I was told I needed hip surgery to fix a torn labrum. This was the worst injury I had ever had, and I found myself asking a lot of questions, not only to the doctors about what was to come, but to the Lord as well. "Why me?" "Why now?" "How does this prove that you are protecting me?" He was supposed to have this amazing plan for me, and for the first time in my life, it did not coincide with the plan I had for myself. I was out of patience. I did not want to wait to feel better, I wanted to feel better immediately. After hitting another delay in rehab, I was at rock bottom, so I prayed and I dove into the Bible for solace, realizing that the only thing that could help me feel better was the one thing I had turned away from.

It should not take us being at our lowest point to turn to the Lord. The one constant we will find in the good and bad times is the Lord, so we need to trust that He knows more than us and can see the bigger picture.

I challenge you to remain patient as you work through the trials of your life, knowing that the Lord is always right on time.

Jordan Pierson
Grand Canyon University Softball
2018-2021

131

May 10

"All Scripture is God-breathed and is useful for teaching, rebuking, correcting and training in righteousness." -2 Timothy 3:16

Everyone in their life is going to "drop a pass" whether that is in actual sports or in life, and you do not accomplish what you wanted. My question today is what are you going to do about it? As a receiver, I look up to many great players, but one thing that I pay attention to is how well those receivers respond when they drop a pass. I believe that a great receiver is a great receiver not only because of their stats, but also because of their ability to handle adversity. The number one reason for success is well managed failure. We will "drop a pass" in our life, but how will we respond?

The best way I have found to help overcome adversity is through using the power of God's Word. When we go through struggles, our ability to quickly shift our mindset to reciting God's Word can affect our performance. When I was a sophomore at Clemson, I remember making a critical error during a scrimmage that led to a punt for the offense. My natural reaction was to get frustrated with myself, but I quickly reminded myself of Philippians 4:13 under my breath, "I can do this. Give me the strength, Lord." Saying a verse is my first reaction now because I made the decision beforehand that I was going to recite God's Word. So, apply God's Word to your life because like it says in 2 Timothy 3:16, it is useful for teaching, rebuking, correcting, and training yourself to be more like Christ.

I challenge everyone to grab onto God's Word and have one verse memorized to apply in the trials we face.

Hamp Greene
Clemson University
2019-2024

132

May 11

"They [Pharisees] came to Jesus and asked: "Is it right to pay the imperial tax to Caesar or not?... "But Jesus knew their hypocrisy. "Why are you trying to trap me? "He asked. "Bring me a denarius and let me look at it." They brought the coin, and he asked them, "Whose image is this? And whose inscription?" "Caesar's," they replied. Then Jesus said to them, "Give back to Caesar what is Caesar's and to God what is God's."
-Mark 12:14-17 NIV

What does it mean to give God what is God's? If we look at a penny, we know its' value because picture of Abraham Lincoln is on it. Whose picture is on you and me? The Bible says that we are created in the image of God, therefore we belong to God. Each one of us is unique and have an extravagant value because God created us. I know that my value is only found in God, but for many years I found my value in soccer. It wasn't until I tore my ACL that God clearly showed me that my value is not found in what I do, but in who I am. The only way for me to truly know who I am, was to know whose I am first. We are His! We are not the sum of our every high and low; but rather we are extravagantly valuable because God's image is on us! We don't have to perform for His acceptance and love, He freely gives it! To give God what is God's is ourselves. Our time, talents, treasures, and our whole lives.

How does knowing that YOU belong to GOD change the way you do sports?

Tijana Duricek
Texas Christian University Women's Soccer
2017-2021

133

May 12

"I pray that out of his glorious riches he may strengthen you with power through his Spirit in your inner being, so that Christ may dwell in your hearts through faith. And I pray that you, being rooted and established in love, may have power, together with all the saints, to grasp how wide and long and high and deep is the love of Christ, and to know this love that surpasses knowledge – that you may be filled to the measure of all the fullness of God."
– Ephesians 3:16-19 NIV

Among the successes, challenges, and failures experienced as a student-athlete, the one constant I could always rely on was God's love for me. Particularly through the tribulations, I had a visual reminder of God's love right in front of me every day at practice and competitions – a swimming pool. Relating this body of water to the ocean was my way "to grasp how wide and long and high and deep is the love of Christ." From Paul's prayer, we know God's love is unfathomable to us on Earth. When I visualize the ocean, I can only see the water up to the horizon. What I cannot see, is the vastness of the entire ocean. The ocean is an analogy to Paul's prayer. The imagery of the ocean was, and still is, my constant reminder of the love of Christ. Although His love cannot be measured or explained, I was experiencing and swimming in His love every day at the pool. Recognizing and experiencing God's love is only the beginning of securing and strengthening an unshakable trust in His promises.

Take a moment today to thank God for His unconditional love. How will you experience the vastness of His love today?

Savanna Townsend
Iowa State University Women's Swimming & Diving
2013-2017

May 13

"For I know the plans I have for you," declares the Lord,
"plans to prosper you and not to harm you, plans to give you hope
and a future." -Jeremiah 29:11 NIV

What does it mean to be 'enough'? Often times as athletes I feel like we are being forced to ask ourselves that question.

It was the summer of 2008. I found myself back in Iowa after the Cubs had signed a Japanese player named Kosuke Fukudome to replace me. I remember asking myself, "What am I going to have to do to prove that I am enough? God what are you doing?" As I wrestled with each of those questions, I will never forget the day that I got back into my car after one of my games in Iowa, with tears coming down my face, I told myself that I had enough. People continued to encourage me to keep going, and though I struggled through the remainder of that year I was able to limp across the finish line of the 2008 season. Fast forward two years to 2010: After accepting a contract to play for the Hanshin Tigers in Japan, God enabled me to break Ichiro's single season hit record and I found myself on stage at Osaka-Jo Hall, sharing my testimony in front of ten thousand Japanese at a Franklin Graham festival. Many people came forward during the invitation to give their life to Christ. God told me, in that moment; Remember the pain that you felt in 2008? Though you may not have felt it then, I was at work. I had a plan for your life, I see you, I love you, and you are "enough" just the way I formed you.

Will you put your trust in His plan for your life? No matter what the world is telling you, He is saying you are enough!

Matt Murton
Chicago Cubs / Hanshin Tigers
2003-2017

May 14

"So let us hold tightly without wavering to the hope we affirm,
for God can be trusted to keep his promise." -Hebrews 10:23 NLT

I remember a few years ago when I was playing professional volleyball in Serbia, and it felt like such a random place to be and a random season of life. I remember asking God, "why am I here? What's the next step for me?". Because, at that time, according to my circumstances, I was not thriving or succeeding both in my job as a volleyball player, but also in my spiritual devotion to God. That was my 3rd year overseas and the separation from friends and family was beginning to weigh on me.

While in Serbia, I was reading through Isaiah and got caught on the word "hope". The Hebrew word for hope used most often in scripture is QAVAH- to wait with tension or with eager expectation. Biblical hope is active, not passive. And it is based in the unchanging and unfailing character of God, not our circumstances.

Now, looking back, I'm reminded that God never wastes anything in our lives. In fact, it's the seasons of life that seem most confusing and relentlessly difficult where He produces the most fruit in us. I didn't see it at the time, but God was pruning all the distractions and comforts I had grown accustomed to. I learned in that season, that God doesn't always change our circumstances, because sometimes He is more concerned about changing our perspective.

The question is, where are we placing our hope? What are we clinging to in hard times? The Bible says God is the source of hope.

Sarah Blomgren
University of South Carolina Volleyball
2012-2016

136

May 15

"For it is by grace you have been saved, through faith—and this is not from yourselves, it is the gift of God— not by works, so that no one can boast." -Ephesians 2:8-9 NIV

It is so easy to get wrapped up in our performances and outcomes. I can't count the amount of times I have wondered about my worth as a result of a bad day on the golf course. I went so many years being blinded by a lie that my performances and scores define me. I remember getting to the point where I was never satisfied with any performance of mine on the golf course. Coming across the quote; "God's love is not based on performance" opened my eyes. Diving deeper into this quote, writing it down everywhere I looked, and eventually living by this quote, I had transformed my entire perception of performance results.

God gave Himself for you to glorify and live through Him, not for you to prove His love for you. He's already made the ultimate sacrifice. Who are we to think our performance will determine His love for us? He loves us no matter how good or bad our performance is. He is blessing us by giving us the ability to play the game we love while also giving us passion and drive.

In your next day of competition, I challenge you to prepare well and give it your all, but also recognizing that no matter the outcome, Jesus never expects perfection. God's love is not based on performance. Let this fact give you peace, allow you to play your sport freely, and decrease the pressure you're putting on yourself.

Libby Winans
University of Oklahoma Women's Golf
2018-2022

May 16

*"The grass withers, the flower fades, but the word of our God
will stand forever."*
-Isaiah 40:8 ESV

Throughout what seemed like a basketball career of constantly falling short, the fear of letting people down crippled me. The realization that I might have failed the expectations my coaches and teammates had of me consumed me. I made the mistake of putting my hope and trust in an outcome, instead of in our constant Provider. I placed value in the approval and affirmation I would receive from a good game. At times, the weight of the pressure I set on myself to measure up to the opinions of others crushed me. But God, in His grace and kindness reminded me that the things I was striving and working for only brought emptiness.

Although a process, I learned to cling to the One who provides true life and hope. When the pursuit of acceptance and glory ultimately failed me, the everlasting truth of the cross remained. The word of our God is living and active – full of redemption and power, deserving of our undivided attention. We can rest in the simple peace that our striving conquers nothing, but the blood of Jesus allows us to live in the fullness of who God tells us we are through His Word.

Ask God to help you fully surrender your trust to Him and His Word.

Rebekah Hand
Marist College Women's Basketball
2016-2020

May 17

"You can make many plans, but the LORD's purpose will prevail." -Proverbs 19:21 NLT

Accepting that the LORD's purpose will always prevail has completely changed my life as a Christian and as an athlete.

Sometimes your plan and His plan line up, but often they don't. I never planned on having multiple coaching changes during college. I never planned to transfer schools. I never planned to switch from football to track and field after my freshman year. But once I recognized who was truly in charge, I found joy and peace in all of the uncertainty and change.

When our plans don't materialize how we want them to, we often say "everything went wrong". Our definition of wrong, however, can turn into God's definition of perfect. God will put us where He needs us, and where He knows we need to be. He can use any person or situation for good. As your relationship with the LORD and your prayer life grow, changes and obstacles turn into gifts from God. Closed doors turn into new opportunities to seek Him in whatever life brings your way.

Think of a time when your plan didn't work. Consider how the Lord was with you in that moment.

Wyatt Rhoads
Iowa State University / University of Colorado Men's Track & Field
2015-2021

May 18

Then Jesus said, "Come to me, all of you who are weary and
carry heavy burdens and I will give you rest. Take my yoke upon you.
Let me teach you, because I am humble and gentle at heart, and you
will find rest for your souls."
- Matthew 11:28-29 NLT

There are many good things that Jesus calls me to while I am here on earth. He calls me to be a leader on my team with my words and my actions. He calls me to give my best in school. He calls me to be a loving husband to my wife. He calls me to serve in my local church. All of these things are good. My life with Jesus is radically different because of the purpose He gives me by enabling me to live a life that can have an eternal impact. However, I am continually reminded of the fact that I cannot do these things on my own.

When I try to accomplish good things without Jesus, I get left feeling overwhelmed, anxious, and frustrated. And Jesus always calls me home.

I plead with you to return to Jesus when you are weary. Give Him your burdens and pray for rest for your soul. Jesus has always met me in that space with open arms and He promises to meet you there too.

Kyle Hiebert
Missouri State University Men's Soccer
2015-2021

May 19

"For God has not given us a spirit of fear and timidity, but of power, love and self-discipline."
— 2 Timothy 1:7 NLT

Paul wrote a very personal final letter to Timothy while he was awaiting his execution in a Roman prison. This letter begins with Paul acknowledging Timothy's firm faith and encouraging him to remain steadfast. He emphasizes that Jesus' grace is the ultimate power source – it emerges as calmness when fear starts to creep in. We should always go to Him in prayer. It takes hard work to follow Jesus, but what a privilege! We must be willing to make sacrifices and press on with our eyes fixed upwards on Him.

My college volleyball experience was a unique one to say the least. It consisted of 5 years and 3 different universities. Moving around like that, it would have been very easy for me to be filled with fear and doubt. However, I knew in my heart that I was planted right where God wanted me. The moving around hasn't stopped as a professional volleyball player over the last 4 years. I still always go to God for guidance and know that His hand is on each move. There are times in life where making decisions will be scary – will God's loving calmness or the fear that is not from Him take over?

Take a prayerful moment to reflect on a time when you had to make a difficult decision. How did you respond? Did calmness or fear arise? Next, think about who has influenced you to continue looking upwards. Reach out and let them know how much of an impact they had on your life.

Andie (Malloy) Baguley
Baylor University / University of Nebraska Volleyball
2012-2017

141

May 20

"His pleasure is not in the strength of the horse, nor his delight in the legs of the warrior; the LORD delights in those who fear him, who put their hope in his unfailing love.
-Psalm 147:10-11 NIV

The daily physical demand of athletics was a burden too heavy for me to carry. My teammates needed a leader and point scorer, my coaches expected an All-American, and yet every workout, practice, and training session left me empty, exhausted, and wondering if I would ever be strong enough.

Suddenly God gifted me with this verse and my entire perspective changed. I was not there to be the strongest, greatest, most talented athlete. I was there to live out every day in such a way that the light and love of Jesus would be put on display for all to see. My physical weakness forced me to declare my absolute dependence on the strength of God alone and in doing so, His name was glorified and made know to those around me. I needed to be brought low so that Jesus's name could be lifted high.

No matter what role you play in your sport, top scorer or third string, God is more concerned about the condition of your heart than the strength of your legs, your performance, or your highest accolade. He is more interested in your dependence on Him and your desire to love others out of gratitude for how much He loves you. Put all your hope in the unconditional overflowing love of God, it will always be enough.

How can you use your position and weaknesses to put the name of Jesus on display for all to see?

McKenna Woodford
Washington State University Volleyball
2015-2019

May 21

*And he said to all, "If anyone would come after me, let
him deny himself and take up his cross daily and follow
me. For whoever would save his life will lose it, but whoever loses his
life for my sake will save it. For what does it profit a man if he gains
the whole world and loses or forfeits himself?"*
-Luke 9:23-25 ESV

As a student-athlete, I thought senior year was supposed to be
filled with fantastic performances as a culmination of life-long
commitment to a sport. Instead, it was constant disappointment that I
wasn't achieving the times or places I had achieved earlier in my
career. I became so consumed with my perceived failure, putting all
my energy into what I thought I could do to save my season.

In Luke 9, Jesus teaches us to put our energy and our lifelong
passion into proclaiming His name, not to make most of ourselves.
Our time on Earth is so short and is truly only preparation for the
wonders of Heaven. We're called to die to ourselves and use our
skills, passions, and gifts for His sake. That means not dwelling on
sports achievements and disappointments but finding ways through
those experiences to glorify Him. Life with open hands for Jesus will
prove to be exceedingly more purposeful and fulfilling than anything
else. For me, this kind of a focus lifted the pressure of performance
and allowed me to be fully engaged in my last swimming
competitions.

**How can you deny yourself in practice or competition today and
take up your cross to follow Jesus?**

Brooke Evensen
Iowa State University Women's Swimming and Diving
2013-2017

143

May 22

"But thanks be to God, who gives us the victory through our Lord Jesus Christ." - 1 Corinthians 15:57 ESV

During my collegiate golf career, I played each week against my teammates in order for our coach to determine who qualified for the upcoming tournament. During my freshman year, I worried that I wouldn't be good enough to qualify and my teammates would replace me on the traveling team. My performance started to tank because I worried so much about the outcome.

Then, after attending an FCA (Fellowship of Christian Athletes) huddle, I learned that my identity wasn't found in my performance, but rather in who Jesus says I am. He is the King of all kings and the Lord of all lords. Ultimately, He's the Coach of all coaches. Knowing this truth freed me up to use my talent to bring glory to Him.

Whenever I need guidance through a difficult situation, or just need to be coached up, I know I can turn to Jesus. He holds an undefeated record against death itself and He recruited us to be on His victorious team. It's a win-win!

Jesus is the ultimate G.O.A.T. (Greatest of All Time). When you give your life to Jesus, you are forever victorious through Him. Live freely knowing you are on Team Jesus and glorify Him in all your actions today.

Christie Emery
Young Harris College Women's Golf
2014-2018

May 23

"Now to him who is able to do far more abundantly than all that we ask or think, according to the power at work within us, to him be glory in the church and in Christ Jesus throughout all generations, forever and ever. Amen." - Ephesians 3:20-21 ESV

Have you ever felt like a misfit or that you didn't belong? Growing up, as well as in the college arena, I didn't always have the confidence in competition which just didn't match up with the work I put in at practice. Feelings of being out of place would plague my thoughts with my lack of consistency and thoughts of comparison. However, the Lord showed me that I was right where I belonged and it was once I took my eyes off myself and put them on Him, things started to fall into place. He unveiled to me what a true relationship with Him looks like with saying yes to what may appear scary and risky, what I did not think I was ready for, and what I thought I was not capable of... but God. By His power, grace and mercy, He did far more than I could every think, ask or imagine with His provision in my sport. Most importantly, His provision in changing my heart.

You may feel out of place where you are right now, but remember that sometimes the Lord will put you in places and spaces that you feel unqualified for. An explanation may not be provided but by saying yes to what He has next and fixing our eyes on Him, He reveals what He has in store for our lives to draw us into a deeper relationship with Him.

Take some time to reflect on where the Lord has placed you, how far he has brought you, and give Him thanks.

Hilary Green
Iowa State University Gymnastics
2014-2018

145

May 24

"For by him all things were created, in heaven and on earth,
visible and invisible, whether thrones or dominions or rulers or
authorities-all things were created through him and for him. And he is
before all things, and in him all things hold together."
-Colossians 1:16-17 ESV

I have always wanted to be the best I could, and I felt this most in my sports, grades, and relationships. These are great things, the Lord gave me passion for them, and I've always wanted to excel in each area. This drove me and helped me get an opportunity to play college football, study a subject that would allow me to get into medical school and maintain a relationship for nearly four years.

My Junior year, my girlfriend and I split, I was told my chances of getting into medical school were 4%, my spiritual mentor passed from pancreatic cancer and I tore my ACL in practice. My world was falling apart, everything I had worked so hard to build was crashing down in the span of a few months and I was defeated. In this season of my life, I continually felt God say to me, "I have something better. I am faithful." I held on to these words and today God has blessed me with community that has lifted me up daily. Our God is so good, and He will always fulfill His promises. The more we lean on Him, the stronger our foundation will be when the storms come. The Creator of all things wants to be involved in your life personally and give you peace when life gets hard.

What are some ways that you have seen God's plan unfold in a way that was better than yours?

Cam Collins
Southwestern University Football
2018-2022

146

May 25

"Faith is confidence in what we hope for and assurance about what we do not see." - Hebrews 11:1

Like Peter, step out in faith and God will not let you drown. Sharing my faith was difficult growing up. I didn't have all the answers about God and was always worried about embarrassing myself. But pursuing God gave me the confidence and understanding that it's okay not to understand everything. If I understood everything, faith wouldn't be necessary. My perspective on life changed when I started caring more about how God saw me rather than how other people saw me.

God is always with you. He is closer to you than you are to your own skin. At my lowest points in life, God showed up when I needed Him. When He lets a situation seem hopeless, He is about to show off in your life. If the timing isn't right, it won't happen yet. Have patience. Remain faithful. God's timing is always perfect.

Slow growth is still growth. If you keep heading in the right direction you will eventually get to where you want to go. My journey in strengthening my relationship with God is daily. A good friend says there are two things you can't live without, air and prayer. I'm thankful for still breathing today, and I can't remember the last day I went without talking to God. God wants to talk to you, and He wants you to talk to Him.

Are you running your own race? Are you faithful through difficult situations? Are you consistent in your pursuit of God?

TJ Holyfield
Stephen F. Austin State / Texas Tech University Men's Basketball
2015-2020

147

May 26

*"For our sake he made him to be sin who knew no sin, so
that in him we might become the righteousness of God."*
-2 Corinthians 5:21 ESV

Growing up the grandson of a conservative preacher, I was constantly reminded to represent our family well. Every Sunday after church, my grandfather would ask his grandkids to see our notes from the sermon. I didn't have a genuine interest in the substance of the message, but purely the approval of my grandfather- so I obeyed out of fear of disappointment. Fast forward to college. I still viewed my relationship with God in the same manner- a duty or obligation to follow the rules, but my heart wasn't in it. I was merely performing for acceptance but felt like a failure. There was no way God was proud of me. I was tired and worn out from religion.

I came across the "Read the Bible in 90 Days" plan on the Bible App and made a commitment to myself that I would follow through with it. I began to read the story of God's chosen people and their history of continually letting Him down. I was amazed at His pursuit of them despite their failures. He wanted their heart. This culminated with God wrapping on flesh in the form of Jesus and being crucified so that He could take their place and credit His righteousness to them. I was wrecked. What a love. I began to obey out of a heart overflowing with thankfulness, no longer for approval. The Father had performed a spiritual heart transplant in my life.

Commit to starting your day in Scripture. It's not always fun, but He always shows up.

Jaxon Shipley
University of Texas Football
2011-2014

May 27

"Then David said, "The Lord who rescued me from the paw of the lion and the paw of the bear will rescue me from the hand of this Philistine." Saul said to David, "Go, and may the Lord be with you." - 1 Samuel 17:37 CSB

Most of us have heard the story of David and Goliath. This was the same for me my junior year as I opened my Bible at the Big 12 Championship. Anxiety was high, the pressure I felt was higher, I had a torn labrum, and to make matters worse I was dealing with food poisoning. At this point, I was grasping for anything.

Reading that morning my eyes were opened for the first time to the fact David "chose five smooth stones from the stream, put them in the pouch of his shepherd's bag and, with his sling in his hand, approached the Philistine." (V41) because he was not used to the armor Saul tried to dress him in.

Many times in our walk with the Lord we try to come to God dressed in armor, when in fact he really wants us to come just the way we are. David chose to do what he knew how to do and be his authentic self. This ultimately led to him defeating Goliath.

Sometimes we will defeat the giant and sometimes we won't. Our God wants us just as we are, His child, and e will be with us. I rejoice in the fact that God allowed me that week to drop the weight and compete for his glory.

What do you need to let go of today to allow you to be authentic with God?

Mary Michael Witherell (Maggio)
Texas A&M University Women's Golf
2011-2013

May 28

"Do everything without grumbling and arguing, so that you may be blameless and pure, children of God who are faultless in a crooked and perverted generation, among whom you shine like stars in the world." - Philippians 2:14-15 CSB

Shine. That one word, now tattooed on my wrist, is a reminder to me that my actions should always point myself and those around me to the Lord. During my time with Iowa State Volleyball, some teammates and I had a weekly Bible study. As we studied *Philippians 2:14-15,* we wanted a way to hold each other accountable to the life transforming lessons we learned that day. We chose to use the word 'shine' as a reminder to each other that all of our actions should reflect Jesus to others and that the Holy Spirit is in us, shining His light to the world. That word shaped the way we treated our teammates, reacted to wins and losses, completed all the reps in the weight room, and respected our coaches, teammates, officials, and so on. As we grow in our walk with the Lord, our hearts change to look more like Jesus in all we do. Sometimes we just need a simple reminder to let God shine through our lives.

As an athlete there are many times where it's easy to grumble and argue about fatigue, teammates, playing time, etc. Give those things to the Lord and invite Him into those struggles, pray that you can shine for Him in everything you do!

Suzanne (Horner) Snyder
LiigaPloki Mestaruusliiga Volleyball
2017-2019

"Indeed, I count everything as loss because of the surpassing worth of knowing Christ Jesus my Lord. For his sake I have suffered the loss of all things and count them as rubbish, in order that I may gain Christ." - Philippians 3:8 ESV

Chasing after success is easy to do in the world of athletics. There is always more that we can do and more success to be had. As a student-athlete, it seemed my eyes were only focused on the next win or award that I could get my hands on. I believed that with a certain level of athletic achievement, I'd sigh in contentment with where my life was at.

As I went to take that sigh, I felt anything but contentment. I was disheartened and full of sorrow. I realized that while I was chasing everything that didn't matter, I left behind the One that did.

It's easy to get distracted with what our coaches, teammates, and fans view as success and value. To push aside what truly matters to gain something we ultimately know will fade and vanish. As followers of Christ, let us run after Christ more than we run after our own achievements. Let us push aside anything that gets in our way of following Jesus and joyfully count it as loss for the sake of gaining Him. Because we know that what we gain from this world is temporary and fleeting, but what we have in Christ is eternal.

Take a moment to reflect on where you spend your best time and energy. Is it spent on chasing the things of this world or gaining Christ?

Caitlyn Merzbacher
University of Minnesota Women's Tennis
2015-2019

May 30

"And we know that God causes everything to work together[a]
for the good of those who love God and are called according to his
purpose for them." - Romans 8:28

My sports career has become a microcosm of my life. The
mental and physical trials I have gone through to get where I am today
have been unpredictable. But Romans 8:28 comforts me in knowing
that as long as I am living for Christ and doing everything I can to
represent Him in everything I do, that all will work out for me in all
aspects of my life.

As a football player, you have to sacrifice the desires of
yourself and put the well-being of the team at the forefront. It is the
same concept as a Christian, as we must give of ourselves for the
well-being of the body of Christ and know that our actions affect a
bigger team.

It is always hard to see the bigger picture when you are in the
frame. As time goes on in life, your sports career, or your journey
after sports, we know confidently that our work is not being left
unnoticed. If we live a selfless life seeking to help others and show
them Christ through our actions, then we know God will work in our
favor for the ultimate good.

**In all situations, good or bad, ask yourself "How is God using me
and what can I learn from this?". There is always a bigger plan at
work.**

Jeremiah Oatsvall
Austin Peay State University / University of Memphis Football
2017-2022

May 31

"For the wages of sin is death, but the free gift of God is eternal life through Christ Jesus our Lord." – Romans 6:23 ESV

As athletes we earn scholarships, playing time, and starting spots. On my college team, nothing was freely given. I remember getting my first collegiate start halfway through my freshman season. I was proud, it felt like I had truly earned the opportunity. This striving mentality is beneficial in athletics, but it was a major block when I was confronted with the truth that no matter how much I do for God, it does not earn me a right relationship with Him.

The concept of "freely given" is hard to wrap our minds around as athletes because we are so accustomed to striving, achieving, and earning everything that we receive. But God's word says that eternal life is a *gift,* more specifically, it is a *free* gift, which means that we did not, and cannot, do anything to earn this gift.

By God's grace, I was able to learn that my performance and works for God could not earn me good standing with Him. In contrast, all I had to do was receive the free gift of Jesus dying in my place. No meddling or performing on my part, just simply believing, and trusting that Jesus' work on the Cross is enough.

Take some time to read and meditate on Romans 6:23 and John 17:3. What are these verses saying? Ask God to show you the ways you have been trying to work for His approval. How can you find rest in the finished work of Christ today?

Laramie Hall
Kansas State University Women's Soccer
2016-2020

June 1

"So do not worry, saying, 'What shall we eat?' or 'What shall we drink?' or 'What shall we wear?' For the pagans run after all these things, and your heavenly Father knows that you need them. But seek first his kingdom and his righteousness, and all these things will be given to you as well. Therefore do not worry about tomorrow, for tomorrow will worry about itself. Each day has enough trouble of its own." - Matthew 6:31-34

In life, we often encounter things that can cause us to stumble during our walk with Christ. My athletic career in general was plagued with injuries. Throughout that journey, I found myself becoming anxious about when I would be able to compete again, or IF I would be able to compete again. The times that I would lean into the Lord and His promises for His children, were the times I would find a surreal amount of peace.

When going through uncertainty and adversity, it can be scary. It can feel like you're at the bottom of the mountain and the top isn't visible. These feelings of anxiety are a part of our sinful nature. However, Jesus defeated death so we can find victory in those moments, *regardless* of our sinful nature. There is nothing to worry about when you invite Jesus into your worries or anxieties. His love is everlasting. He calls you by your name. He knows every hair on your head. Seek first His kingdom, and just take a deep breath; It is already finished!

Next time you are at the bottom of a mountain looking up, invite Jesus to climb it with you. "Faith is a journey, not a destination."

Gavin DeWitt
Iowa State University / Maryville University Wrestling
2016-2020

June 2

"For where two or three gather in my name, there I am with them" - *Matthew 18:20 NIV*

Imagine making it to the NCAA tournament, or any other major collegiate championship. It's a big deal! My junior year, we had made it to the NCAA tournament and were about to play the University of Florida in the second round. My teammate and I planned a Bible study in our hotel room the night before the biggest match any of us had ever played. We had twelve out of the fourteen of us total in that hotel room. It was SO EVIDENT God was in that room with us. Every time I read this verse in Matthew, I think of that night in that hotel room. Each of us was from a different part of the world, let alone the country. California, Florida, Texas, Georgia, Greece, Russia, and more were represented. I remember sitting there in awe of the moment and how this verse came to life right before my eyes. "Where two or three gather in my name, there I am with them." God continued to lead us throughout that season as we prayed with our opponents before matches, even our rivals, highlighting yet again, regardless of the circumstances, God is with us when we gather together in His name.

Reflect on moments in your story where this verse also came to life. Pray for God to lead you into more opportunities to gather in His name with others, whether that be teammates, friends, etc. Coming together with other people impacted my faith immensely and I pray that for you too!

Kolby Bird
University of Miami Volleyball
2015-2019

155

June 3

"Yet to all who did receive Him, to those who believed in His name, He gave the right to become children of God." – John 1:12 NIV

Who am I? Ask yourself that question.

For my first two years in college, I was a starter for the Texas A&M football team. I believed those words made me something important, and meant I was a part of something that people cared about. I had reached my dream of being a starter, and I knew it made me a big deal. Unfortunately, that title got taken away from me after I broke my foot in a practice, and you know what happened? The team went on the road, won the game, and my name was never mentioned.

I reached the pinnacle of college football, and I was forgotten. I did not even want to go do things when the team traveled because I did not want to be seen as not being a part of the football team. I allowed myself only be known as Austin Frey the football player. A saying I have heard many times allowed me to see who I truly was in the mirror, "when you are what you do, and what you do gets taken away, who will you be?" I had to change my identity from Austin Frey the football player to Austin Frey a child of God. I realized that being known as only a football player was too small of an identity, and I needed something that could never leave me or forsake me.

As athletes we will all be replaced at some point. Who will you be at the end of your career? What is your identity now? Right down who you want to be and read it daily and watch how that affects the way you live.

Austin Frey
Texas A&M University Football
2014-2018

156

June 4

"As the heavens are higher than the earth, so are my ways higher than your ways and my thoughts than your thoughts."
-Isaiah 55:9 NIV

We so often try to put boundaries or limits on what *we* think God cares about or what *we* think God can do with our circumstances. I used to not think that God really cared about volleyball. I was unhappy and disappointed with how volleyball was going, at the time, and I questioned why God would allow things to go so differently than I expected. Satan wants nothing more than for us to have a wrong view of God and His power. I allowed lies to control how I felt about God, and I doubted that He really had good plans for my life. But over time, God has used volleyball to humble me and show His great love and power. I never thought a game could be used like that.

God doesn't think the same way we do. His ways are *higher than our ways*. If we try to put limits on what God can and cannot do with our lives, we rob ourselves of seeing Him work in incredible ways and we rob God of the glory He is worthy of. There is no one that God cannot reach and no story that God cannot redeem. Don't allow lies to place limits on a limitless God. Grace itself, displayed on the cross through Jesus Christ, shows us that God's thoughts and ways are not like ours. There is grace, there is power, and there is peace in trusting in the power of the One who holds our lives in His hands.

What limits have you put on God? What areas of your life do you need to learn to trust in God and rest His infinite power?

Tori Dilfer
University of Louisville Volleyball
2019-2022

157

June 5

"Humble yourselves, therefore, under God's mighty hand,
that he may lift you up in due time. Cast all your anxiety on
him because he cares for you." – 1 Peter 5:6-7 NIV

The Lord has been so clear at laying these verses on my heart in my recent years competing professionally. God is always reminding us to be humble and to realize how He desires to lift us up— reminding us we aren't where we are today by our own strength. It is so evident God loves doing sports with us, He loves showing Himself to us on and off the field of competition, but He also loves to be intentional. When we are struggling, He leans into our problems or concerns, and guides us to community to help us endure the hills and valleys.

As athletes, the limelight can distract us from our purpose of The Great Commission and being a true light for sharing the gospel on our teams. We can carry so much anxiety to perform and a desire to succeed, but we can't let that overpower our true goal as Christ-followers. Therefore, we are not here to perform for man, or to even perform for Christ; He loves us and even while we were still sinners Christ died for us. Despite our abilities or failures, Jesus wants to use us for His Kingdom building, not for building a bigger following on social media. Let's keep running after the real eternal prize and seek first His Kingdom and His righteousness over the things of this world!

.

How can we be more conscious of competitive pride and not let it distract us from the ultimate goal of making disciples?

Jade Hayes
P1440 Professional Beach Volleyball
2018

June 6

Then Jesus said to his disciples, "Whoever wants to be my disciple must deny themselves and take up their cross and follow me. For whoever wants to save their life will lose it, but whoever lose their life for me will find it." – Matthew 16:24-25 NIV

God is sovereign over all things. He is in control. It took me a lot longer to understand that than I'd like to admit. Growing up, I dreamed of being a scholarship athlete at the Division I level. I had worked hard for three years to shed my walk-on status my senior year, but God had other plans. Although I was crushed, the Lord was stretching me. He was asking me to surrender to His will for my life and to stop clinging so tightly to my will for my life. I spent 25 years thinking my plan was better than the plan the Creator of the universe has for me... Not anymore. There is beauty in surrender. Christ surrendered His life on the Cross, so that we could be forgiven of our sins - past, present, and future.

My prayer is that as you and I grow closer to Him, we can live our lives in obedience to who He has called us to be. Seek our loving Father and root yourself in community with other believers. We've been on teams our entire lives, don't go solo now.

We find rest, peace, and joy in the Lord when we let go of our longing to be loved by the world. We can't truly love others until we embrace the love, grace, and mercy we receive through relationship with Jesus Christ.

Clark Lammert
Texas Tech University Men's Basketball
2011-2015

159

June 7

"For it is by grace you have been saved, through faith- and this is not from yourselves, it is the gift from God- not by works, so that no one can boast. For we are God's handiwork, created in Christ Jesus to do good works, which God prepared in advance for us to do." - Ephesians 2:8-10 NIV

Just as most college athletes, I was the topic of many conversations, interviews, articles, and accolades in high school. I thought "this is what living feels like." Then I got to college. Last man off of the bench, receiving no praises for the one thing that I thought would always give me worth and praise.

I was unbelievably frustrated. The Lord orchestrated my life to have some of the highest highs in basketball, where I thought my worth laid, just to take it all away. I remember thinking "God, I am working so hard. Why is it not enough?" I remember His response so clearly. "My child, you have always been enough."

My thoughts on basketball, and life in general, dramatically changed since finding Christ. My worth would never be found in basketball. It has always been through Christ. This realization allowed me to play the sport I loved in such a freeing way. Did things always go the way I wanted? No. But what never changed was His faithfulness in and through my life. The ball will stop bouncing for everyone. Once that happens you will search for worth in something. Turn your eyes and your hearts to the One that will never fail.

Where does your identity and worth lie? Praise God always and ask Him to show you how to truly find your identity in Him.

Ashley (Gomez) Hankins
Xavier University Women's Basketball
2016-2020

160

"Physical Training is good, but training for godliness is much better, promising benefits in this life and the life to come."
-1 Timothy 4:8 NLT

As athletes we put heavy emphasis into physical training. We lift weights daily, condition, work agilities, and are detailed about which items we allow to be put into our bodies. These are all good things to do, but as much time and diligence as we put into our physical training, are we doing the same for our spirit? Do we train for godliness? Again, there is nothing wrong when we train for the physical, yet we see that it's much better to train for godliness. Unfortunately, at some point, sports come to an end and physical training does not have as much importance as it once did. However, training for godliness provides 'promising benefits in this life and in the life to come'. Training for godliness sets us up to reflect Christ, gives us eternal mindsets and conditions us not to put our identity in sports, but rather, place our identity in the Lord. I can understand why Paul says in Colossians 3:2 "Think about the things of heaven, not the things of earth". Though godliness does not make this life the most comfortable, it undoubtedly is the most fulfilling life one can live in this world.

So, I leave you with this...how hard are you really training? We should be training for godliness just as much, if not more, than training for the physical.

Geremy Davis
New York Giants / San Diego Chargers / Detroit Lions
2015-2020

June 9

"Therefore, my brothers and sisters, stand firm. Let nothing move you. Always give yourselves fully to the work of the Lord because you know that your labor in the Lord is not in vain."
-1 Corinthians 15:58 NIV

I played five years of college volleyball with the sole goal of winning a conference championship or national title. Neither of these goals came to fruition during my time at the colleges that I attended. The year after I graduated, the university I had played for finally won a conference title. In a way I felt slighted, cheated, and left out.

For the next year I wrestled with this frustration. And as I sought the Lord through my questions, I started to understand how I was a part of building a healthy program which is more important than a Championship.

I believe one of the many lessons we learn as college athletes is that we must give ourselves fully to our team with the hope of a physical reward at the end of the season. But I believe that God wanted to teach me that laying a strong foundation, building healthy culture, and leading by example is more important than standing on a stage gaining recognition at the end of a season. As I have moved into my professional career, I strive to give myself fully to the Lord in my work. To help lay a foundation for healthy culture whether I see a physical reward. We must remind ourselves what we do with our life is not our own, it's the Lord's. He deserves the glory, not us.

Ask the Lord to shift your perspective from a me to a we mindset. Meaning you and Him.

Tori Ortman
California Baptist University Volleyball
2013-2016

June 10

"For God is working in you, giving you the desire and the power to do what pleases him." -Philippians 2:13

As a college athlete, there are a lot of pressures which are a part of the game. Not until I finished playing college volleyball while receiving my Bachelor's in Nursing, did I realize how much these external pressures truly affected me.

To play at the highest level you can't just be good at volleyball, you have to also stay mentally tough through the 5th set, be a player that can put the ball away during a long rally, and you also have to block out the external pressures of the crowd. Making errors is a part of any athlete's game. It's when these errors become consuming negative thoughts about yourself, talents and skills and God wants us to use those gifts to bring honor and glorification to His name.

During matches and practices, I began to take moments to praise His name and recite truths that are in His word over myself. Doing this kept me shielded from the negative works of the enemy. I believed that I could achieve any outcome because of Christ, but the truth is, regardless of the outcome, I could rest at night and be content BECAUSE of Christ. Giving up complete control was the best thing that I ever did, and it showed when I played. The Lord seeks a deeper relationship with each and every one of us, it is not always about the big prayers before games, and the verses written on athlete's shoes or the tattoos to show your devotion to Christ, but the small daily efforts that we make to keep Christ at the center of all that we do.

How will you keep Christ your center?

Sarah Peterson
Newman University Volleyball
2014-2018

163

June 11

"Three times I pleaded with the Lord about this, that it should leave me. But he said to me, "My grace is sufficient for you, for my power is made perfect in weakness." Therefore I will boast all the more gladly for my weakness, so that the power of Christ may rest upon me." -2 Corinthians 12:8-9 ESV

In this passage Paul is begging God to take this hardship from him. Instead of satisfying that request through the removal of the hardship, God used it as an opportunity to remind Paul of who his God is. Our God is sovereign, strong, and powerful even when all we see is our own weakness.

In sports, weakness is never something that is valued. My sophomore year of college I struggled with a chronic knee injury. The whole season I played never feeling that I was at my best. I lamented, struggling to understand where God was in my weakness. Through this, God reminded me of my brokenness and my undying need for Him in every aspect of my life. God does not look upon our weakness with disappointment because He knows the fragility of our human state. We are constantly in need of His strength.

In Christ, weakness is not something to hide or dismiss. God uses these moments to reveal what is in our hearts and to strengthen our relationship with Him. Not only does this humble us before our Creator, but it puts us in a position to witness more of His greatness. We can boast in our weakness knowing that anything that is accomplished is a true reflection of God's goodness and power.

Reflect on past times when His strength has carried you through.

Ayoka Lee
Kansas State University Women's Basketball
2018-2023

164

June 12

"… 'God has shown me that I should not call any person common or unclean. So when I was sent for, I came without objection. I ask then why you sent for me.'" -Acts 10:28-29 ESV

Jesus was reviled for His table-fellowship with sinners and tax collectors. Peter found himself in a potentially similar situation when he entered the home of Cornelius, a Roman soldier. Even though Cornelius' household was a God-fearing one, the cultural standards of the time made it an uncomfortable place for him to be. Yet, Peter obediently went where he had been sent.

Dugouts and locker rooms might be some of the most spiritually toxic places that athletes enter. Yet, our athletic gifts from God have practically sent us into these places. Jesus promises that we are sent like sheep among wolves, and He demands that we be wise as serpents, innocent as doves. Indeed, some teammates will be positively repulsive to your Christian sensibilities. And while you work to distance yourself from the debauchery, you may also be tempted to join in on some level – and you will.

Peter learned from the Lord that he should call no man common or unclean, and he learned that he could expect to be sent to anyone, anywhere. We, too, are sent to bring healing and mercy in unlikely, uncomfortable, and even unseemly places. Jesus teaches us that the Father desires mercy, and He promises that the Spirit will guide us in all truth – everywhere and at all times. That includes dugouts and locker rooms.

How are you sent to bring mercy, healing, and truth into your dugout or locker room?

Graden "Grady" W. Dahlberg
University of Texas at San Antonio Baseball
1998-2000

June 13

"...But God, being rich in mercy, because of the great with which he loved us...by grace you have been saved—..."
- Ephesians 2:1-10

Pride often hides the barriers in our lives that are limiting us from growing. For too long, I found my identity in football and it was my pride that hid it from me. In my senior year of college, when I knew that football was coming to an end, God used those around me to rebuke me about what I found my identity in. My initial reaction, my pride, was being offended. "They don't really know me." "Who do they think they are?" "I definitely don't idolize football." As the season came to a close and it was all over. The dust finally settled and by God's grace, I saw it. That I was a wretched sinner, walking in pride. Knowing there was nothing I could do to be saved. "But God" in His providence, His own timing, His own chiseling away at my heart of stone covered in pride, God humbled me.

It is sinfulness, like pride, that often blinds us from the light. It is nothing that we do that causes us to grow. It isn't even those around us. Like dead men at the bottom of the sea, it was God who pulled us out and breathed life into us. By grace, we are saved and God makes us low so that He might be high. All thanks to the sacrificial act of Christ on the cross, those who were "dead" are now made alive through Him. Praise be to God!

What is your identity in? I challenge you to think about that in a convicting manner. What eternal weight does that hold?

Chance Pierce
Abilene Christian University Football
2016-2020

June 14

"But one thing I do: Forgetting what is behind and reaching forward to what is ahead" -Philippians 3:13a

It is so hard to forget what is behind us and reach forward in times of adversity. God presented this verse to me at a time during my baseball season when I really needed it. I was going through a rough patch during my season and lots of negative thoughts began to creep into my head. I prayed that God would give me the strength to finish the season strong, but nothing was really changing. I kept praying and trusting in Him and the last week of my season was the best week of my baseball career. That was no coincidence to me.

Baseball is very similar to life in a way where it knocks you down over and over again. You must have a very short-term memory in order to reach forward for what is ahead. It is very easy to get wrapped up in what happened yesterday. God presented me this verse to help me leave yesterday in the past, good outcome or bad, and reach forward to the next challenge ahead.

Pray that God gives you the strength to let go of the past and reach forward to the future!

Bryce Teodosio
Clemson University Baseball
2018-2021

June 15

"So, whether you eat or drink, or whatever you do, do everything for the glory of God." -1 Corinthians 10:31 ESV

For many years my idea of success as an athlete was based on stats and awards. I sought recognition from everyone, and that was where my identity and motivation as a player were found. I came to know Jesus my sophomore year of college and God quickly showed me how I had been seeking my glory rather than His. I began to learn what it meant to glorify God in every aspect of my sport. First, in my effort, not just in games and practice but in the warm-up and on the sideline. Second, in my attitude, to pray in moments when I felt myself getting frustrated, challenging myself to be mindful of my complaining. Lastly, in my communication with teammates, coaches, and officials. The words that came out of my mouth needed to be ones that were giving life to others. I sought accountability from those that were able to recognize my selfishness and redirect my thought process on what was most important.

As an athlete, there are many moments that we will be tempted to make much of ourselves, pushing aside the reality that apart from God we are nothing. We have been given a unique platform in sports to shine the light on God, the gift Giver, in every outcome and circumstance. Whether we have our best game or our worst, we win or lose; God is worthy to be praised!

What are some ways that you and/or someone else can help point you back to God and His glory rather than your own?

Aleah Dillard
University of Texas at El Paso Women's Soccer
2012-2017

June 16

" Rejoice always, pray continually, give thanks in all
circumstances; for this is God's will for you in Christ Jesus. "
-1 Thessalonians 5:16-18 NIV

At the end of chapter 5 and in these verses, Paul is reminding the Thessalonians how to act and be prepared for the second coming of Christ. These verses still apply to us today because we are eagerly awaiting the return of Christ. I love these verses because Paul is reminding us to take the focus off ourselves, and put it on Christ.

I remember a pastor speaking on thankfulness once, and he said this; "Having a thankful heart shows where our focus is." If we have a thankful heart, we are less focused on ourselves, and we are more focused on God and what He provides. A thankful heart shows that we trust God no matter what is going on around us, because we recognize that He is in control. Having a thankful heart does not mean just being happy all the time. It means that we turn our hearts to God to recognize Him in every walk of life. God is working for His glory. He knows and wants what is best for us, and when we are thankful, we show that we know He is in control. I love the end of verse 18, "for this is God's will for you in Christ Jesus. We can rejoice always, pray continually, and give thanks because it is God's will for us through His son Christ Jesus. His will be done!

Look at your life right now and share with God all the things you are thankful for.

Brian Klein
Washington Nationals / Atlanta Braves Organization
2020-Present

June 17

"Trust in the Lord and do good; dwell in the land and enjoy safe pastures. Take delight in the Lord, and He will give you the desires of your heart. Commit your way to the Lord; trust in Him and He will do this: He will make your righteous reward shine like the dawn, your vindication like the noonday sun." – Psalm 37:3-6 NIV

As athletes, what you do seems to be all that matters: the spot you earn, the game you win, and the accolades you attain. These things are praised by our world and so easily consume our minds and efforts. In reality, the only thing that matters in our lives is doing what we're called to do by Jesus. We are called to work hard, but we must remember that we work hard to resemble the nature of Jesus, not in a reflection of ourselves or as an attempt to gain worldly approval.

Jesus gives us our athletic ability so that we may carry out His plan for a greater purpose. We are powerful, strong, talented, and confident; however, we are given these things that allow us to succeed by Jesus and Jesus only. We are called to work hard, and we are given the tools to do so. The key to building potential is remembering that we are here to do the kingdom work of the Lord. When adversity hits, when the spot isn't earned, when the game or accolade isn't won, we need to think of why we are in this place: for our ultimate purpose to change the lives of the people around us in an upward direction. When we win, we must remember that it is for His glory, not ours. Our victories are set in place just as our losses are. Our goal is to commit our ways to Him and know that He will act in accordance to His plan.

Commit your ways to Him, trust in Him, and He will act.

Bella Easton
The College of William and Mary Volleyball
2021-2025

170

June 18

"The second is this: 'You shall love your neighbor as yourself.' There is no other commandment greater than these."
-Mark 12:31 ESV

What are your goals for this season?

If I had a dollar for every time I heard that question, I could pay my rent for this month. It's great to have goals, but I want to shift our focus to Christ's goals for us. After all, His goals are better than ours. Jesus commands us, in John 15, that we should "love one another as He has loved us."

Based on this verse, and several others like it, our mission as athletes is to love our teammates. We are called to love ALL of our teammates, including the ones who are hard to deal with. At the end of the day, our athletic careers will not be defined by wins and losses, but by the souls we've interacted with.

We have an AMAZING opportunity today to go and love our teammates well. Go buy a meal for teammate and intentionally ask them how they are doing. Your teammates are never going to care how much you know and love Christ until they know how much you know and love them.

Make loving your teammates the #1 goal for this season. Invest in them, even if they don't invest back.

Your teammates are never going to care how much you know and love Christ until they know how much you know and love them.

Jordan Brown
Texas A&M – Commerce University / Paris Junior College
2014-2018

171

June 19

"The grass withers and flowers fall but the word of our God endures forever." - Isaiah 40:8 NIV

My freshman year of college I was on a tennis team with 9 girls, 5 of which were from out of the country. I realized school was going to be rough and most of my time would be spent playing tennis or working out. We were up for 6am workouts and in the afternoons we were practicing until 4 or 5. After that was done I then had tutoring until around 9. My days were crammed and at the time I didn't even like my sport. Everything about it was frustrating me because I didn't feel like I had a purpose. I felt like every decision I was making was based on what would better my tennis and this team.

Although I struggled through my first year at school, I realized I was there for greater purpose. I was blinded by the grind of my sport at the opportunity I had to truly reach the world. I was so focused on myself and what I could be doing to get better and help myself in times of hurt and frustration that I missed the whole reason of why I was on the team. It wasn't to just get better. I was the only one who knew Jesus and realized if I share Him with these girls who come from all over, they then could go and share Him and His goodness with the entire world. Once I was able to discover my purpose for playing my sport, it freed me from the daily frustrations.

My challenge for you today is this...Do you find yourself focused solely on you at your sport or do you focus on the people you are with?

Alee Clayton
University of Georgia Women's Tennis
2018-2022

172

June 20

"Then the Lord said "You feel sorry about the plant, though you did nothing to put it there. It came quickly and died quickly. But Nineveh has more than 120,00 people living in Spiritual darkness, not to mention all the animals. Should I feel sorry for such a great city?"
- Jonah 4:10-12 NLT

As athletes we pray for our health, for strong bodies and for the opportunities to showcase our abilities for God's glory. Those prayers to an extent have always been answered as we have moved from one practice to the next, one game to the next and one level of competition to the next. We pray for our teammate's health and our teams' successes. We pray for those athletes and coaches around us to all be blessed.

We don't always pray for our opponent's health, success and ability, yet they deserve God's blessings just as much as we do. What I love about the book of Jonah, is that it speaks to the human spirit. We often rebel against God, because what He asks of us sometimes makes us uncomfortable. When we do give in to His will, we do it thinking that God will meet *our* expectations of what He should be doing through us. Jonah fights going to Nineveh because it's uncomfortable, when he finally arrives in Nineveh, he gets upset because God has decided to show mercy to Nineveh and its people. As God gives Jonah a tree for shade, and then kills the tree, Jonah becomes upset. Which leads God to ask, that if Jonah can feel sorry for a plant, shouldn't God feel sorry for a great city (Jonah 4:7-12).

How can we as athletes show and share our blessings with our opponents?

Kaeman Mitchell
University of Illinois Football
2009-2012

173

June 21

*"I came to you in weakness with great fear and trembling.
My message and my preaching were not with wise and persuasive
words, but with a demonstration of the Spirit's power,
so that your faith might not rest on human wisdom, but on God's
power." - 1 Corinthians 2:3-5*

The dilemma between accepting ill-advice from our peers, coaches, or parents and trusting in our ultimate potential is constant for athletes. Throughout my career, I've had countless situations where I sought advice, and it resulted in me questioning my ability to reach my next level goals. The two factors I identified as essential are faith and focus. I allowed my faith to sway away from God's power and the bigger picture to the wisdom of people who may not have understood the vision. That resulted in a less focused, less confident pursuit. I began to consider alternatives more than I considered ways to make my vision come true. The reassurance of God's power enabled my focus to realign just in time. Without it, I would have sold myself short and never pursued a collegiate, nor professional career.

There's real value in understanding the difference between man's wisdom and God's power. People can only give you perspectives based on their own understanding, fears and perspective. God's power, and our faith in Him, enables us for far more achievement, despite our current situations.

Write down what goals you're pursuing and identify two perspectives with each that are limited to the wisdom of your peers, parents, coaches, etc.

Austin Rettig
University of Tampa Men's Basketball
Manchester Giants Basketball Club
2012-2017

June 22

"And he died for all, that those who live should no longer live for themselves but for him who died for them and was raised again."
-2 Corinthians 5:15 NIV

"Who am I?" I had worked so hard to be where I was. I gave up everything for softball: my time, my heart, and my life only to find out something was missing. It was my sophomore year of college that I found myself completely lost, broken, and empty. I remember crying out to God for help because I didn't even know who I was anymore. I was in pursuit of the world, and all my attention was focused on my image and my success in my sport. It was my escape and my identity. In time of questioning, God revealed what was missing: Jesus.

I had known of Jesus my whole life, but nothing in my life changed because of that. It was easy to chase the world and success, but until I chased after Jesus and made Him the Lord of my life, there would have always been something missing. Sports are not a bad thing. Yet, when they consume who we are that's what they become. There is more to life than success. There is more to life than winning. There is more. You can have a relationship with God through Jesus and experience greater joy, peace, and fulfillment than this world could ever give you. Fulfillment that lasts eternally. Whatever you are in pursuit of right now, know that God is in pursuit of you. He wants your heart, not just now but forever.

Evaluate your heart and dig deep. Where is your identity?

Kinsey Koeltzow
University of Oklahoma / Grand Canyon University Softball
2019-2023

June 23

"Blessed be the God and Father of our Lord Jesus Christ,
who according to His great mercy has caused us to be born again to a
living hope through the resurrection of Jesus Christ from the dead."
-1 Peter 1: 3 NASB

While trying to find the perfect uplifting, awe-inspiring verse that every athlete could rally around before every game/meet/match/etc., I was led to this verse in First Peter by the Holy Spirit. One that has no significance in the context of sports. But a verse that starkly reminds us of the foundation on which we stand as Christians. One that fixes our eyes back on Jesus, not ourselves.

God wants us, as Christians, to do great things for the kingdom of God, and as athletes, that can be a bit overwhelming. But God doesn't define these great things as achievements and accolades in this world. He gives us the good news of the gospel and wants us to not lose sight of where our identity, joy, and hope are rooted. There are many distractions in this world that want to take our attention away from our identity in Christ, and sports can be one of them.

Remind yourself of the Father's love for you as a child of His and allow the Holy Spirit to fill your heart with the living hope that is afforded to us through Jesus Christ life, death, and resurrection. Take that unwavering hope with you to your arena and your teammates.

Remind yourself as a Christian athlete, that your identity on this earth is not in how well you perform on your stage, but that you are first and foremost a child of His and He loves you dearly.

Rob Blackwelder
Augusta University Men's Cross Country
2010-2012

176

June 24

"Better is a little with righteousness than great revenues with injustice. The heart of a man plans his way, but the LORD establishes his steps." – Proverbs 16:8-9 ESV

We have all heard the saying, "Let go and let God". I believe we can also agree that this is much easier said than done. Letting go and taking advice has never been one of my strong suits. I was the guy who always wanted the ball in my hand and always wanted to control every aspect of my life. This is all well and good until you encounter struggle, and you can't dig your way out. Then the question becomes clear: Who or what do you submit to? Who do you lean on when things get tough? You see, I made baseball my identity and I believed that I could just "WILL" my way into whatever I wanted. In this process, I lost sight as to why God had put me there in the first place. I couldn't fathom that His plans for me were much bigger than baseball.

Drive and work-ethic are very good things, but if man is at the wheel, they can be misdirected and ill-guided. God has a plan for your life and it may not be what you think it is. Are you willing to submit to that plan?

What aspect of your life are you currently struggling in? Have you given this to Christ? Are you trying to write your own narrative? Take some time in prayer to reflect.

Garrett Kelly
Tarleton State University Baseball
2012-2014

June 25

"Therefore, my beloved brothers, be steadfast, immovable, always abounding in the work of the Lord, knowing that in the Lord your labor is not in vain." - 1 Corinthians 15:58 ESV

One of the best habits an athlete can develop is consistency. When you understand the power of showing up every day, especially when you don't feel like it, you start to appreciate the grind. You understand why it is necessary to show up when you aren't motivated, and you see your biggest gains during those periods of consistency.

The same is true in our walk with Christ. There are times when we are on fire for God and devoting our life to Him feels easy. But there are even more times when it's hard. It's hard to be different and live a life of devotion to Jesus. On those days when it is difficult, but you show up anyways, you often grow the most. It is on those days that you understand you can't do this life on your own.

Marathoner Des Linden sums this idea up perfectly after winning the Boston Marathon… "Some days it just flows, and I feel like I'm born to do this, other days it feels like I'm trudging through hell. Every day I make the choice to show up and see what I've got, and to try and be better. My advice: Keep showing up."

During periods of your life when it's hard to pray, study Scripture, or live a Godly life, choose to keep showing up. Stay devoted even on the days when it feels like you are trudging through hell. You'll thank yourself later.

Christian Fagerlin
Grand Canyon University Men's Cross Country / Track & Field
2018-2023

June 26

"And my God will supply all your needs according to His riches in glory in Christ Jesus." -Philippians 4:19

In western Christianity, we tend to see God as a "wish grantor". Our society loves to take Philippians 4:19 out of context. We see this verse as if it were to say God will supply all of our "wants" and not our "needs". Those are two vastly different things. Many times, we ask God for tangible things that only benefit ourselves for self-glorification. Then when our wishes are not granted, we blame God, get mad at Him, or even worse other believers claim we did not have enough faith.

Quick story, my senior year at South Carolina I was benched in the middle of the season. Never to see the field again the rest of my career. I had aspirations of the NFL and finishing out my career as QB1. I was a "believer", who went to church, did the right things, but was very upset with God when I did not get what I wanted. Shortly after, I began to see the Lord working in my heart. Then a few years later, I began to see God's path for my life unfolding right in front of my eyes. He led me to coaching and mentoring young men who aspire to play collegiate athletics just as I did.

I can honestly say, I am making more of an impact for God's kingdom coaching than I would be if I played in the NFL. That is where the end of verse 19 came together for me in my walk with the Lord. "According to His riches in Glory in Christ Jesus".

God supplies everything we NEED when we follow His plan and purpose for our life. Not our wants.

Perry Orth
University of South Carolina Football
2013-2016

179

June 27

"Humble yourselves, therefore, under God's mighty hand,
that he may lift you up in due time. Cast all your anxiety on
him because he cares for you." -1 Peter 5:6-7

I grew up hearing these two verses quoted a lot. I recently realized they were said one after the other. As athletes, and especially Christian athletes, we are told regularly that humility is key when trying to represent Christ in our performance. If we're honest, that can be a real struggle. Pursuing our dreams and goals can feel like it's riding on the "right person" noticing us at the "right time". However, God's Word tells us that it is His timing that truly matters, and it is Him who brings the favor we so desperately search for.

When I realized verse seven follows up a very challenging responsibility on our part in a society of Instagram fame, blue checks, and a "God helps those who help themselves" mentality – it changed the way I understood this verse. God knows staying humble will, at times, create a sense of anxiety, because we feel the need to make things happen on our own. Working hard and living righteously can seem like it isn't enough to get where we dream of being. Let me encourage you today - if you feel the pressure to orchestrate your own story - to relinquish control to the God who knows you better than you know yourself. His plan is good, pleasing, and perfect for what He has created you to do. "The steps of a good man are ordered by the Lord".

God, give us the faith to believe You wholeheartedly when You say You care for us.

Austin McBeth
Iowa State University Basketball
2010-2013

"And he took the children in his arms, placed his hands on them and blessed them." -Mark 10:16 NIV

Physical touch is powerful. Daily we use it to self-soothe when we're uncomfortable or feel insecure, express love to one another, greet each other, etc. Biologically, touch releases all our feel-good hormones and can serve to lift our outlook on our self, life, and circumstance. Touch is communication, and if used rightly, can heal.

As a former athlete, I know the power of touch and nonverbal communication. As a coach throughout COVID, I have seen the lack of connection in athletes and teams today because of the isolation that resulted from lockdowns, quarantines, and the like. Isolation leads to increased feelings of anxiety and depression. We need to regain our connection.

God gave us touch as a tool to lead when words and prayers might not be enough. We can comfort our teammates in distress with a silent hug or a literal shoulder to lean on. We can convey confidence and encourage one another with strong, undistracted eye contact in the heat of competition. Ultimately, we can imitate Jesus by touching and agreeing in prayer for one another. We can help to heal people's hearts who feel unseen through seeing them as Jesus does. Jesus performed around 37 miracles by touch, so let us imitate Him in our locker rooms, on our fields and courts, and in our homes.

Something so small as a high five or fist bump or smile, can communicate so much. Ask God to reveal how you can communicate His love for the lost and found using your touch.

Vincent Croce
University of Virginia Football
2011-2015

181

"So now *give me this mountain of which the Lord spoke on that day, for you heard on that day how the Giants were there, with great fortified cities. It may be that the Lord will be with me, and I shall drive them out just as the Lord said." – Joshua 14:12 ESV*

Caleb first entered the land of Canaan as a dispatch of 12 scouts under Moses' authority instructed to spend 40 days in reconnaissance of its occupants. Upon returning, Caleb was ready to accept his divine inheritance; however, ten other scouts trembled in fear at the thought of overcoming the giants who possessed their land; they failed their first faith test as a team forcing them to wander for 40 faith-strengthening years.

When the Lord fulfilled his prophecy granting him the promise land, Caleb requested the roughest, most difficult terrain to farm with his family. The Amalekite giants had fled into the hills and mountains for refuge, where Caleb requested to reside. Caleb knew his limitations. He wanted the most difficult section of land to ensure he remained **God-dependent** rather than self-reliant. He did not see himself as entitled to the fertile valleys as we may assume.

Strength comes through trials, where faith is fluent and requires constant attention. Allow your dependence on God to be strengthened by letting the Lord carry your burdens. As an athlete, use your training as your ministry, focus on improving your weaknesses rather than complacently working on your strengths.

Train on your mountain to help promote dependence & intimacy with the Lord throughout today. Pray for the mountain not the valley.

Josh Jones
Texas Christian University Football
2001-2004

"Do not be conformed to this age, but be transformed by the renewing of your mind, so that you may discern what is the good, pleasing, and perfect will of God." -Romans 12:2 HCSB

I've heard it said that love is spelled T-I-M-E, and if that's the case, I loved Basketball. I watched it, played it, spent hours watching highlights of my favorite players to try and mimic what I saw. My favorite movies were basketball movies or sports movies in general. I had trained and programmed my mind to be focused on basketball. I constantly thought about what I could be doing to get better, or just simply thought and longed to get in the gym and get shots up. When I got to college and I began to pursue a relationship with Jesus, it wasn't long before I figured out that my thoughts were more concerned with this world than with my King and Savior.

We are shaped and molded, whether knowingly or unknowingly, by the things we consume. In a world that fights for our attention, God can easily slip through the cracks. Living for Jesus is often difficult, and it gets even more difficult when we don't give Him time to shape the way we think. Many would say they want, like the verse above states, to know God's will, but what are we consuming more of, the world (via social media, video games, tv, etc.) or God? Let's allow God to renew our minds with His Word, worship, prayer, and time with fellow believers.

Think through how you can begin to give God more of your time and attention today. It all starts with small steps.

Zach Glotta
Austin Peay State University Men's Basketball
2015-2019

July 1

So we can confidently say, "The Lord is my helper; I will not fear; what can man do to me?" - Hebrews 13:6

My time at Baylor as a student-athlete taught me that I had POWER in Christ that had gone untapped my whole life. When I got to campus as a Freshman, I had no idea what it meant to be a "Christian-Athlete". I went to private school, I grew up in the church, I prayed before matches, but my game and my faith were always separate. Shortly into my freshman year, a woman named Marci Jobson (Formerly Marci Miller on the USWNT), who would later become my mentor, taught me that Christ could completely change my game, and that my purpose on the Baylor Soccer team could be for so much more than the fleeting glory of winning championships and getting time in the spotlight. I learned I could use my time as a student-athlete as a "training grounds for life". I was taught how to invite the Holy Spirit in to play with me on the field, to empower me to play with freedom, to help me be a great teammate, and to be my legs and voice when they were giving out.

We often use the phrase "Drop the Chains" on my team. When I walk in the freedom and joy Christ offers me, I can run, compete, serve, and push myself to my breaking point with no anxiety and complete freedom to pour out my cup every time.

Where do you need to "Drop the Chains" in your game? Invite Christ in, let Him transform not only your heart, but watch Him take your game to a new level through freedom in Him.

Ally Henderson-Ashkinos
Baylor University Women's Soccer
2017-2021

"Look among the nations and see; wonder and be astounded. For I am doing a work in your days that you would not even believe if told." - Habakkuk 1:5 ESV

2020 and 2021 were years filled with fear, anxiety, and change. During this difficult season God revealed to me how faithful He is through surrendering all parts of my life to Him. It can be so easy as an athlete to wonder and try to figure out why things happen and for what purpose they serve. God's desire for us is to let that go and stop asking why. His desire for us is to cling to Him regardless of the situation. He knows what we need because He created us. He knows when we need it because He planned out our very lives. And He has a reason for absolutely everything we go through because we are worth it to Him.

Understanding this changed the way I experienced hardship because I began to see the beauty in why God wants us to let go. I started to see that maybe I wouldn't find the answers to all my questions, and maybe I didn't need those answers to know, love, and grow closer to Him.

I am guilty of this every day, if we won't understand things even if they were told to us… Why do we try so hard to?

What situation do you keep trying to figure out on your own? What questions are you trying to answer that only God can answer? What are you not giving to the Lord? Whatever it is find joy in where you are because He has you there for a reason far better than one you can come up with.

Kennedy Pedigo
Southern Methodist University Women's Golf
2017-2022

July 3

"For in him all things were created: things in heaven and on earth, visible and invisible, whether thrones or powers or rulers or authorities; all things have been created through him and for him."
– Colossians 1:16 ESV

In competition, my purpose and self-worth were derived solely from my success as a player. My sport was created by God, but I was selfishly competing, instead of glorifying His name. The uncertain and changeable outcomes of "success" in sports often turned the hours of training into a discouraging cycle of insufficiency. Seeking purpose through worldly affirmations is a dead-end street.

Our sinful desires cause us to move further away from Christ. If you're starting off on the wrong road, any attempt to move forward will just move you further from your desired destination. I found myself on the wrong road often in my collegiate volleyball career. I was only able to recognize this, and redirect my life on to the right road, once I found sufficiency in Christ alone.

As I refined my volleyball skills on the court, I too had to refine my relationship with the Lord. This relationship provides a peace that surpasses all understanding, even in an imperfect and flawed world. Sports are a gift from God, created through and FOR Him. I pray we give Him credit for the work He is doing in our hearts as we put our entire worth in His sufficiency.

Is God with you in the game or have you left Him on the sidelines? My prayer is that we would use our gifts FOR God, to glorify His name and advance the Kingdom of God.

Katelyn Vander Tuig
Washington State University / California Baptist University
2015-2019

July 4

Pray then like this: "Our Father in heaven, hallowed be your name. Your kingdom come, your will be done, on earth as it is in heaven." - Matthew 6:9-10 ESV

God's will is simple: love God - love others. In 2007 I transferred to Baylor University, and walked onto the softball team. Following God to Texas taught me how to love Him and love others.

Being on a division I softball team felt like a dream come true, then reality quickly set in. Once a starter, now I sat on the bench. Once a straight "A" student, now I was struggling. My spot on the team was in jeopardy. My goals of becoming an athletic trainer were derailed. I had to change my major if I wanted to stay on the team. I prayed that God would show me His will, and He told me that this was His will. I switched from Kinesiology to Education. I thought I would never become a teacher because teaching scared me. Study hall was the tool He used to show me that His team needed a teacher.

God was up to something. If I wasn't on the bench, I never would have learned that a good teammate is not about being a starter but wanting the best for the team. I did not know that this was the mission field I was called to.

God will use what you have to position you where He needs you in His kingdom. He used my athletic ability, and He will use yours if you allow Him. Nothing is ever wasted.

What has He gifted you with? What is He asking you to do? Obey Him! Success comes through obedience to God.

Sophia Lujan
Baylor University Softball
2008-2009

187

July 5

"For our light and momentary troubles are achieving for us an eternal glory that far outweighs them all. So we fix our eyes not on what is seen, but what is unseen, since what is seen is temporary, but what is unseen is eternal." - 2 Corinthians 4:17-18 NIV

Finding purpose and motivation in the midst of a dark season of life is extremely difficult. This is coming from an athlete who has faced a tale of two halves in my college soccer career. My freshman and sophomore season I started and played every minute in every single game. Then, come junior year, nothing. No starts, no playing time. Nothing at all.

At the time, it's very hard to label this trial as "light" and "momentary". We all know that would devastate any competitive athlete. So how do we find *joy* in the midst of this?

Just as 2 Corinthians tells us: By fixing our eyes on eternity. By looking to the cross of Christ, we can know the One who has victory over every sin, disappointment, and loss that life has to offer. When we fix our eyes on Jesus, the ultimate Comforter, the woes of life fade to the background.

Troubles by no means disappear. Life will always have trouble. However, we get to have an eternal hope that will always remain. We can know that these trials are achieving an eternal glory as we continue to lean into Christ and trust Him with our lives. These "light" & "momentary" troubles are temporary, but God is forever.

What trials are you facing right now? How can you shift your perspective by fixing your eyes on eternity?

Shae Turner
Kansas State Women's Soccer
2019-2023

188

July 6

"Rejoice in the Lord always. I will say it again: Rejoice! Let your gentleness be evident to all. The Lord is near. Do not be anxious about anything, but in every situation, by prayer and petition, with thanksgiving, present your requests to God."
– Philippians 4:4-6 NIV

"Play where your feet are" – the five words that inspire me daily, led me to start a podcast and write a book, find new purpose, be grateful in my circumstances, and build a connected community.

As a junior in college, I was devastated when injured and forced to medically retire with Post Concussive Syndrome. I seemingly lost my identity and purpose. Dealing with brain injuries and a new life ahead, I learned to Play Where My Feet Are; to do and be my best no matter what, no matter where – coaching, in the studio, reteaching my brain, and embracing my new role.

Paul, the author of Philippians, is an excellent example of Playing Where Your Feet Are. Our joy is not rooted in circumstances; it is rooted in Christ. Christ never changes, never waivers, and is always good. What if I told you Paul encouraged the people to "rejoice in the Lord always" while standing in chains, imprisoned? His feet were in the worst place and position limited by chains on his ankles. Still, he played where his feet were!

Take some time today to ask God to push you to Play Where Your Feet Are, embracing your role by being present in each moment, intentional with spaces you occupy, joyful with those you encounter, and thankful in all circumstances.

Cameron Dobbs
University of Miami Volleyball
2017-2021

189

July 7

"...Walk in obedience to him, and keep his decrees and commands, his laws and regulations, as written in the Law of Moses. Do this so that you may prosper in all you do and wherever you go."
-1 Kings 2:3 NIV

Being on a sports team is one of my favorite parts of life right now. The road trips, the team dinners, going to battle together, there is nothing like it. I care deeply about relationships and believe that we were put on earth to be in relation with others. However, sometimes I question my ability to disciple others and make selfish excuses. In 1 Kings 19, Elijah flees to the wilderness out of fear for his life. He is exhausted and feels as though his work did not result in revival. God brought Elijah out of discouragement by giving him a mission and assuring him that God's work on earth is not dependent on his success or lack thereof but his willingness to walk in obedience.

Maybe you need to find your wilderness to get away, be in solitude, physically rest, and remind yourself of the mission. Listen for God in a still, small voice or maybe in the way the leaves change color to see that God is working in and around you. In order to have a strong faith that endures failure, we need a strong sense of the mission and know that God's plan for the world transcends any of our efforts.

When you find yourself feeling discouraged about not inviting that friend to lunch or that your testimony won't change someone's life, pray for God to remind you of the mission and that He is bigger than all of your successes or failures.

Haylee Swayze
Rice University Women's Basketball
2018-2022

190

July 8

"I can do all things through Christ who strengthens me."
-Philippians 4:13

While playing golf, I am constantly having to hit different shots. A round of golf is never the same, even on the same golf course. Before each shot, I try to focus simply on my target. I remind myself right before each shot that I know the shot because I have God by my side and this brings me comfort. Playing golf is mentally tiring and can drain you if you're not mentally prepared or ready. Having a constant reminder of being able to do everything because God is near strengthens you and is always comforting.

If you are scared of doing anything in life, then you will live in constant fear. This quote that I randomly thought of one day comes to my mind: "You can't do anything with fear or else you would be afraid of life". If you live in fear, then nothing would be possible. You have to be fearless and when you have God on your side, then you can overcome fear. Knowing fear is something that I think can stop you from achieving your goals. There will always be goals that you are trying to reach. To achieve those goals, always remember that God is on your side, so take comfort and be fearless.

When you are facing challenges in your life, take time to thank God that you have been placed in that position and then know that you can conquer that challenge with God on your side.

Bentley Cotton
University of Texas Women's Golf
2020-2024

191

July 9

"For this world is not our permanent home; we are looking forward to a home yet to come." -Hebrews 13:14 NLT

I lived at 5 different addresses in college. I've lived at 12 different addresses since moving out of my parents' house after high school. While each of these homes have had their different advantages (free gym, fun roommates) and disadvantages (loud neighbors, no AC), none of them has ever truly felt like home. There is always something missing, some lack of peace or true rest or perfect belonging. And actually, Scripture tells me this feeling checks out. Because we're not home yet. Peter uses the words "sojourners and exiles" to describe how we as God's people live in this world (1 Peter 2:11). The author of Hebrews speaks of seeking a homeland and desiring a better country (Hebrews 11:13-16). We live right now in the world that God created to flourish and thrive but is currently sick with the disease of sin. It's not supposed to be this way. Thankfully, we have hope. Jesus said he was going to prepare a place for us and that He will come back for us (John 14:2-3). Paul assures us that those who trust in Jesus are members of the household of God (Ephesians 2:19). John tells us that one day God's home will be with His people and all sadness and pain will be gone forever (Revelation 21:3-4). We are not home yet, but one day we will be.

Do you believe that we have a hope and a future to look forward to? What would change in your life now if you knew you had a guaranteed future home with God?

Caitlin Boon
University of Minnesota Women's Rowing
2008-2012

July 10

"Consider it pure joy, brothers and sisters, whenever you face trials of many kinds, because you know that the testing of your faith produces perseverance. Let perseverance finish its work so that you may be mature and complete, not lacking anything."
— James 1:2-4 NIV

I've grown to know that trials and adversity are a part of life. At first, this wasn't something that was easy for me to understand and I would frequently ask God "why me?" From the injuries in college and the NFL, to being released multiple times, I would find myself wrestling with that question. It wasn't until I really sat down in my still moments to hear from God, to seek for clarity and discernment on the trials I was facing. And in those moments, it was something unexpected that God asked me a question in return, "why not you?" Why can't you be the one to face these trials and some day boast in the fact it was God that brought you out of all fire.

I then realized that all those things were building my faith, making me stronger, wiser, able to stand in that fire knowing I had a real way out. That's when I started to feel the joy from all those times of confusion and pain; it was in those trials that I was building a real foundation through Christ. I began to feel freedom from my own mind knowing those trials weren't for nothing, it built my faith in Him.

Ask yourself that question: why not you? Why can't you be the one God uses to show that when we have faith and stand in the fire with God, nothing is impossible. You're going to make it out.

Marcell Ateman
Las Vegas Raiders
2018-2021

193

July 11

"Whatever you do, work at it with all your heart, as working for the Lord, not for human masters, since you know that you will receive an inheritance from the Lord as a reward. It is the Lord Christ you are serving." - Colossians 3:23-24 NIV

Growing up, sports were my world. Coming into college I knew how to put in the hard work and saw rewards from this, but these rewards were not satisfying. I would play well in a tournament or win an event, and that joy would quickly fade. Then I would chase the next thing just to feel that sense of joy again. Seeing who God truly is by reading His word gave me a different perspective on why to work hard at golf (or really anything in my life) and what that looked like. I started to pray in between shots, write down verses in my yardage book and ask God to continue to change my perspective. My heart wants to work hard for God because of who He is.

Working hard for the Lord is not a chore, it's a response from our love of God. We are here to glorify God and serve Christ as best as we can. Working hard for approval of man is not going to sustain our needs. If we work hard in all that we do as we are working for the Lord, God will reward us.

Take a moment to ask yourself if you work hard as you're working for the Lord. Write down one way you can start to glorify God in your hard work.

Heather Fortushniak
Kansas State University Women's Golf
2018-2022

194

"As for man, his days are like grass; he flourishes like a flower of the field; for the wind passes over it, and it is gone. and its place knows it no more. But the steadfast love of the Lord is from everlasting to everlasting on those who fear him.." - Psalm 103:15-16

When competing, the athlete has a chance to attain what seems like immortality. Whether you're a professional athlete or trying out for the team for the first time, every one of us has walked those school hallways lined with retired jerseys of the greats who came before us. These relics honor the past while setting hopes for the future. But in reality, we athletes have a love affair with greatness and fame that I think is really a craving for immortality.

It's fitting that we honor the excellence and hard work of athletes who have achieved greatness in their sport. But there's also a dangerous corner in the human heart that longs for attention, adoration, and even God-like immortality apart from God Himself. Psalm 103 describes our days on earth as temporary and fleeting but God's love is described as steadfast. This term 'steadfast' means His love never ends, never wavers, and doesn't turn its back after a poor performance. When we chase after the world's 'immortality', we're chasing a false promise. When we live sustained and energized by God's steadfast love, we get heavenly immortality AND His peace that prevents us from chasing the world's false promises.

Why do you think worldly immortality is so attractive as an athlete? What is one way you might be seeking worldly immortality over God's steadfast love?

Austin Carr
New Orleans Saints / New England Patriots
2017-2021

July 13

"For everything there is a season, a time for every activity under heaven." – Ecclesiastes 3:1 ESV

We are surrounded by seasons, whether it's in our sport, the changing of the weather, or even the highs and lows of life. Preseason starts strength training. Fall brings the changing colors of the leaves. In our Christian walk, we experience seasons that are amazing and difficult. After my 17-year career ended early due to an injury, I found myself in a season of loss and physical, mental, and spiritual pain. Feelings of frustration in the change of my plans, while not fully trusting in His plans for me. During this time, I realized how seasonal my relationship with God had become. I only ran to Him when I needed Him and placed Him in the background when my life was going my way.

Just like practicing for our sport through the seasons, we must daily practice and pursue Christ to build a strong relationship with Him. Regardless of what season of life, learn to be content in every season by trusting God's plan and embrace the changes when they come. This passage shows us that even in the trials of life, highs, and lows, God is using those times to grow us. There is a time and purpose for every season and the best part is that God is holding your hand through them all.

When we learn to be content through every season of life, we can boldly move forward with confidence knowing that God is in control.

Courtney Middelkoop
Iowa State University Gymnastics
2014-2018

"Whatever you do, work heartily, as for the Lord and not for men." - Colossians 3:23 ESV

Before I gave my life to Christ, I was focused on everything around me. When I stepped onto the court my mind was overwhelmed with thoughts of playing to get the approval of whomever was watching the game: my coaches, family, the media, the list goes on. I was unable to focus on the task at hand, and the outcome of my performance became a part of my identity.

When I gave my life to Jesus, the most freeing aspect was that I no longer had to perform for anyone. The volleyball court became my sanctuary where I was able to worship God by giving thanks for the body God gave me, the ability to play volleyball competitively, and work whole heartedly to worship God without focusing on how people will judge my performance. I know that God defines who I am, not spectators, coaches, media, or family. Inviting God into my daily practice, games, and other training sessions through prayer and reading His Word allows me to focus the most important aspect of life, worshiping and spending time with God in all that I do throughout the day.

Take time to meditate on Colossians 3:23 today, ask the Holy Spirit what areas of your life are you seeking the approval from others and how you can invite God into the daily rhythms of your life.

McKenzie Jacobson
University of Arizona / Suhl Lotto Thüringen / Vandœuvre les Nancy
2013-2021

July 15

"A new command I give you: Love one another. As I have loved you, so you must love one another." -John 13:34

Today, the word love is often used as an emotion: I love pizza, I love football, I love my girlfriend. Within these sentences, love is being used as a noun - a passionate, emotional feeling about someone or something. As a result, when we read about God's love in scripture, we understand it as this emotion. Rather, in the verse above, Jesus uses the word love as a verb, not a noun. Jesus is commanding to *do* love, not *feel* love. What does that look like?

Earlier that night, Jesus washed his disciples' feet during the Last Supper. In Jesus's day, washing someone's feet was a selfless act of honor and service. With that modeling in mind, Jesus is telling His disciples to honor and serve others. Loving people in this way does not require you to feel a certain way towards someone. You can serve and lift others up regardless of how you 'feel' about them; whether you are strangers or have known them your whole life. This kind of love, when modeled as Jesus did, captures the hearts of the world. This isn't just great in theory. It is actually my story. Not growing up in a Christian home, I first began to understand who Jesus was as I saw how my Christian teammates treated and loved others. This was radically different than anything I had ever experienced. This drew me in close to them. Thus, when they shared with me about Jesus, their message was authenticated by the love they had previously exhibited.

Identify someone in your life who is far from God, but close to you. How can you love him or her this week?

Vincent Paolucci
Wake Forest University Football
2014-2016

July 16

"He said to me, "My grace is sufficient for you, for my power is made perfect in weakness." Therefore, I will boast all the more gladly about my weaknesses, so that Christ's power may rest on me."
-2 Corinthians 12:9 NIV

I've always struggled with perfectionism, especially as a collegiate athlete. I used to think leading the match in digs and having a notable box score would truly satisfy me. But what happens when we acquire those things, and we still are not fulfilled? Even more importantly, I contemplated my own value as a person when I came up short of those expectations. I always thought my mistakes and failures on the court defined me. I was wrong. Despite our doubts and fears, God shows up for us every time. He continues to display His unconditional love and care regardless of our mistakes and failures. You do not need to try and perfect yourself for God to love you. He already does, immensely!

When I accepted Jesus into my heart and knew my worth came from being His, I had the freedom to play without a fear of failure. I started playing for His glory and not my own selfish gain. All of the accomplishments and accolades from our sport will fade away, but God's love and grace is forever.

Take some time today and thank God for His unconditional love. Think about the grace He shows us on a daily basis and practice showing that grace to those around you, and yourself.

Christa Branson
Lubbock Christian University Volleyball
2011-2014

July 17

*"Through Him we have obtained access by faith into this
grace in which we stand, and we rejoice in hope of the glory of God.
We rejoice in our sufferings, knowing that suffering produces
endurance, endurance produces character, and character produces
hope." - Romans 5:2-4 ESV*

Endurance - the fact of enduring an unpleasant or difficult process or situation without giving way. As athletes, we are constantly trained on endurance. Hours and hours are spent on the field to achieve peak physical stamina and the ability to endure on the biggest of stages. As Christians, we are also called to endure our sufferings. Suffering can look many different ways - a mistake in a big game, a poor relationship with a coach, feeling alone in the locker room.

When I arrived at college, I was shocked at how dark of a place the locker room was. I remember feeling heavy about some of the conversations that went on in there. In the midst of the darkness, I felt a call to be an agent of change. By the grace of God and four years of caring for the people around me, God produced so much fruit. Teammates accepted Jesus and lives were changed, but not by my doing. The truth is, my endurance probably failed more often than not. The beauty of our faith in Jesus is that no matter how many times we fail, His love endures. And in enduring suffering on the cross, Jesus paved the way for everlasting hope.

Take some time to consider where your faith is lacking endurance.

Aaron Thomas
Stephen F. Austin State University Football
2011-2015

July 18

"Now set your heart and your soul to seek the Lord, your God." - 1 Chronicles 22:19

Sometimes it may be difficult to commit your entire self to the Lord. I have found myself many times being extremely nervous and anxious before tournaments or stressful days of golf. In my early years of high school, my nerves and anxiety towards the game almost took me to the point where I wanted to completely quit golf to better my mental health. With a lot of different thoughts going through my mind at this tough time, I knew I could not let all of my hard work and talent go down the drain. This is when I fully committed myself to God to get me through the downfall and uplift me to continue what I loved to do.

I relate my situation to when David is on his way to fight one who is almost unbeatable. David put his mind and soul fully to the Lord alone and with this, he was able to conquer and overcome adversity in his way. When we commit our entire self to God, everything in life will fall into the correct place.

When you wake up with uncertainty and discomfort, pray that the Lord would help you fully commit to Him and show you how things will naturally fall into place when your full trust is in *the Lord, your God*.

Meagan Winans
University of Oklahoma Women's Golf
2021-2025

201

July 19

"I am the good shepherd; I know my sheep and my sheep know me— just as the Father knows me and I know the Father—and I lay down my life for the sheep. I have other sheep that are not of this sheep pen. I must bring them also. They too will listen to my voice, and there shall be one flock and one shepherd."
—John 10:14-16 NIV

Early in college, I did not have a meaningful relationship with my faith. As I grew more comfortable being at a new school, in a new city, with new football teammates, I started to realize something was missing and I was determined to figure out what "it" was.

My life changed for the better once a classmate introduced me to church. He understood my hesitations to attend church were rooted in not growing up in the church, fear of not being accepted, and that my lifestyle did not coincide with the church. Once I finally attended church with him and started to volunteer in the children's ministry, I began to find my identity. I cultivated a church family and connected with my teammates and other student athletes who were strong in their faith through FCA. I quickly realized that Christ meets us where we are at despite how far we may have strayed away from the flock. Those reading this should find comfort knowing that our Father is resilient.

Consider if you have strayed from the flock, and if so, make a conscious effort to listen to the voice of the Good Shepherd.

Miles Johnson
Baylor University Football
2014-2016

July 20

"For you created my inmost being; you knit me together in my mother's womb. I praise you because I am fearfully and wonderfully made; your works are wonderful, I know that full well."
    -Psalm 139:13-14 NIV

For the longest time, one of my greatest fears was letting people down. This was especially true in lacrosse; my mindset while playing was to avoid disappointing my coaches, teammates, or even strangers in the stands. More often than not, it seemed that my performance on the field wasn't meeting their expectations, and I quickly became crippled by the weight of my shortcomings. I had put so much pressure on myself to perform for others and let it rule my life.

During that time, I had lost sight of the simple truth of the Gospel. Christ's death secured me from the judgement I deserved for my sin, let alone the judgement from people on the sidelines. His death plainly stated that I was enough regardless of my performance, both on and off the field. From then on, I needed to accept that others' perceptions of me should have no influence on my identity as that was already secure through Christ's work on the cross. This understanding allowed me to play with freedom knowing that I was playing for His glory and unwavering faithfulness, rather than others' approval. Though failures and shortcomings are always inevitable in sports, only in Christ could I find comfort.

When you face criticism and shortcomings in your sport, take a deep breath, and remember that Christ died for you to perform free from judgement and for His glory.

Christian Cropp
Yale University Men's Lacrosse
2017-2022

203

July 21

"Whom have I in heaven but you? And earth has nothing I desire besides you. My flesh and my heart may fail, but God is the strength of my heart and my portion forever."
-Psalm 73:25-26 NIV

One week before my senior season of beach volleyball at the University of Hawaii, I slipped and fell off a fifty-foot waterfall. I broke ten ribs and fractured my scapula, and my left lung collapsed. My hopes of having a killer senior season and helping my team win a National Championship had fallen and shattered with me right off that waterfall.

In the months and years after my accident, God showed me that my hope was severely misplaced. All my life, I had hoped for certain achievements in my sport and was always crushed when things didn't turn out how I'd hoped. I would get frustrated, go back to the drawing board, and set newer and loftier goals for myself. Finally, I realized that nothing in this world would ever be able to satisfy the hope I long for. No amount of success on the volleyball court will ever satisfy me if that's all I hope for; I will only keep wanting more.

Miraculously, I fully recovered from my accident and am still playing beach volleyball professionally. Because I have placed my full faith in Jesus, I have learned to live with a forward-thinking, eternal hope that I know will surpass all my expectations. When my earthly life seems to be falling apart, I can still live with joy knowing God will always keep His promises.

Where is your hope placed—in the things of this world or in a strong and mighty God?

Heather Friesen
Professional Beach Volleyball Player
2017-Present

204

July 22

"Draw near to God and He will draw near to you."
-James 4:8

Having faith is hard. Keeping the faith is harder. Athletics make it hard. The noise of busy schedules makes it hard. On top of all that, projecting your faith in a culture where society tells you to "fit in" or when it is not the norm makes it even more difficult. Within all the trials, it is easy for our time with the Lord to be the last thing on our to do list. Busyness is the enemy of reflection and reflection is crucial to a fulfilling and life-giving relationship with Jesus.

For me, college culture and the busyness that comes with being a collegiate athlete was something that pushed me to break out of the ordinary ways of culture and look to the One who had complete control over my life. This time revealed things to me about Jesus and how crucial our time in His word is. My quiet time every morning motivated me to live life in accordance with His truth. Not the average way. Not the fun way. What WE think is best will always be narrowed to God's best for us. Schedules and commitments test this mindset. I had to surrender daily and CHOOSE to seek the Kingdom and not the approval of culture. The fulfillment of worldly things will never compare to the fulfillment of falling more in love with Jesus. As believers, we need to be better about finding the time to sit in stillness and turn our eyes to the Creator. If we want to experience a life with Jesus, we must first center ourselves to rest in a lifestyle with Him.

Find ways within your busy schedule to give your attention to the only One who can give you rest and fulfillment.

Megan Harrah
Randolph-Macon College Field Hockey
2017-2021

205

July 23

You were taught to put away your former way of life, your old self, corrupt and deluded by its lusts, and to be renewed in the spirit of your minds, and to clothe yourselves with the new self, created according to the likeness of God in true righteousness and holiness.
– Ephesians 4:22-24 NRSV

As an athlete it was easy for my identity to become focused on my playing time, my stat line, or what my coach thought of me. Over the years, this endless cycle of looking for worth in fleeting things became tiring and never led to the love and fulfillment I was searching for. These verses speak to the life those who love Jesus are called to live. Through Christ, we are given new life. We are chosen as God's children to walk alongside, to learn from, and to be loved by Him. There is nothing we must do to earn this love. He has chosen us, even though we are sinners and continue to conform to the ways of the world we seek satisfaction in.

Paul's life in Ephesians is a beautiful and redemptive story of how Christ has chosen us. He gives new life when we are undeserving of redemption. God's love is not dependent on playing time or championships. Instead, His love is free. In Christ, your worth is not found in the fact that you are an athlete. You are a new creation in Christ, loved deeply and transformed fully by the work of the Holy Spirit. What an amazing gift!

God yearns for you to love Him deeply, taking the place of the fleeting successes of this world. Today, how can you live in the fullness of God's love for you in a revolutionary way?

Shelby Livingstone
Rice University Women's Volleyball
2014-2018

"As for you, the anointing you received from Him remains in you, and you do not need anyone to teach you. But as His anointing teaches you about all things and as that anointing is real, not counterfeit – just as it has taught you, remain in Him."
– 1 John 2:27

What if we recognized and believed that our greatest strength could be standing firm in the fact that God gave us an individual anointing that our team needs from us that no one else can contribute? Instead of spending many seasons of my soccer career wondering why it wasn't going the way that I hoped and planned after I had put my training and passion for the sport above everything else, I wish I could have leaned into God's anointing for me earlier.

We were never made to be identified by the sport that we played, however we have been given a platform to fight for and spread God's kingdom through our sport. You are set apart – marked by a distinction through the anointing that separates you from everyone else. This anointing qualifies and equips us to serve a role that our team needs beyond statistics - a role that is worth more than any number of goals scored could ever be. Circumstances may be out of your control, but God will make a way when there seems no way.

Spend some time thanking God for the gifts that He has given you to be able to compete in the sport you love. Ask Him for help in stepping out in faith and obedience while leaning into His anointing for you and how you can best use it in your sport to glorify Him.

Alison Walls
Drake University Women's Soccer
2018-2022

July 25

"Remain in me, and I will I remain in you. For a branch cannot produce fruit if is severed from the vine, and you cannot be fruitful unless you remain in me. Yes I am the vine; you are the branch. Those who remain in me, and I in them will produce much fruit. For apart from me you can do nothing." -John 15:4-5 NLT

In a world that encourages you to boast your highlights and statistics, it is important to take a step back and realize that, without the Lord, we could not produce any of it. Apart from Him we are nothing. It is easy to get caught up in our own accomplishments and the limelight that comes with them, but we can give the glory back to God by showing those around us that the fruit we are producing is not of our own doing.

In addition, one of the biggest challenges in our time and age is remaining in Him, especially in our circumstances. Locker rooms and training tables are difficult places to sometime create and have "fruitful" conversations and actions. It is our job as Christians to be an anomaly and stick out and to go against the flow of what is normal and popular. Being a part of the vine looks different, and your fruit will be a testimony to that.

Ask God and take time to reflect in areas where you can work to be attached to the Vine. Additionally, in areas where fruit is being produced, ask how you can give God the glory for it.

Dalton King
Air Force Academy Football
2018-2021

July 26

"Better is the end of a thing than its beginning, and the patient in spirit is better than the proud in spirit." -*Ecclesiastes 7:8 ESV*

As athletes, we set individual and team goals that we strive to achieve. Whether these goals are in the weight room, on the playing field or in the classroom, attaining these objectives will take time, hard work and endurance. You may not see the progress you are making each day as you put forth the effort. However, you must remain patient and trust that the discipline, perseverance, and effort you are putting into your training will ultimately pay off.

Like the diligence we need to achieve our athletic goals, we must learn to be patient with God for the plans He has for us. Often, we pray with an expectation of an immediate answer to prayer requests. We go so far as expecting Him to give us exactly what we want and now. However, this is how God builds discipline and trust in Him. The Lord answers our prayers in His perfect timing and answers them in ways that He knows is best for us. It may be hard to wait for what God has in store for us, but we should never be discouraged. Instead, we should rejoice and remain faithful because His hands are constantly at work in our lives. (Phil 1:6) Just as fans do not see the hours of work athletes put in to reach their goals, we may not always see God at work. (Romans 8:28)

Being patient and waiting for the Lord's perfect will for our lives will always result in greater success and contentment than any plan we could envision for ourselves. (Isaiah 40:31)

Mason Laurence
University of North Carolina Football
2017-2020

July 27

"Go therefore and make disciples of all nations, baptizing them in the name of the Father and of the Son and of the Holy Spirit, teaching them to observe all that I have commanded you. And behold, I am with you always, to the end of the age."
– Matthew 28:19-20 ESV

It's hard to deny that sports can take you places, but the question is how are you representing your Creator as you compete in these places? My freshman year of college I stepped onto campus overflowing with faith, but hesitant to share it. I cared more about fitting in, being liked and performing athletically than representing Christ on and off the field. As I worked my way into playing time, I became obsessed with my identity in soccer rather than my identity in Christ. I felt an emptiness which was soon filled as I learned what it looks like to compete for Christ.

As athletes we have a platform, and we choose how we use it. Whether you realize it or not, you are always in the spotlight; people look at who you represent, how you represent them and how that translates into your performance. When I began to represent Christ rather than myself, I found a joy that changed the way I played the game. This joy translated into me becoming the best competitor, teammate, and advocate for the sport which has taken me so many places.

Boldness in faith translates to great representation of Christ. Take some time to think about how Christ is evident in your life on and off the field.

Grace Piper
Texas A&M University Women's Soccer
2016-2019

"Jesus said to her, "I am the resurrection and the life. The one who believes in me will live, even though they die; and whoever lives by believing in me will never die. Do you believe this?"
– John 11:25-26 NIV

July 3rd, 2019, my life changed dramatically for the worse, or so I thought. My father, who was the University of Louisiana at Lafayette head baseball coach for 25 years, passed away from a sudden heart attack. I was in the Bahamas at the time with my wife and friends when I got the news of his heart attack and all I could remember was asking "why him God"?

I assumed that since my father was a servant leader and a warrior for Christ that he was just magically invincible, and I immediately went to blaming God. Fast-forward to now, 3 years later, and I am stronger in my faith than I ever have been before. Now, how could that even be possible? After losing a father and multiple years later, I can be at my strongest with my faith. It is exactly like Jesus says in this verse, "whoever lives by believing in me will never die". It took me a while to realize it, but my father is not dead. He lives through all the people he impacted through the years and lives through me with his teachings of how to be a servant leader. So yes Jesus, I do believe this.

When things tend to not go your way, are you one to also immediately ask God "why me"? Next time you are faced with a hurdle in your life, grab ahold of your faith and pray it out because God always has a reason for what He does in your life.

Austin Robichaux
Los Angeles Angels Organization
2014-2018

July 29

"The end of a matter is better than it's beginning, and patience is better than pride." - Ecclesiastes 7:8

Throughout my years of playing football, I often found myself battling adversity on my own, thinking I was the one who would produce the solution to whatever stood in my way. From working my way up the depth chart, to bouncing back from injuries, at times I put all my faith in myself to get where I wanted to be.

Occasionally as athletes, competitive in nature, we have trouble setting our pride aside to let God come in and work in our lives. We get so caught up in the grind that we forget who got us there in the first place. Eventually, we find ourselves in a place where we have nothing else to give. The beauty of being in that place though, is what comes next and why having a relationship with the Lord is so powerful. He promises to never leave us or forsake us. Even through our trials, especially those that come in the life of an athlete, God is immutable which substantiates the peace that covers all tribulation.

Paul tells us to be patient in affliction. As an athlete, you are bound to face some hardships at some point in your career. Life could get loud, but God always speaks louder! Just be still and seek Him through the chaos. Do not let the distractions of life distract you from hearing from the omniscient One who is full of good will.

Take some time today to ask God to prepare and soften your heart for what He has planned for you.

Barrett Cain
McMurry University / Stephen F. Austin State University Football
2012-2016

July 30

"Do not be anxious about anything, but in every situation, by prayer and petition, with thanksgiving, present your requests to God...Finally brothers and sisters, whatever is true, whatever is noble, whatever is pure, whatever is lovely, whatever is admirable- if anything is excellent or praiseworthy- think about such things."
- Philippians 4:6,8 NIV

So many of us struggle with anxiety and I'm no stranger to that fight. Especially as a student-athlete you have a lot on your plate- staying healthy and injury free, fueling your body in the right way, making sure to get enough sleep, excelling in your classes, nailing that internship, earning the playing time you want, maintaining relationships, the list goes on and on. It doesn't get any easier after college either! The reality is, life is stressful, but the Bible shows us how we can move from distracting anxiety to intimacy with God. In Philippians, Paul gives us a three-step process to dealing with anxiety. First, we should be honest about what is burdening our minds and release those worries to God, the One who is strong enough to carry them and loving enough to want to. Second, we should practice gratitude; reflecting on what we can be thankful for even in the hard times and more thankful that we can approach the all-powerful Creator of the universe with our concerns. Finally, once the weight has been lifted off our hearts, we need to replace it with the truth and goodness of God's Word.

During quiet time, tell God how you feel, thank Him for who He is and what He's done, and then read His Word and meditate on it.

Gabby Muncy
Virginia Commonwealth University Women's Soccer
2012-2016

213

July 31

"And without faith it is impossible to please God, because anyone who comes to him must believe that he exists and that he rewards those who earnestly seek him." - Hebrews 11:6 NIV

There is a story in the Bible that has helped take my faith to another dimension. In Genesis 22, God ordered Abraham to take his son Isaac and sacrifice him. This command sounds absurd in any circumstance but especially when God had already told Abraham that Isaac was the son that He would fulfill His promise through. Abraham obeyed and got to the place of sacrifice when he said to his servants that accompanied them "Stay here…We will worship and then we will come back to you." We? I thought he was going to sacrifice his son, why would he guarantee the return of both? Abraham did not know what was going to happen, he just knew SOMETHING would happen. He knew God already said Isaac is the son of the promise and that God is not a God that goes back on His word. He believed that God is who He says He is, so he obeyed when it did not make sense. God required Abraham to sacrifice the promise (literally) in order to truly receive the promise. There will be times in your career or life when you will have to make decisions, in those moments remember that faith is required to please God and His promise is to reward those that seek Him in obedience.

What part of your career or life do you need to trust that God is who He says He is?

Anthony Egbo Jr.
Abilene Christian University Football
2018-Present

214

August 1

"Whatever you do, work heartily, as for the Lord and not for men," - Colossians 3:23 ESV

What's your why. As a college freshman, I came in started my first few games, passed all the fitness tests and was at the top of my game. Slowly after the first few weeks my play started dropping, my mistakes became more evident, and my playing time decreased. I started losing joy in the game.

I then caught myself, I was playing to not mess up, playing that my coach would notice all the good things I did, playing that people would notice me and think I was the best. I had lost sight of the joy of working hard and playing to bring glory to God not for man. For all of us, this can be a struggle: to play or live our lives with freedom knowing that our Identity is in Christ, that our performance (on the field, at our job, in our relationships, in our schoolwork) does NOT define us. Our identity is in the death and resurrection of Jesus Christ. Because of that freedom, we can play and live life to the fullest, with reckless freedom, and not be afraid to fail but able to learn from mistakes.

After I was reminded to play with freedom in Christ and that my failures and mistakes don't define me, my season turned back around quickly and the joy that I got to experience playing college soccer with freedom is a testimony of Jesus' love!

What's your why? What is motivating you? Is it to please man? Or to bring glory to the One who created you?

Lydia (Frierson) Radcliffe
Charleston Southern University Women's Soccer
2014-2018

215

August 2

"Let us not become weary in doing good, for at the proper time we will reap a harvest if we do not give up."
- Galatians 6:9 NIV

I have been tried and tried again throughout the past seven years of my CrossFit career. I have been at the cusp of failing to qualify for the big stage multiple times, but became known for having a comeback. I have been cut early from the CrossFit Games for a very minor technical mistake. I have had a competition ending injury that took me out of the Games with only three events of 15 left during my best performance yet. Why do I keep coming back? Why do I want to keep giving everything I have day in and day out to something that seems to never go my way? Because I know and trust that this is all a part of His plan. I have faith that God's plan is bigger than mine, even when things do not seem fair. I'm not finished yet because God's not finished yet. I will not give up, and will reap what I harvest when God is ready.

Through these tough times, it would be easy to question "why me, God?" But instead, I use this time to refocus my energy on Him. Have I gotten too caught up in making CrossFit the center of my world?

Think back to a time when you felt cut short of your potential. Did you blame God, or use this time to refocus your energy on what is most important? Your relationship with God should always come first. This could be a sign to reevaluate.

Brooke Wells
Professional CrossFit Athlete
2015-Present

216

August 3

"Let us know; let us press on to know the Lord; his going out is sure as the dawn; he will come to us as the showers as the spring rains that water the earth." -Hosea 6:3 ESV

As an athlete there are a lot of things you are expected to know. Expected to know every play that coach calls. Expected to know to show up to an "optional" practice. Expected to know to schedule classes around your practices. This list goes on and on but as a Christian, there is one thing you are expected to know and that is the person of Jesus Christ. Without knowing who Jesus is, we do not know who our God is. The question I want to pose to you today is do you truly know Jesus? Are you pressing on to know Him? Knowing Jesus is the priority that trumps all other priorities because knowing Him changes everything. It changes the way we live, it changes the way we love, and it changes the way we play sports.

Sports will fail you. School will fail you. Your career will fail you. But Christ will never fail you. He is consistent, unchanging, and forever. He is as sure as the dawn, and He will come to you as spring rains that water the Earth to change you, bear fruit in you, and show you His unconditional love. God is for you and knowing Him changes everything.

I encourage you to press on to know Him, to truly know Him, so that you may experience the magnitude of His love for you. Seek Him in the quiet places. Go to Jesus – just you and Him and spend 30 minutes with Him.

Mary Kathryn Harrah
University of North Carolina
2015-2019

217

August 4

"The earth is the LORD's and the fullness thereof, the world and those who dwell therein" - Psalm 24:1 ESV

Something I grew up thinking was that God had no place in my life outside of my spiritual life. I only allowed Him in on certain parts while blocking Him out from others. In fact, I didn't even think God cared about any other aspects of my life outside of church and my own personal time with Him. However, I learned that nothing could be further from the truth. The older I became, the more I realized everything is His. According to this verse, not only is creation His, but everything in the earth is as well. Once I allowed the Lord to open my eyes to the magnitude of that truth, I began to see that everything about me is His. Everything in my life is the Lord's. My money is His, my home is His, my marriage is His, and my career is His. Once I understood this, I began to invite Him in on those aspects of my life that I previously wouldn't have. I learned very quickly that He not only cares about those parts of my life, but He's the one empowering me to succeed in those spaces. His Presence extends far beyond the church walls and reaches both the field and floor we play on. He desires to play with us and through us, and once we as athletes realize that, we will begin to play with the fullness of joy, how the Lord intends.

What part of your sports career do you need to let the Lord partner with you more in?

Jayson Hopper
Professional CrossFit Athlete
2021-Present

August 5

"Trust in the Lord with all your heart, and do not rely on your own understanding. In all your ways acknowledge Him, and He will make straight your paths." - Proverbs 3:5-7 RSV

As a track athlete, I felt like I was constantly on the go. If we were in season, each workout or race was intended to help us get stronger, faster, and fitter for the next workout or the next competition. The whole season was about building momentum. If I was injured, the focus became receiving the appropriate treatment and doing the proper strengthening exercises. Once again, the focus was building momentum. While the processes of each circumstance differed, both instances left room for fear, doubt, and mistrust. Am I fast enough? What if I'm not ready in time? Will I ever get healthy? Amidst the constant mental and physical demands of sport, God longs to give us what the mind, body, and soul truly desire –rest. Within the successes, failures, and uncertainties of sport, God calls us to be still. To be present with Him in whatever season of sport or life we find ourselves in. God calls us to invite Him into these spaces so He can give us peace, help us find rest, and make straight our paths.

In what areas of sport and life, do you need to invite the Lord into? In what ways is it difficult to find rest in the Lord amidst the perpetual momentum of athletics?

Jasmine Staebler
Iowa State University / University of North Carolina Women's Track
2015-2020

August 6

"When he has brought out all his own, he goes on ahead of them, and his sheep follow him because they know his voice. But they will never follow a stranger; in fact, they will run away from him because they do not recognize a stranger's voice." -John 10:4-5 NIV

Jesus uses the analogy of a good shepherd in this passage. He is the Good Shepherd who goes before us and we are His sheep. Sheep follow the good shepherd because they recognize His voice. As an offensive lineman, I rely on the voice and cadence of my quarterback to start every play. After countless plays in practice, my teammates and I pick up on the voice of our quarterback and lock in on his specific voice. If we don't, the defense will simulate the snap count and we'll have false starts, hurting ourselves and the outcome of the game.

Following Christ is just like this. We have to listen to the Holy Spirit each day as we pray and read God's word. Spending time with Jesus helps us to know His voice and truly follow Him! Throughout my life the fake cadence of the enemy often sounds like the truth, but the devil lies and even uses half truths to get us to jump offsides. When I dive into the word, and pray for guidance, God makes clear to me the truth of following Him and teaches me to know His voice.

"…his sheep follow him because they know his voice." Can you recognize God's voice over the lies of the enemy? Take time to pray and ask the Holy Spirit to help you to know Jesus and His voice!

Koda Martin
Arizona Cardinals / New Orleans Saints
2019-Present

220

"...train yourself for godliness; for while bodily training is of some value, godliness is of value in every way, as it holds promise for the present life and also for the life to come."
– *1 Timothy 4:7b-8 ESV*

I'm not the first to relay the importance of pursuing God's heart before anything else. If it sounds like a familiar theme, it's because it is a familiar stumbling block to many of us. For myself, sports were seldom more enticing than God. I was humbled enough in my sport to quickly realize I couldn't place my value there. It didn't hold. I'd also "tasted and seen" the Lord to a degree that left no question as to whether God or sports were more glorious. Sports, and all of life, however, can be one great distraction.

When heavy questions of faith loom overhead, it's easier to go practice a superfluous skill like volleyball. Although my cognizant self knows there's no hearty answer in this diversion, it allows for momentary escape. It's easier to avoid hard things than to come before Almighty God, ask your questions, and seek Him when it's painful. But this is the work God asks of me (John 6:29). Active faith.

Similar to sport, training yourself for godliness is not passive. Godliness doesn't come "with age" in the absence of careful tending, or after years of distracting yourself. Don't squander God's good gifts by turning them into ultimate things or distractions. I need this reminder as much if not more than anyone reading this.

In the end, which crown is more worthy and lasting? Spur one another on toward these things.

Elizabeth Gilley
California Baptist University Women's Volleyball
2016-2020

August 8

"But God demonstrates His own love towards us, in that while
we were still sinners, Christ died for us."
-Romans 5:8 NKJV

God intervenes the moment you need Him. I experienced the most trying year and season of my life when I was a sophomore in college. I fractured my back, had two family members diagnosed with stage 4 cancer, and I had put God on the back burner and began choosing myself. I had spent so much of that time trying to control situations I had absolutely no control over and not trusting that God's plan was better than my plan. I began to cripple under the pressure, and lack of control until it simply got too heavy for me to bear alone. And I chose to fix my gaze on Jesus.

It is so easy to praise God when life is good and you're performing well on the field, the court, whatever your competition place is. It is NOT so easy to praise God during your trials and tribulations, however, it is so important. God is so good and works for YOUR good in every way. I am forever grateful for that season of my life because it changed my heart and ignited my relationship with Jesus. I was broken down to be built up in Christ.

Are you praising God in all walks of your life or only when things are falling in your favor? Take a deep breath and ask God to reveal areas of your life, if any, that could benefit from more praise.

Megan Friend
East Texas Baptist University Women's Soccer
2015-2019

August 9

"Am I now trying to win the approval of human beings, or of God? Or am I trying to please people?" - Galatians 1:10 NIV

"Do not be anxious about anything, but in every situation, by prayer and petition, present your requests to God. And the peace of God which transcends all understanding will guard your hearts and your minds in Christ Jesus." - Philippians 4:6-7

It always feels good when your coach is pleased with the way you perform. For many years of my athletic career, I thrived off coaches singing my praises after a well-played match. When I got to college, every team was so competitive that the difference between a win and a loss could be just a few small errors. I became terrified to mess up, fearful of the response from my coach. The pressure to perform perfectly left me with crippling anxiety nearly every day in the gym. But God has not given us a spirit of fear, He gives us peace, love, and a sound mind.

Your coach might expect perfection, but God doesn't care what the stat sheet or scoreboard says. He is pleased when we use the gifts He has given us to the best of our ability, and point the glory back to Him, regardless of the outcome. God promises us an overwhelming peace when we come to Him in our most anxious moments. We can compete freely, knowing that the victory was already won by Jesus defeating death on the cross.

When performance anxiety sets in, invite God into that moment and ask Him to replace it with the peace only He can provide.

Paige Whipple
University of Arizona Volleyball
2017-2021

"Then I heard the voice of the Lord saying, "Whom shall I send? And who will go for us?" And I said, "Here am I. Send me!"
- Isaiah 6:8

This was the verse that God put on my heart going into college. Servant leadership is something so often mentioned in our culture, but it is so hard to do as humans. The number one enemy of servant leadership is pride. Let me take you to a time where pride is tested: after practice cleanup. Nobody wants to go through a long hard practice and then have to clean up after. "That's the freshmen job… Someone else will do it… starters don't "have to". I would have these prideful thoughts and then this verse would come to my mind, and I would be convicted of not being a good leader. So, I determined that any time there was a job to be done, getting foul balls, fixing the field, tarping the field, moving heavy stuff; I would take the hardest one and do it with a smile on my face. I ended up seeing change on my team, instead of people complaining or not doing their job, we would compete to get the hard jobs first and see who could do them the fastest. It turned into older guys teaching younger guys so much more than how to clean the field.

Jesus came down from heaven, put aside all pride and glory, and lived His entire life as a servant; to give us an example of how to live and how to love people. This is a life verse for me now, and I find myself always taking the hard job with joy, knowing I will reap a heavenly reward and will lead people with my actions.

I challenge you to do the work no one else wants to do.

Jacob Ashkinos
Baylor University Baseball
2017-2021

"Everyone who competes in the games goes into strict training. They do it to get a crown that will not last, but we do it to get a crown that will last forever." -1 Corinthians 9:25 NIV

Achieving success in athletics can be gratifying, yet when the success becomes an athlete's sole focus it can leave one wanting. In my first collegiate season, I swam on relays and even finished top ten in an event at my championship meet. However, it wasn't until my season was over that this unsatisfied feeling washed over me. I questioned the purpose of all my training because the feeling of joy I experienced had already faded. Through this, God revealed that my identity was wrongly rooted in success in the pool, which shackled me to the unpredictability of my emotions and performance. That's when I realized only God provides the freedom to leave it all in the pool and walk away knowing my value is rooted in my identity as His child rather than in the fleeting moments of athletic success.

We can compete boldly knowing our real success has eternal roots. We put all our effort into our sport and leave the results behind because our identity lies in the hands of our Maker, not in our results. It's only when we understand this that we can comprehend the true joy of competing and experience the truest form of success—the ability to compete free from the chains of ephemeral achievement.

When we play for God and not ourselves, our success becomes everlasting —an eternal crown is not contingent on the results of our performance. Pray that God reveals the source of your identity.

Ophelia Pilkinton
Yale University Swimming & Diving
2019-2023

August 12

"But by the grace of God I am what I am, and his grace to me was not without effect. No, I worked harder than all of them – yet not I, but the grace of God that was with me." - 1 Corinthians 15:10 NIV

Did you know that Paul, author of 1 Corinthians and one of the most well-known apostles of the early church, spent much of his early life persecuting Christians? And yet what the enemy intends for evil, God can use for His glory. Paul's accolades for Christ are matched by few, but what I love about this verse is, Paul could have claimed his conversion as his own righteousness, yet he understood that it is *only* by God's grace that he is what he is.

Within my first two weeks as a freshman, I was diagnosed with an injury that would keep me out of competition for the next year. But, over the course of the next four years, God has continued to teach me, remind me, and then remind me again, that I am what I am *only* by the grace of God. And His grace never fails.

Before I ever step onto the field, I know that God's grace to me is not without effect. Therefore, I no longer operate under the stressors of my success and failure to determine my identity, but rather, Christ's power shows through me by my life, not by my performance. And how much more freely can I perform, when the Almighty, the God of the universe, is with me.

What area of your performance are you still holding onto that God is asking you to surrender to Him?

Ryan Metz
Virginia Tech Baseball
2017-2022

August 13

"I know what it is to be in need, and I know what it is to have plenty. I have learned the secret of being content in any and every situation." —Philippians 4:12

It was my super senior year of college, I had battled back from 4 knee surgeries, including a complete reconstruction. Preseason All-American, lofty goals displayed all around my house—the stage was set and I was ready for my storybook season.

Nine games in, I blew out my other knee. All of it gone. I ripped those goals down so fast. Angry, battling identity— what the heck was it all for? That was the moment I began the most beautiful death walk into true life with Christ.

If I truly wanted to be used by God, I had to die to me. All of me— MY goals and MY dreams. He slowly began to teach me that **whatever I create, I must sustain; but what He creates, He sustains.** It's in this place of total, authentic surrender that we unlock the peace that Christ died for. All that I am is His: instead of naming what I want and inviting Him to bless it, my job is to draw so close to the heart of God that I can partner with what HE wants—HIS goals and HIS dreams.

We serve the King of Kings! The Creator of the universe! Trust, through ALL circumstances, that He's good and He's equipping you for everything He created you for. Rejoice! None of this will be wasted.

What might He be asking you to release to Him? How can you partner with God today?

Whitney Jones
University of Oklahoma Women's Basketball
2008-2013

227

August 14

"You must not have any other god but me."
– Exodus 20:3 NLT

As an athlete, this may be one of the most challenging lines of Scripture to apply to your life. Reaching the top in any sport means more sacrifice than anyone will see or know. When we strive to reach new heights, we can easily lose sight of whom we are serving and who truly holds the crown we are pursuing.

Growing up with dreams of playing on the PGA Tour, I lived out the highs and lows of chasing an idol I had created in my mind. I believed that my life would reach its full purpose once I made it to the PGA Tour. Through the tough times, it became difficult for me to understand God's purpose in my life. It became clear that my existence had to be worth more than the results of each shot, round, or tournament. How do you handle adversity when it is thrown your way? Do you lose sight of your purpose, or do you lean into God? God wants us to reach our goals and He encourages us to run to win the race. But if our goals are self-centered and not God-centered, we are chasing after the wrong trophy. God has a perfect purpose for your life, continue to seek and glorify Him through the wins and the losses.

Today, ask God to help you align your desires and talents with His plan for your life. What an amazing impact He can make in our life, as well as in those around us when we choose to put God above everything else.

Matt VanCleave
Kansas State University Men's Golf
2002-2005

228

"So, whether you eat or drink, or whatever you do, do it all for the glory of God." - 1 Corinthians 10:31 ESV

How can our lives look like Jesus if we do not know Him and how He lived? The best thing we can do is give Him the simplest thing we have to offer. It is of high value and everything and everyone is constantly jostling for it, yet we give it away so flippantly.

Sports, like so many other things can be used for the glory of God, but only if we use them how God intended. Once sports, a job, a relationship, etc. become something else other than what God designed them to be, they have our attention, and our lives can easily drift to look more like the world. We worship the gifts God gives us instead of God Himself. We often let the urgent overtake the ultimate.

I remember coming out of high school and all I wanted to do was get a scholarship to play college basketball. I did, and it felt good for about a month. Then I was left with another feeling of want that nothing in this world can fulfill.

Our attention is constantly drawn away from God which causes ups and downs in our spiritual lives. So, the next time you feel like you're drifting from God, do an inventory on what you have been paying attention to lately. Try incorporating God and other believers in everything you do, whether that be eating, drinking, or sports.

Make a list of the things that currently have your attention and ask yourself how and why you put these things above your relationship with Jesus.

Kellan Turner
MidAmerica Nazarene University Men's Basketball
2014-2019

August 16

" 'For I know the plans I have for you' declares the Lord, 'plans to prosper you and not to harm you, plan to give you hope and a future.' " – Jeremiah 29:11

Growing up reading the Bible, this verse used to put a smile on my face. I had the impression that it was a promise for things to come for that Jesus would provide all that I needed. For He would direct my path not allowing me to be derailed.

As I grew and became a professional athlete, I quickly realized that the verse was in fact a promise. A promise that would only manifest itself on His time and not mine. My patience and willingness to trust Him when I could not see my next step would make that Scripture come to life.

My senior year in college I was faced with a situation in which this exact verse resonated in my life. After the evaluation period, I had not received the feedback I had hoped for. In that exact moment I believed my dreams of getting to the NFL was shattered. As I sat in the darkness of my room, I got on my knees cried, and prayed. As I was doing so, I bitterly said "Lord, Your plan not mine" and as soon as I spoke those words, a peace filled me up allowing me to get up. Suddenly, the burden and disappointment I was feeling vanished.

3 years later I glorify His name, for what I once thought was shattered, He made whole again. I look at the past 3 years and through the trials I can now see the work He was doing in my life.

Write down the things you are struggling with, pray over them "Lord, your plan, not mine", and give them to the Lord.

Hergy Mayala

Calgary Stampeders / Montreal Alouettes / Hamilton Tiger-Cats

2019-Present

"He must become greater, I must become less."
– John 3:30 NIV

We pour so much time and effort into our sport to not just be good at it but great at it. Many athletes (including myself) fall short of what they sought out to accomplish. However, our sports' journey many times gives us an expedited snapshot of who we are as people. Especially with baseball being a game of failure, it quickly teaches you a lot about yourself.

Like most sports, baseball is a numbers-driven game regarding statistics. You are tied to your numbers for better or worse. As current and former athletes, you may feel tied to your careers (good or bad) and at times it can subtly become your identity. What your role is on the team, are you all conference, are you a role player may be some of the questions that you've asked or are asking yourself currently. Working and striving to get the most of your ability is not just permissible, but it is what we are called to do as Christians. But for all Christians, whose we are is the most important question we can be asking ourselves. Having our identity rooted in Christ is the single most important thing to strive for in our lives. Much like our sport, we must be intentional in preparation and practice to become more rooted in Him. There will be ups and downs but keep your eyes up and "set your mind on things above".

How can you become more intentional in your walk with Christ today?

Luke Murton
New York Yankees Organization
2009-2013

August 18

"Not that I am speaking of being in need, for I have learned in whatever situation I am to be content."
– Philippians 4:11 ESV

4 years. It took 4 years full of injuries for the Lord to teach me that my worth, identity and joy were all dependent on the game of soccer. So, from my senior year in high school all the way to my senior year of college, the Lord stripped soccer from me. I was angry, confused, and bitter as to why He would take something away from me that I loved and that He gifted me with. But that alone was the problem – I loved soccer more than the Lord, and I was using the gift He gave me for my glory instead of His.

Every single injury I faced required nothing but rest, and I know the Lord was intentional here in teaching me how to sit back and find true rest and fulfillment in Him. The Lord wants us to desire Him above all else and find true joy and contentment in Him. Although my college career didn't look like I had originally envisioned, I wouldn't change a thing. The joy that comes from a relationship with Jesus is eternal and far greater than any temporary award or accomplishment I could've gained through soccer.

The Lord allows us to go through spiritual valleys so He can feed us, mature us and grow our desire for Him. Take some time to reflect on the spiritual valleys you have gone through and what the Lord was trying to teach you through it.

Nicole Neuwirth
University of North Carolina Women's Soccr
2015-2019

"Trust in the Lord with all your heart and lean not on your own understanding; in all your ways submit to him, and he will make your paths straight."
– Proverbs 3:5-6 ESV

It's very hard to surrender things to God. In high school and into my freshman year of college, I had become very good at "telling" God where He could act in my life and where I did not need Him as much. Most notably, I tried to leave God out of baseball. I would go to FCA and I would go to church, but once I got on the field, I would pretty much tell God, "Don't worry about it, I got this" (kind of ridiculous telling that to an all-powerful God). That mindset is easy to keep when the going is good, but when everything started to crumble around me, I began to think that maybe I do not have this under control. I played the worst I ever had that fall and was probably 1-2 players away from being cut, but I would not change anything that happened.

Through that fall, I learned the valuable lesson of surrendering things to God. At times, we feel that it is so much easier to try to use our own knowledge to get through things instead of a reliance and trust in God. However, it is the complete opposite. By leaning on the knowledge of the all-powerful Creator, we can have the comfort and freedom in knowing that He is looking out for us, and He has a plan for our lives.

What are some things in your own life that you feel you are unwilling to surrender to God?

Matthew Siverling
Virginia Tech Baseball
2019-Present

August 20

"When you pass through deep waters, I will be with you ..."
– Isaiah 43:2 ESV

As athletes, we live in a world where society constantly pours into us that we can do anything we put our minds to. We have conditioned ourselves to rely only on self. So, it's only natural that our sinful hearts also believe we both struggle and achieve all on our own. But God is an amazing God. He gives us talent, opportunity, support, passion, skill sets, work ethic, motivation, and drive as tools for our sports. This all comes from Him. He is not limited to only getting us started, but He also follows through in our journeys.

"Deep waters" meant the literal deep waters I felt like I was drowning in as a division 1 swimmer. "Deep waters" meant struggling with temptation of drugs and alcohol throughout my college career. "Deep waters" later meant experiencing the ups and downs of relationships through the years. "Deep waters" meant experiencing depression after losing loved ones. No matter what sport, what position, what level of competition, or who you are, God is leading you through these deep waters despite our inclination to do it alone. And when it is finished, it is not our achievement alone but God's pursuit and love of us that is the ultimate achievement. God was there in the beginning, the middle, and most certainly will be there in the end. He deserves all the credit and all the glory. He deserves for us to see Him in those deep waters right beside us.

What are the deep waters in your life? Ask God to reveal Himself in these times and know that He is right there beside you.

Morgan Johnson
James Madison University Women's Swimming
2010-2014

"For whoever wants to save their life will lose it, but whoever loses their life for me and for the gospel will save it. What good is it for someone to gain the whole world, yet forfeit their soul?"
-*Mark 8:35-36 NIV*

Ever since I started playing softball, it was always about what was next. My purpose in life was to get a scholarship to play in college. Once I got to college, my purpose was to earn a starting spot. It was always about what I could earn next. Softball wasn't enough. I was doing well by the world's standards, yet I felt so empty. I wanted everything the world had to offer, but in turn, I put my Bible down. I was placing false expectations in the game of softball. However, it was impossible to play for the glory of God when all I wanted was to receive glory from man. I wanted to control my life and achieve more.

It's hard to put it in perspective, but it almost seems ridiculous to care about my performance on the field. What good is my athletic ability if in turn I forfeit my soul? If I give up on God because He isn't a priority? The Lord shifted my perspective drastically through an injury, and in turn, I can play to my full potential and stop worrying about the standards of man. While it seems like it at the time, nothing of this world will ever be important enough to forfeit your relationship with the Lord. I am thankful I have a God who is powerful enough to change my priorities. I am now free to play the sport I love instead of being consumed by it.

Where in your life have you forfeited your soul to the world? Pray the Lord makes that known to you and releases you from it.

Hannah Hollander
Furman University Softball
2020-2024

August 22

"All athletes are disciplined in their training. They do it to win a prize that will fade away, but we do it for an eternal prize."
– 1 Corinthians 9:25

Discipline is a trait we have as athletes to show up to practice even when we don't really want to be there. In my experience, on most days, practice was daunting, and it was hard. I really didn't enjoy the physical and mental pain I knew I had to push myself through in practice. However, I knew if I was disciplined, I would make it into a racing boat. I would be fast enough to row with the upperclassmen. I achieved all my goals in rowing, but the endless hours I spent practicing only earned me one day of feeling on top of the world before I had to earn my place again. The feeling of accomplishment for my own glory was fleeting. It left me empty every time because after one day, nobody cared.

When we are disciplined in our walk with the Lord, we gain everything. He will bring us through challenging times. We will experience trials and pain. However, if we keep our focus on the Kingdom of Heaven, that feeling of value and worth we worked so hard for in practice, will be handed to us -not because we earned it. If you are willing to train your body for race day, train your spirit in The Word. Be ready to go with God.

When we are disciplined in our walk with the Lord, we will never lose. He already won it all. You do not have to earn your place. The gift of salvation is everlasting.

Hattie Doherty
University of North Carolina Rowing
2017-2020

August 23

"For our light and momentary troubles are achieving for us an eternal glory that far outweighs them all. So we fix our eyes not on what is seen, but on what is unseen. For what is seen is temporary, but what is unseen is eternal." -2 Corinthians 4:17-18

There is a greater hope ahead of us. As a college athlete, it can be hard at times to keep our eyes fixed on eternity in the midst of challenges, losses, feeling unworthy; the list could go on. As a freshman, how my day was going depended on the success I was having with soccer and school. It was a roller coaster of emotions. However, during my sophomore year God began teaching me that I have a greater hope in Him eternally and all that is going on around me is temporary, whether good or bad. I learned the balance of wanting to work hard and be the best teammate I could be for the glory of God and not be controlled by the success I was having.

Christ remains constant in His character as our solid rock. As followers of Christ, it seems when things are not going the way we plan in our mind it can feel like the end of the world. Being a former athlete, I can confidently say that what your teammates, coaches, and peers will remember most is your character as a player and heart for God.

Keep your eyes fixed on eternity and the eternal impact you can have on those around you.
What are your eyes fixed on? Take some time to meditate on who God is and that your worth is completely in Him.

Ashley Zane
Kansas State University Women's Soccer
2016-2020

August 24

"Don't forget to show hospitality to strangers, for some who have done this have entertained angels without realizing it."
-Hebrews 13:2 NLT

I think we can all relate to being in a scenario where there's room for the "new guy" to show up on the scene—especially in our athletic careers! A teammate, a coach, a manager, whoever! Whatever the case may be, we all deal with strangers on a regular basis. God tells us to be "hospitable" to strangers—friendly and welcoming. Do you find this is something you practice on a regular basis? If not, ask yourself why. Don't you appreciate when someone is kind to you in passing or comes alongside you when you're the new guy? Is your excuse something along the lines of "I don't feel like it," "I'm not really a people person," "They're kind of weird." Better yet, is it something along the lines of "they're taking my spot!" "They're going to slow me down," "They haven't earned their place yet." NEWS FLASH: IT'S NOT ABOUT YOU!!! It's about loving and serving God. He first asks us to love Him. He THEN asks us to love others above ourselves. With that being said, can I suggest that you can't truly love God without loving others? Even if they are taking your spot—we're called to love, be hospitable, and trust that God will have His way. Don't miss that opportunity!

Is there someone in your athletic space that you could be more hospitable with?

Jessica Cahoy
Professional CrossFit Athlete
2015-2021

238

August 25

"You did not choose me, but I chose you and appointed you so that you might go and bear fruit - fruit that will last - and so that whatever you ask in my name the Father will give to you."
- John 15:16 NIV

Performing poorly is a tough thing as an athlete. It is easy to become defeated, discouraged, and feel like a failure. I struggled with feeling like my purpose was to please my coaches and perform well every single day. But having a relationship with the Lord has given me so much freedom. Our purpose is to love and serve those around us well, and to glorify the Lord in all that we do and with all that we are. I can walk onto the court everyday knowing that I can glorify God in how I love and serve my teammates regardless of my performance. I have confidence in knowing that Jesus defined my value when He died on the cross for me. So no matter how I perform athletically, my value is untouched.

You were chosen on purpose and for a purpose. And this completely changes how you live. God did not choose you by accident, and He has called you to a greater purpose - to love and serve others one at a time. However, just because we are chosen does not mean we are qualified. We have been chosen out of His abundant grace for us. Fruit grows through prayer and a relationship with Jesus - a connection to the vine.

How can you use your sport in the good and the bad to glorify the Lord and pursue the purpose He has given you?

Brie Postema
Virginia Tech Volleyball
2020-2024

239

August 26

"We love each other because he loved us first."
-1 John 4:19 NLT

God is love, and we love because of Him. Everything we do in life should be done as an act of love because we have God's love in us. We should let this drive our decisions, relationships, and desire to be better. God's love is all around us. It's in the little moments and all the beautiful things in life. We must remember to cherish it. Cherish the beautiful sunrise, the moments of laughter with a loved one, the challenging workout that leaves you feeling revived, and even the mundane tasks that fill your day-to-day. Because what is life without love? It's empty, full of disappointment, and driven by selfish ambition. That's life without God.

Life with God gives us peace through the ups and downs. It gives us hope that we can endure all of life's seasons. If we can wake up every day and remind ourselves that God is with us and His never-ending love is inside us, then we can see the world in a different light. We can choose to accept that every day is a blessing and a new chance to share God's love with every person we encounter. Whether it's our spouse, our siblings, our kids, our coworker, or a stranger on the street. We can use every moment as a challenge to shine God's love and share it. We are here to love and be loved. Now we must accept this gift and share it with the world.

I challenge you to make the choice to be filled with love today. Because God chose to love you and will always choose to love you no matter what.

Amanda Barnhart
Professional CrossFit Athlete
2018-Present

240

August 27

"Love one another with brotherly affection. Outdo one another in showing honor." -Romans 12:10 ESV

I was always timid to share my faith in college with my teammates, coaches or other athletes. I knew I was to be bold in proclaiming the gospel and making disciples as Jesus commissioned us to do, but having those conversations instilled fear in me.

Since graduating, I've recognized and learned the value of being a Christian with my *life*. With my actions, words, intentional conversations, serving, giving, and by *not* participating in the negative norms of complaining that often surround us, I can best demonstrate Jesus' love and the gospel to others. When my faith is evident through my life's actions, when conversations arise about Jesus, they are less surprising to others and less uncomfortable for me because they've already seen a difference in me and I can give an explanation as to why.

When your daily life reflects Jesus, conversations about Him will be naturally brought up, either by you or others. Take advantage of your platform. You have daily opportunities and interactions as a teammate, role model, student and friend. Be bold for Jesus, strive to look like Him with your life by loving and showing honor to others and He will place people and conversations in front of you so you can grow His kingdom. After all, our athletic achievements are irrelevant and minuscule compared to the backdrop of eternity.

Are you more focused on outdoing others in your sport or outdoing others in love and honor?

Carly Blackwelder
University of South Carolina Women's Soccer
2012-2015

241

August 28

"Not that I am speaking of being in need, for I have learned in whatever situation I am to be content. I know how to be brought low, and I know how to abound. In any and every circumstance, I have learned the secret of facing plenty and hunger, abundance and need. I can do all things through him who strengthens me."
- Philippians 4:11-13

I must be honest. I am writing this in a moment where Paul's words are especially hard to believe. How is it that Paul was able to be content in whatever situation he found himself? How is it that he could write a letter of joy in prison? What is the secret of facing plenty and hunger abundance and need?

My Junior year of high school was the year I suffered an injury that changed the direction of my life. In a place of despair, I cried out to God in anger, pleading with God to change my circumstances. Instead, He changed my heart. As I prayed, He slowly showed me that He knew what He was doing, and I could trust Him. He showed me that in my weakness, I had the opportunity to rely on His strength and be okay. And I was more than okay, I was saved. When I finally began to trust God enough to depend on Him, I was able to experience the contentment that Paul describes.

Take a second to write down where you are relying on your own strength; admit this to God; and ask for His help. His hands are the safest place to rest our lives in.

Reighan Childers
University of Missouri Kansas City Women's Soccer
2015-2019

"This book of instruction must not depart from your mouth;
you are to recite it day and night, so you may carefully observe
everything in it. For then you will prosper and succeed in whatever
you do." -Joshua 1:8 CSB

With practice, school, work, and the overall stress of life it can be easy to push our time in the word aside. Joshua tells us here that "this book of instruction" (the Bible) "must not depart from our mouths", thus meaning that our devotion to God through reading His word should be constantly on the forefront of our minds. Now this isn't just a once-a-week type of thing Joshua is talking about. By saying that our time in the word should be both day and night, Joshua makes clear our devotion to God is not something that we should just rush to get through like a chore. It should be something that our spirit thirsts for.

The most amazing part of this piece of Scripture that Joshua tells us is that when are constantly in the word that we will prosper and succeed in whatever we do. This is something that I like to call "Hugs from God". It's so reassuring knowing that if we put God and His word first, that we will be successful at whatever we do in life. No trials, tribulations, hurdles, walls, or barriers will stop us if we stay near to God and His word.

30 for 30 Challenge: Let's spend 30 minutes in the word for 30 days straight.

Elijah Green
Northwest Missouri State University Football
2018-2022

August 30

"And Jesus came and said to them, "All authority in heaven and on earth has been given to me. Go therefore and make disciples of all nations, baptizing them in the name of the Father and of the Son and of the Holy Spirit, teaching them to observe all that I have commanded you. And behold, I am with you always, to the end of the age." -Matthew 28:18-20 ESV

"God's calling is His equipping". As athletes, our whole lives are spent working towards goals and striving to be our best. As a result, we develop a performance mindset. This is where I found myself as a college football player. My identity was wrapped up in my performance on the field. I saw my value in "what I do", not who I am. The truth is we are made in the image of God and He sees us as "very good" (*Gen. 1:31*). This is where our value comes from! Once we understand this, then we can take to heart what Jesus commands the disciples to do in this passage.

The disciples were a rag tag group of men. They were not educated, wealthy or well respected in their communities. The least "equipped" in the worlds' eyes. However, Jesus didn't care about their resume because He knew God called them and equipped them through His calling. Jesus charges them to "Go" and make disciples; the calling I believe He has for all of us. The last few years I have been discovering what this means for me and I invite you to do the same. LET'S GO!

GO ask God where He wants you to GO. Far or near, be obedient to the call and know where your value comes from!

Carter Roberts
Wheaton College Men's Football
2015-2019

244

"Are you tired? Worn out? Burned out on religion? Come to me. Get away with me and you'll recover your life. I'll show you how to take a real rest. Walk with me and work with me – watch how I do it. Learn the unforced rhythms of grace. I won't lay anything heavy or ill-fitting on you. Keep company with me and you'll learn to live freely and lightly." -Matthew 11:28-30 MSG

"Are you tired? Worn out?" As athletes, we probably laugh at these questions from Jesus. Of course, we're tired! We have nagging injuries, sore muscles, and tired minds from hours of practice. We have strained relationships and the exhausting burden of performing well. So, of course we're tired. And when we express our exhaustion to coaches, friends, and relatives we are often met with responses like "don't be lazy" or "there's no off season for champions." So, we continue in our exhaustion.

But that's not how Jesus responds to our exhaustion. Instead, Jesus says: "Come to me…I will show you how to take a real rest." What a beautiful and enticing sentence. Most of us athletes don't know how to take a real rest, but Jesus' words in this passage offer true rest and peace. I'm not just talking about a day off from our sport. I'm talking about real, true rest. I'm talking about real rest that allows us to "live freely and lightly." Athletes, resting does not make you lazy. We all need rest. You don't have to live tired and worn out. Go to Jesus. Learn from Jesus. He will teach you how to take a real rest.

Are you tired? Worn out? What is exhausting you right now? Where do you need to go to Jesus for rest in your life?

Abby Lee
Columbia University Women's Basketball
2015-2019

September 1

"Even as the Son of Man came not to be served but to serve, and to give his life as a ransom for many." — Matthew 20:28

A pastor was on his way to church to deliver a sermon one Easter morning. He passed a boy with a sinister look, carrying a bird cage. Rattling around inside were three sparrows. The pastor asked the boy, "What do you plan on doing with the birds, son?"

The boy replied, "I'm gonna have some fun. I'm gonna tie them up and see if they can fly, then I'm gonna see how long they can go without food, and then I'm gonna feed them to my cat."

The pastor asked, "How much for those birds?" The boy responded, "You don't want these birds, they are field birds; they're worthless." The pastor asked again, "How much for those birds?" The boy thought he was kidding, and told him $500. The pastor's response: "Done. Deal. I'll take 'em."

Isn't that crazy? Well, in the same way the pastor paid an incredible amount for the birds, Jesus paid an incredible amount for us — He paid with His life. He was willing to be tortured, beaten, and scorned, nailed to a cross until He died, because He loved us. He wanted us and was willing to give everything so that we can be in Paradise with Him for eternity.

That's the God we serve, one who will do anything for us. In Matthew 6:26, Jesus says, "Look at the birds of the air; they do not sow or reap or store away in barns, and yet your heavenly Father feeds them. Are you not much more valuable than they?"

Above all else, God loves and cares for you at all times.

Nik Pry
University of North Carolina Baseball
2019-2022

"But regarding anything beyond this, dear friend, go easy. There's no end to the publishing of books, and constant study wears you out so you're no good for anything else. The last and final word is this: Fear God. Do what he tells you."- Ecclesiastes 12:12-13 MSG

Have you ever walked into the gym and set your bag down only to let out a heavy sigh from feeling tired and worn down? Yeah, me too. Probably more times than I'd like to admit. Competing in sports can oftentimes feel more like a marketing campaign than an outlet for the gifts and talents God has given us. Pressures come at us from all angles. Expectations from coaches, hopes from family and friends, social and brand requirements, and our own personal dreams weigh on the heart. However, we've been invited to "Fear God" - to be in complete awe and wonder of His presence in our life. Each day we can seek Him first; not scroll our feed, land a new sponsor, plan the next workout, or win the next game, but instead "go easy."

I believe we, as Christian athletes, should have a different countenance and feel to our presence. If we are truly standing in awe of God, shouldn't we have a deeper peace about ourselves and a never-ending grace for teammates, coaches, and athletes around us? Our focus should be on what He told us to do: Do it out of love. Do it with all our strength and might. Do it humbly and with a cheerful heart. Endure the hardships. Sacrifice our comfort and trust in Him. Be patient - the work will pay off. Give it all back to Him and let Him make all the difference.

What has God done in your life that you are in awe of?

Cole Sager
Professional CrossFit Athlete
2013-Present

September 3

*But the LORD said to Samuel, "Do not look on his
appearance or on the height of his stature, because I have rejected
him. For the LORD sees not as man sees: **man looks on the outward
appearance, but the LORD looks on the heart"** -1 Samuel 16:7 ESV*

As athletes, we have been given the opportunity to train our
bodies to do some truly incredible things. Take a moment to thank
God for that. We spend hours and hours perfecting our craft and
pushing our bodies to the limit, yet we often end up more critical of
how we look than thankful for what our resilient bodies can do. *If only
I could gain weight. If only I could lose weight. I wish I was more
muscular. I wish I was less muscular.* Thoughts from all sides of the
spectrum infiltrate our minds daily. Our God hears these cries and has
a response – your worth is not based on your body.

When we place our identity in our appearance, we are always
left empty-handed and wanting more. We are certainly called to take
care of and nourish our bodies (1 Cor. 6:19-20), but Scripture states
that physical training is only of *some* value, while godliness is of
value in every way (1 Tim. 4:8). Therefore, when you are tempted to
place value in your appearance, be reminded that God places value in
your heart. When you are inclined to be critical of your body, choose
to be thankful that your identity is not in the temporary, but in the
eternal God whose love is not skin-deep, but soul-deep.

**Our goal on this Earth is not for people to remember the way we
looked or performed, but to remember the way we treated, cared
for, and loved others with the love of Christ.**

Jenna Pfeiffer
Baylor University Track & Field
2012-2017

248

September 4

"Consider it pure joy, my brothers and sisters, whenever you face trials of many kinds, because you know that the testing of your faith produces perseverance. Let perseverance finish its work so that you may be mature and complete, not lacking anything." -James 1:2-4

It seems weird to consider it pure joy whenever you face trials of many kinds, right? However, I don't recall Jesus ever saying this life would be easy! I came into college so excited to play basketball. However, my college career went the opposite of how I imagined it. After not getting the playing time I wanted and then having to undergo not one, but two hip surgeries, I felt completely worthless and empty. I always thought that I was only as good as my production as an athlete was, and when that got taken from me it was just awful. Jesus began to open my eyes to see a new perspective on basketball, life, and most importantly my relationship with Him. I wasn't empty because I couldn't play basketball, I was empty because my life wasn't fully rooted in Jesus.

I found a new role for myself on the team. I became a better encourager, friend, and teammate. This life is only temporary. All our accolades, stats, and earthly possessions will pass, and we have eternity with Jesus to look forward to. Once I figured that out and fully believed it, my life was changed. I am thankful every day and I do consider it pure joy that I have faced trials of many kinds, because my identity is found in Jesus Christ and Jesus Christ alone.

When reflecting on your experience, have you ever been dissatisfied with the story that is being written for you?

Gracie Simpson
Lipscomb University Women's Basketball
2018-2021

September 5

"I, Nebuchadnezzar, lifted my eyes to heaven, and my reason returned to me, and I blessed the Most High, and praised and honored Him who lives forever" - Daniel 4:34 ESV

This moment takes place after King Nebuchadnezzar has spent the previous seven years of his life living as an ox. A curse from God that occurred because of his pride and refusal to repent and obey. In humility, the king finally lifts his eyes toward heaven realizing his purpose is to glorify God not his own majesty.

"All glory to God" is a phrase most athletes are quite familiar with, but many misunderstand. The more we become like God, the greater our capacity to glorify and therefore enjoy Him is. As King Nebuchadnezzar shows us, lifting our eyes towards heaven, focusing our hearts on our eternal purpose to exalt and glorify God, cultivates the humility and surrender necessary for sanctification. Humility is not something we can discipline ourselves into, but rather a byproduct of living in the presence of King Jesus.

As I continue my football journey, through injuries, insecurities, struggles with self-worth, and loss of motivation to continue, the Lord has pressed on my heart the redemptive power of lifting my eyes toward heaven. By striving to live in Jesus' presence fueled by thankfulness of His blessings, an ability to live satisfied and sanctified in God's presence has come through the continued renewal of my mind.

Take some time to think about how you can better glorify God in your daily life.

Nick Cannon
Furman University Football
2020-2023

September 6

"Consider it pure joy, my brothers and sisters, whenever you face trials of many kinds, because you know that the testing of your faith produces perseverance." - James 1:2-3 NIV

During my time as a collegiate athlete, it seems as though I have been more prone to injury than I have in my entire life. With soccer being something that I found my identity and worth in, when it started to get its own trials through different hindering injuries, I was left feeling down, not knowing how to trust God with soccer or how He was using it in my life. I was lost. God eventually revealed to me that He didn't bring me to Northwest to play soccer, receive a bunch of accolades, and have my identity be in who I was as a soccer player, but to make disciples of the very girls that I spend everyday with and to become more rooted in Him. With that perspective change, I was able to give even more effort and put forth a new energy into my trainings, workouts, and even into the friendships that I was building within the team.

When trials come in our given sport, it is vital to press into God and seek Him through it all. When we don't seek Him first, we begin to feel empty and unfulfilled in our purpose. All trials that we face as athletes will produce perseverance to continue walking deeply with God through every and any circumstance.

How is God using your sport to produce perseverance in your faith? Ask God to reveal that to you, and press into those trials.

Atiana Stratman
Northwest Missouri State Women's Soccer
2019-2023

September 7

"For to set the mind on the flesh is death, but to set the mind on the Spirit is life and peace. For the mind that I set on the flesh is hostile to God, for it does not submit to God's law; indeed, it cannot."
-Romans 8:6-7 ESV

I spent much of my athletic career worrying and waiting for breakthrough and victorious moments. Looking back, I now realize I wasted much time seeking earthly success that promised fulfillment, but instead left me disappointed and unsatisfied. One quote that resonates with me says, "If our happiness terminates on it, we are idolaters." I was turning a good thing (running/sport) into an ultimate thing that drove my emotions and identity.

Through setbacks, failures, and a career-ending injury, I quickly learned that God cares substantially more about the person I am becoming and the eternal impact I am making than any earthly accolade I could ever obtain. I have found that releasing my tight grip on the world does not lead to an unfulfilled life. Instead, God promises that we will experience joyous and abundant days when our eyes are fixed on Him (John 10:10). Let God leverage your life for His kingdom and glory and do not throw away today wondering if you are where you are supposed to be. Trust God's timing that He will guide and provide for you, and delight with confidence that you are living in His "Plan A" for your life!

What practical strategies can you employ this week to set your mind on the Spirit and experience life and peace through a relationship with Christ?

Elyse Prescott
University of Minnesota / University of Iowa XC/Track & Field
2016-2021

September 8

"Two are better than one, because they have a good return for their labor: If either of them falls down, one can help the other up. But pity anyone who falls and has no one to help them up."
- *Ecclesiastes 4:9-10 NIV*

Here I am again, lying on the soccer field, looking up at the sky, and wondering why God would let this happen again. Having been in this situation before, I knew the inevitable. I would soon be under the knife for another surgery. However, this time was different. I was a senior, and I knew that not only was my season over, but so was my soccer career.

I was devastated, depressed, and unable to come to terms that something I dedicated my entire life to was over.

I ended up isolating myself from my team and friends. I stopped going to practices and games. After a few weeks of self-pity, my coach approached me and told me I needed to come back and be a part of the team again. I asked him why it mattered when I would not be able to play again. He said, "Your contribution to this team is more than what you as a player can accomplish on the field. We need your leadership, encouragement, and accountability. Your teammates need you." Until that moment, I did not truly realize the impact of being on a team. We are not created to walk through this life alone. As athletes, we are blessed with a community of coaches and teammates that can build us up when we are down.

How can you look beyond yourself and be a positive impact on your team today, regardless of your individual circumstances?

Molly (Bray) Elliott
Lipscomb University Women's Soccer
2012-2016

253

September 9

"who Himself bore our sins in His own body on the tree, that we, having died to sins, might live for righteousness—by whose stripes you were healed." - 1 Peter 2:24 NKJV

A walking miracle. That is a statement I heard quite a bit during my last collegiate year of volleyball. Being a 22-year-old with a broken back, multiple disc issues, nerve issues, and legs going numb, took its toll on my body; mentally and physically. I am a walking miracle; you are a walking miracle. Not because of a traumatic experience, but simply because of Christ's love for us, what He did on the cross, and that we have been born again as believers in Christ. That is the ultimate sacrifice and miracle.

Jesus took on the most brutal death: emotionally, physically, and mentally. He was mocked, spat at, and beaten. He had the crown of thorns put on His head, which most likely penetrated through the skull bone. He was scourged, tearing off flesh on His body. Once on the cross, for every breath He had to take, He had to push His body up; with nails in His wrists and feet, while His exposed back was rubbing against the cross, which caused agonizing pain. On top of all of that, He had the weight of the world's sin on His shoulders.

I pray we remember daily what Jesus went through for us. He defeated death and now is alive today to save us. We suffer for a sport we love; He suffered because He loves us.

Continue to show Christ's love to others, taking up your cross daily, and know you are an awe-inspiring, walking miracle because of Christ.

Amy Pflughaupt-Williamson
Texas State University Volleyball
2017-2019

254

"Obviously, I'm not trying to win the approval of people, but of God. If pleasing people were my goal I would not be Christ's servant." -Galatians 1:10 NLT

Trying to understand the difference between playing for people's approval and playing for the Lord was really hard for me. I gave my life to Jesus in the second semester of my freshman year and up until that point everything I did was for the approval of man. I wanted everyone to know that I was the best. I thrived on words of affirmation and my volleyball prowess. It took two years for me to live out what it looks like to play for the Lord and for His glory and not my own.

Before every game I would visualize where Jesus was going to be sitting and anytime I got out of character or tried to give myself the glory, I would look at that spot and could see Jesus and whether I was making Him proud. This became an every-game-thing and I even got some of my teammates involved. By no means did I get this right every time, but I finally began to understand the difference between playing for the approval of man and playing for an audience of One.

The Lord is patient with us and always more gracious than we deserve. I found the most success when I truly glorified Christ. That is a thing that has stuck with me in my relationship with Jesus far beyond the volleyball court.

Take some time to repent to the Lord if you have been glorifying yourself over Him. Ask Him to help make this verse real.

Ashley Slay Glotta
Austin Peay State University Volleyball
2014-2017

September 11

"Don't copy the behavior and customs of this world, but let God transform you into a new person by changing the way you think. Then you will learn to know God's will for you, which is good and pleasing and perfect." *-Romans 12:2 NLT*

In an inconsistent, broken world there are not many things that I can guarantee with certainty. However, there is one thing that I can: You will not regret putting your full effort in following Jesus.

When I look back on my college career, my biggest regrets are the times that I spent loving the things of this world more than I loved my Savior. Our Lord knows you by name. He knows the number of hairs on your head. He loves you more than anyone else ever will. Nothing compares to his embrace. Make the decision today to give Him EVERYTHING you have. You will have regrets in your life, but I promise you that devoting yourself to Christ will not be one of them. Let him into the dark parts of your life, only then will you be truly changed.

Speaking to the people reading this who have already given their lives to Christ, I challenge you to reevaluate your day-to-day life and identify the areas where you haven't yet fully surrendered. What're you holding on to? Don't compartmentalize your life. Be the same Christ-like man/woman everywhere you go. Speaking to those who have not yet given their lives to Christ, I want you to ask yourself what you're waiting for. There is no better day than today to begin.

Don't hold back. God has incredible things waiting for you. Surrender.

Jamie Ricksecker
Pima Community College / Arizona Christian University Volleyball
2016-2020

September 12

"But seek first his kingdom and his righteousness, and all these things will be given to you as well. Therefore do not worry about tomorrow, for tomorrow will worry about itself. Each day has enough trouble of its own." – Matthew 6:33-34 NIV

It's challenging to accept the truth as a college student-athlete when you think you have it all together because your grades are good, you're competing well, and you attend small groups and church. My Junior year was my first major injury in my running career. I wondered why God would allow that happen to me but during my 4-month rehab, He revealed a lot to me. God made it clear that I was seeking social media first every single morning by scrolling instead of reading my devotional and spending time with Him. He made it clear that I was seeking partying on the weekends, attending church religiously not faithfully, and not being a true disciple for Christ.

I made it a priority to strive to seek God first and not worry about the next day. After all of this, my relationship with God was great but I wasn't performing the same and running the times I wanted. God revealed to me again that, despite seeking Him first, as I should've been doing anyway, there would still be trials and tribulations. Keep seeking God first regardless of the season.

Ask God to reveal to you what you're seeking daily. At times you don't realize the chaos you've created in your own life while things are going well. God will show you what needs to stay and what needs to go.

Desmond Pierce
East Tennessee State University Cross Country and Track & Field
2010-2014

257

September 13

"You will keep in perfect peace all who trust in you, all whose thoughts are fixed on you! Trust in the Lord always, for the Lord God is the eternal Rock." - Isaiah 26:3-4 NLT

Each day we are given is a new opportunity to honor God. Like life, sports always seem to bring us unpredictable situations. It can be hard to see God in those moments, nevertheless, honor Him. Day after day we train and sacrifice, all for an unpredictable career-ending injury, semifinal loss, or rough season. I've been there and have walked through the pain uncertainty brings. It can be so easy to question God and begin an endless cycle of 'what-ifs'. It's okay to be frustrated or not know how to pray in those moments. God sees you, hears you, knows your heart, and your circumstance.

The God that created you with such a unique purpose, knows your circumstance and has a perfect plan for your life. God doesn't need a starter, gold medalist, or championship title to demonstrate His glory. He wants to use you right now in your current situation. Be honest with yourself and with God. Pray for God to change your perspective to one of gratitude. An attitude of gratefulness (especially in a time when it doesn't make sense) allows for peace and joy to flood your heart and mind no matter your present reality. Put your hope in His unfailing love. Who knows… maybe in the future your story will change the life of someone who will be in a similar position. Let His love and faithfulness be your lifeline.

How can you honor God through your current situation? Write it down and practice it today.

Kristie Jones
Old Dominion University Field Hockey
2015-2019

258

September 14

"Above all, keep loving one another earnestly, since love covers a multitude of sins. Show hospitality to one another without grumbling. As each has received a gift, use it to serve one another, as good stewards of God's varied grace." -1 Peter 4:8-10 NIV

I have played tennis since I was little, and I have been blessed by the way my parents have poured into me through the sport. My mom and dad both used the gifts that the Lord had given them to teach me how to steward my own gifts. They showed me how the game of tennis could make me a better person on and off the court. I have learned how to work hard, stand up for what is right, and fully embrace the gift the Lord has given me because of their guidance.

I am sure my parents would get frustrated with me at times, but they never stopped serving me. My parents followed the Lord's command of showing hospitality without grumbling. They taught me how to serve my teammates throughout college. The Lord has called His followers to encourage one another. By all means, I am not perfect at this, but I believe that we should be striving to serve our teammates in a way that honors the Lord. It could be a simple "How are you today?" or telling a teammate how proud you are of the way they competed. The Lord is rejoicing in heaven when He sees teammates cheering for one another to embrace their gifts.

I challenge you to text a teammate and tell them how thankful you are for them this week.

Allison Stewart Brown
Abilene Christian University Women's Tennis
2018-2022

September 15

"Abraham believed God, and it was credited to him as righteousness…he did not waver through unbelief regarding the promise of God but was strengthened in his faith and gave glory to God, being fully persuaded that God had power to do what he had promised." – Romans 4:3, 20-21 NIV

My collegiate career had been quite rocky with injuries and performance anxiety, self-doubt bombarding me with discouragement. Finally, my senior year, my heart understood what my brain had been telling me for so long – how to compete for an Audience of One.

When we place our faith in God, it does not return void. He is full of power and fulfills His promises. He doesn't promise success or a perfect routine. He does promise that whoever trusts in Him will be justified and their faith credited to them as righteousness. Righteousness is right standing with God, and I can only be with God if I am free from sin – perfect and holy. That's why Jesus must give us *His* righteousness – I cannot earn it by works or performance. If I score well at one competition, the same pressure remains at the next – I must keep earning perfection. Not so in Christ. I didn't need to perform well to be loved and accepted. I needed to allow myself to receive Jesus's righteousness. In Him, I am released from perfectionism, I am confident in my identity, and I am free to joyfully do what He created me to do – worship Him through my sport.

Are you living with faith in the righteousness of Christ as your own? Ask God for faith like Abraham and walk confidently in this new life of freedom in Jesus, knowing God fulfills His promises.

Jamie DeCicco
University of North Carolina Gymnastics
2015-2019

September 16

"But because my servant Caleb has a different spirit and follows me wholeheartedly, I will bring him into the land he went to, and his descendants will inherit it." – Numbers 14:24 NIV

Saying no is something I had to get good at as a freshman in college. Especially as an athlete, there is pressure to go to that party, sip that drink, or break that rule in order to feel accepted. Oftentimes it was tough to turn down invitations to events where it seemed everyone would be, but God placed incredible friends in my life whose goals and convictions are aligned with His and mine. That circle of accountability constantly reminds me that it is possible to have a great time without jeopardizing my reputation or testimony. God didn't give us Scripture as a restrictive rulebook, but as an access code to the joy and fulfillment that comes from following Jesus.

In Numbers 13, twelve spies are sent to investigate Canaan. Of the twelve, only Caleb and Joshua were willing to speak up and trust that the Lord would provide for them in the frightening land. Through it all, they were rewarded for choosing to seek God's will rather than being pressured and deterred by the conformity of others. Caleb's boldness is a daily reminder that God is faithful to every promise. The decisions you make and the actions you take speak volumes about who you are. A testimony of "different spiritedness" has the potential to spark powerful conversations about the Gospel.

God blesses those who follow His ways rather than the world's. Learn to be content with taking the road less traveled.

Julian Ashby
Furman University Football
2020-2024

261

September 17

"How then will they call on him in whom they have not believed? And how are they to believe in him of whom they have never heard?3 And how are they to hear without someone preaching?"
-Romans 10:14 ESV

How did you come to know the Gospel? Think about it. Whether you were raised in the faith or came to know Christ later, someone preached the Gospel to you. Your teammates might not know this Gospel. They might not know the perfect love of Jesus that turns the darkness into light, raises the dead to life, and redeems the sinner into the saint. We cannot add anything to this love because it is perfect. But as this love comes into our hearts, it slowly fills our every desire. Our passion becomes His; to have others taste and see the beautiful love of our Savior. Now consider, the Lord wants to do the same in the life of your teammate...

This can be a daunting task, a new endeavor much harder than any of your hardest days in athletics. Please remember, if you know enough to accept it you know enough to share it, just ask Him for boldness. Get lunch with them, ask intentional questions on the bus, speak truth whenever you can, pray for them, find truth in God's word, but in everything be faithful to speak this Gospel we have been entrusted with. Do not do this alone, find other believers and do this work together!

Start small and find one teammate. Share the Gospel with them. Pray over them daily. Love them well. Find another and repeat. When they come to Faith, disciple them in truth.

Zac Robbins
Oklahoma State Track and Field
2020-2022

September 18

"You, Lord, hear the desire of the afflicted. You encourage them and you listen to their cry." -Psalm 10:17

In the middle of my sophomore soccer season, my dad suffered severe brain damage from a stroke. That year, I spent long hours in the car driving to and from class, the ICU, and practice. As hard as it was, during those car rides, I cried out to the Lord. I expressed how angry I was. I even told God I was mad at Him. I'm not sure what I expected, but I didn't think I'd end up with a stronger relationship with Christ.

Ultimately, though, that's exactly what happened. By giving Him my heart, I drew nearer to God. It didn't happen overnight; It took me months to see the effects. But eventually I learned a big lesson- God wants authenticity. Even Jesus himself cried out to God (Luke 22:44; Mat. 27:46)! He doesn't want our watered-down prayers. He just wants us, messiness and all.

As followers of Christ, we will all face affliction at some point. Maybe you're stressed about a game or upset about a coach. Maybe your sport is causing you stress when it used to be fun. Maybe life is just hard and confusing. No matter what you're going through, let God in. Tell Him how you feel. Rest assured that the Lord hears the afflicted; He encourages them; He listens to their cry.

During your prayers with God today, come to Him with every burden on your heart, even if it's messy. Don't hold back- He wants to hear from you.

Kassie Newsom
University of Central Missouri Women's Soccer
2019-2021

263

September 19

"Let the morning bring me word of your unfailing love, for I have put my trust in you. Show me the way I should go, for to you I entrust my life." – Psalm 143:8

Throughout college and my professional career, I constantly sought to know and control the result or outcome. If I did more, worked more, and sacrificed more, I hoped to perform at the highest level and win. To know that through adversity, injury, and difficult times if I put in the time everything would end up working out. This constant desire to anticipate success left me feeling stressed and chaotic. Placing my identity in my actions and results rather than in the Lord.

There finally came a point where I realized we never have control over the outcome, the Lord's perfect plan will always persevere. Every day I work to grow in trust to realize that His plan for each one of us is greater than we could ever imagine.

The Lord is constantly fighting for you. Take some time to reflect on areas of your life you are searching to control the outcome rather than placing trust in the Lord.

Audrey Alford
University of Oklahoma / Michigan State University Volleyball
2015-2019

September 20

"Whatever you do, work at it with all your heart, as working for the Lord, not for human masters, since you know that you will receive an inheritance from the Lord as a reward. It is the Lord Christ you are serving." - Colossians 3:23-24 NIV

Every day we are chasing a goal or dream. This is different for most people and different for most athletes. The one goal most people have is wanting to be at the top. The Best of the Best. As athletes we work so hard and strive for this goal of being the best that we forgot sometimes who we are working for. Is it for our own glory or for Gods glory? This is a question we can ask ourselves daily before we go into any workout, practice, or game. How can I give all the glory to God today in how I live my life daily and in my sport?

Playing baseball all my life and growing in understanding of what God has called me to do, I have battled with trying to trust myself and thinking that I can do things on my own. God showed me His plan was so much better when I leaned on Him fully and made me prayers known to Him. That He has guided me all throughout my career of how God wants us to grow closer to Him. Whether that is playing our sport or living out another plan that God has for us. He loves and cares for us so much. We can be confident knowing that when we are putting our heart to it and serving God, He can guide us for whatever He has planned for us. We surrender the moment to God and then we go give it our all.

Keep seeking God and His purpose for your life. He says it will be better than anything we ask or think, and it is so true.

William Saxton
University of Central Florida Baseball
2018-Present

September 21

"Go on your way. Eat the fat and drink sweet wine and send portions to anyone who has nothing ready, for this day is holy to the Lord. And do not be grieved, for the joy of the Lord is your strength."
-Nehemiah 8:10

As athletes, discouragement comes in a wide variety of ways. Injuries, bad games, lack of playing time…you name it! When my head coach, Pat Casey, brought me to church for the first time in my life my sophomore year, my entire outlook and trajectory changed forever. Once I gave my life to Christ and found a true, rock-solid identity in Him, any failure, struggle, or trial that I faced was second to how can I glorify God with this situation?

Nehemiah has always inspired me with how he approached the task of rebuilding the walls of Jerusalem. He is the definition of a servant leader and a leader worth following. The thing I admire most about his leadership style is his ability to not let discouragement bring him down. By allowing the joy of the Lord to be our strength, we have an eternal perspective on everything we face. We seek the best of every outcome knowing that we have the opportunity to glorify Christ with our sport, and, most importantly, our lives.

Any obstacle or adversity that we face has a lesson and challenge for growth. Sit down and reflect on any recent obstacles and ask God for wisdom of what He is trying to teach you.

Morgan Pearson
Oregon State University Baseball / Texas Rangers
2014-2018

September 22

"Many are the plans in a person's heart, but it is the Lord's purpose that prevails." – Proverbs 19:21 NIV

Sports have a way of humbling us. Often the team that deserves to win does not, regardless of their preparation, work ethic, and desire to win. I am too familiar with being let down by sports. My senior year of high school, we lost in the state championship. Every season in college we lost in the quarter or semi-finals of our conference tournament. Those losses were especially frustrating when poor calls and bad luck were involved.

As I had more time to reflect on my un-fulfilled victories, the Holy Spirit convicted me that my anger and frustration in these circumstances stem from my deep desire for control and a sense of entitlement. The truth is that my need to control the outcomes in my life is simply replacing God as my King and Ruler with myself. While the desire to win is a good and motivating thing, we are wrong to believe that we always deserve the outcomes that we want.

In reality, we do not deserve anything—especially the grace of God and the gift of salvation. Even when success gives us a false sense of control, God is in control, and He will not fail to accomplish His purposes. Ultimately, God cares most about the attitude of our hearts. Our aim should be to glorify God through our responses in all circumstances, and to have a humble and thankful heart.

Ask the Lord to reveal the places in your heart where you feel entitled, and where you resist surrendering control back to God.

Leah Hoffman
Trevecca Nazarene University Women's Soccer
2016-2020

267

September 23

"For from him and through him and to him are all things. To him be the glory forever. Amen." -Romans 11:36 NRSV

One time a sweet, old lady grabbed my hands, looked me in my eyes, and recited a prayer: "I'm not what I do. I'm not what I have. I'm not what other people say about me. I'm the beloved of God. It's who I am. No one can take it from me. I don't have to worry. I don't have to hurry. I can trust my friend Jesus and share His love with the world."

Obviously, it stuck with me. So much so that I wrote my own version for athletes: "I'm not how I play. I'm not my position. I'm not what fans, friends, family, or coaches say about me. I'm uniquely gifted and loved. THAT'S who I am. No matter my playing time, mistakes, or accolades. I don't have to worry. I don't have to earn love. I can play freely and glorify God with my game."

I was the player whose self-esteem rose and fell based on my performance. Bad practice, bad mood. Lost a game, lost my worth. I wanted to believe that my self-worth was secure in Christ, but it didn't always feel that way. How do you train yourself to believe something? You spend daily time in God's presence so He can remind you.

Pray a Prayer of Examen:
(1) What am I grateful for today?
(2) What emotions did I feel today, and where was God in those?
(3) What did I do today in alignment with my core values?
(4) Who is God leading me to pray for?

Elizabeth Perkins Bounds
Hope College Women's Basketball
Hope College Women's Soccer
2013-2017

September 24

"I keep my eyes always on the Lord. With him at my right hand, I will not be shaken." -Psalm 16:8 NIV

I'm not going to be one to say I've had to deal with the hardest hardships when it comes to sports because I haven't. But I will say I've been through my fair share of trials. I've had to sit 2nd string for the first half of my high school senior year, and in college there have been times where I've really struggled because I just felt I couldn't do anything right, get anything right, or perform the way I should. As an athlete, there's a lot of pressure and a lot of expectation you are supposed to "live up to." It does a lot to your brain and your body. But one thing that I've always found to be true is that God's plan never falters, so trust in it and stick it out.

It is easy to quit or take the shortcut path that might lead to initial happiness, but God has so much bigger plans for you than you can ever imagine. When you feel down, turn to His word, and memorize His truth. Know the promises He has for you, the perfect will that He has for your life, and that in Him you won't be shaken. Trust in His plan because it is perfect. He will never leave you, forsake you, or give you something you can't handle. Have faith in that and know even on your worse day, He's developing you for a time to shine in the future. Stick it out.

When you feel like things aren't going the way you feel they should in sports or in life, continue to stick it out and keep your eyes on the Lord.

Taylor Bell
Furman University Football
2020-2023

269

September 25

"He restoreth my soul: he leadeth me in the paths of
righteousness for his name's sake."
-Psalm 23:3 KJV

Being an athlete is not everything. Don't get me wrong, God blessing you with athletic abilities is an AMAZING gift that you will cherish for the rest of your life. But, like I said, it's not everything. I know… crazy right?

My whole identity was wrapped up in how I performed on the field. On the outside, I was always having fun and never taking anything too serious. On the inside, I was burdened with living up to past accomplishments and overcoming past failures. It was hard for me to stop caring so much. After coming to the realization that I was filled with an unhealthy amount of pressure to perform, I didn't really do anything about it. I tried to just go with the flow and endure the anxiousness I had on the field. If only I knew then what I know now. I'm here to tell you… GIVE IT TO GOD. While in college, I had heard of this before, but never truly embraced it. Now, through this I have learned that He is the only one that can give you peace. He is the only one who can open your eyes to what really matters. He will help show who you are without the sport. He will restore you in a way you never knew possible.

When you find yourself caring too much about your performance, whether it's successes or failures, GIVE IT TO GOD.

MaKray (Odom) Ferris
Trevecca Nazarene University Softball
2016-2021

270

September 26

"Do not love the world or the things in the world. If anyone loves the world, the love of the Father is not in him. For all that is in the world—the desires of the flesh and the desires of the eyes and pride of life—is not from the Father but is from the world. And the world is passing away along with its desires, but whoever does the will of God abides forever." - *1 John 2: 15-17 ESV*

I was a walk-on track athlete in college. My greatest desire was to prove my worth to my team. While I tried to find purpose in my pursuit of earning a scholarship, I was set free by the truth of this verse. Losing a race is nothing compared to the eternal loss it would be to not know Jesus as my Lord and Savior.

The scholarship I received was exciting, but I was left wanting more. I was investing all my time into something that was temporary. This problem doesn't escape us when our athletic career ends. Earthly desire will always be gaming for our attention. However, when you commit your life to Christ, you unleash the freedom of finding your purpose in being a key player in His eternal kingdom, in glorifying God, and enjoying His presence forever.

While pursuing excellence in our sport is good, we lose sight of God's eternal goodness if we hold our worldly aspirations as our main priority. God calls us to follow Him wholeheartedly and put our trust in Him by giving up our earthly desires.

Pray and thoughtfully consider what earthly desires are competing with your desire to follow Jesus and glorify God?

Janie Unkefer
Point Loma Nazarene University Track & Field
2013-2017

September 27

"Let us consider how to stir up one another to love and good works, not neglecting to meet together, as is the habit of some, but encouraging one another, and all the more as you see the Day drawing near." – Hebrews 10:24-25 ESV

As a Sophomore on the Baylor Baseball team, I was having a solid year. Then, 30 games into the season, I tore my ACL. That season-ending injury would end up being an amazing gift from the Lord. Throughout that year I had slowly begun to isolate myself. When I tore my ACL, God opened my eyes to the spiritual desert I was in due to the lack of Christian community in my life. In Hebrews, God lays out three key reasons we need community. First, to stir up one another. Godly community awakens us from our spiritual slumber and helps us to recognize our need for the Lord. Second, to fellowship with those who make us more like Christ. Meeting together we share a common lifeblood and purpose in Jesus. A common and true saying is that we become more like those who we spend time with. Third, for encouragement. The Christian life is not easy, God says throughout scripture there will be challenges. By His grace He has given us the Holy Spirit to guide us, but don't forget that He's also given us each other. We are a family of believers, called to sharpen and build up one another.

Consider the Christian community you have right now. Are you surrounded by men and women who make you more like Christ? If not, be passionate about finding the kind of community that God calls us to in Hebrews.

Levi Gilcrease
Baylor University Baseball
2014-2018

September 28

"Not only that, but we rejoice in our sufferings, knowing that suffering produces endurance, and endurance produces character, and character produces hope, and hope does not put us to shame because God's love has been poured into our hearts through the Holy Spirit who has been given to us." - Romans 5:3-5 ESV

When I dislocated my knee the day before my first game of senior year, I was NOT rejoicing in my suffering. I also wasn't rejoicing a few weeks later when the doctor told me I needed two surgeries. I rejoiced a little when they told me I could possibly get back to playing in between surgeries. But I definitely did not rejoice when I watched the clock run down to 0 at our last game and had still played 0 minutes of my last season.

However, I still trusted God. Not only did I endure that difficult season (thanks to the Holy Spirit), but God also showed me things I would have never known without my injury. He allowed me to empathize with other hurt athletes, see my teammates and coaches as humans deserving of His love more than success, and ultimately, experience more of His love. And it was through that character development that I was able to have hope and rejoice knowing that God will always show up in my suffering. And He wants to show up in yours too!

If you are currently in a season of suffering and in need of hope, think back to when God showed His love to you in a tough time. Tell Him "Thank You", then ask Him to do it again.

Adaeze Obinnah
Rice University Women's Basketball
2013-2017

273

September 29

"Let us not become weary in doing good, for at the proper time we will reap a harvest if we do not give up." -Galatians 6:9 NIV

During college two things happened to me that I know brought me closer to God and helped me grow in my faith.

I had my real true taste of having to face adversity in college when it came to soccer. It took me a while to embrace my role while still working hard and having a positive outlook on my experience. However, I was able to when I finally decided to trust God and truly listen and apply the messages that were being sent my way. By letting go of control and trusting my journey, I was able to truly embrace and feel my true purpose of where I knew I was supposed to be.

Listening to Him and having faith changed my entire college experience. I became a better teammate and person because it was the right thing to do, not because of playing time or status. Naturally, when I became that better teammate, I was also finding that my performance and my relationships were improving at the same time.

The second thing that happened was I lost my church pastor unexpectedly. He encompassed love in every way possible. He was the one who showed me what it looked like to live passionately and to have a true zest and joy for life. As a person and teammate, I wanted to make sure people around me felt as special and loved as he made me feel. He showed me what it meant to "Be Love."

God says "Don't be anxious about anything, but pray about everything. Be patient, my timing is perfect. I have something bigger planned for you and TRUST me, you're going to love it."

Avarie Howard
University of Nebraska-Omaha Women's Soccer
2018-2022

September 30

"So now I am giving you a new commandment: Love each other. Just as I have loved you, you should love each other."
– John 13:34 NLT

I have always struggled with wondering if I'm doing enough, whether that be in school, soccer, or my spiritual life. Was God pleased with me? Have I shared the gospel enough? I wanted my teammates to know Him because I knew the joy to be found in Jesus, but I also put immense pressure on myself to see others come to Christ. I assumed the best way to achieve that was to invite them to church and Bible studies, but it would result in one or two showing up, leaving me discouraged.

When I read John 13:34, I felt God prompting me to let go of my expectations and to love my teammates the way Jesus had loved me. Ultimately it was not up to me to get them to receive Christ; that was never my job, but the Lord's. Rather than getting them to attend, I started trying to meet them where they were. I spent more time listening, caring, praying, and letting go of this performance mindset. God was and always is in control, so I trusted Him with their salvation, because it was never mine to control, and spent my time trying to be the hands and feet of Jesus and letting God move as He always does.

Even if you don't see the fruit of your labor, God is using you for His glory by the ways you're reflecting Jesus to your teammates. How can you love and care for your teammates well in this season?

Brooke (Dunnigan) McAtee
Stephen F. Austin State University Women's Soccer
2013-2017

October 1

"For Christ's love compels us, because we are convinced that one died for all, and therefore all died. And he died for all, that those who live should no longer live for themselves but for him who died for them and was raised again." - 2 Corinthians 5:14-15

Motivation isn't always a hard thing to find when you are an athlete. For me, I always had a chip on my shoulder that I was going to prove to everyone that I could be the best at whatever I was doing. My motivation for the longest time was rooted in that mindset. The problem with this is that it is a selfish mindset, and my motivation would be dependent on my performance.

My sophomore year of college, the Lord changed my perspective through injury and disappointments with playing time. I realized that the one thing that should motivate me in athletics and in life is the fact that Christ died for me so that I should live for Him. I wanted everything that I did from that point on to be an act of worshipping the Lord. How I prepared, practiced, and played was to honor Him and not myself. When I made that switch, athletics became so much more fun. It was no longer about my performance but about giving my all for Him who gave His all for me. The outcome of my performance no longer mattered because I knew I had given my all for the Lord.

Our motivation should come from wanting to live for Christ. Does your effort aim to honor the Lord or yourself?

Zeth Barron
Hardin-Simmons University Football & Track
2010-2014

276

October 2

"I have said these things to you, that in me you may have peace. In the world you will have tribulation. But take heart; I have overcome the world." - John 16:33 ESV

I am here to share the good news of HOPE. Hope keeps you going. It helps you dig deeper, try a little harder, and keep moving forward. Hope = **Hold On, Pain Ends**!

As Christians, we are people that believe in the end of the Story. We do not just believe in happily ever after; we believe in happily FOREVER after! We believe that He who began a good work will carry it to completion. We believe the best is yet to come. In fact, we believe that no eye has seen, no ear has heard, and no mind has conceived all that God has prepared for those that love Him.

I think we can all agree that life is hard. Sports are hard, school is hard, whatever you are walking through is hard. I am not sure what you are going through as you read this but, I am here to encourage you to hold on to Hope, the best is yet to come.

My lasting word is to leave you with what Jesus said to that effect several thousand years ago: He said, "In this world, you will have trouble!" In other words, life is hard, you must confront those brutal facts. But that sobering reality check comes with a promise of Hope. He said, "Take heart, I have overcome the world!" Jesus Christ came to earth, He died for each of us, and conquered death for us to have Hope always!

Jesus defeated the Hard and overcame the Hard in your life so that you can live each day with Hope for an amazing future!

Drew Maddux
Vanderbilt University Men's Basketball
1994-1998

277

October 3

"It is for freedom that Christ has set us free…"
-Galatians 5:1 NIV

If you knew before stepping on the field that you would win the game 2-0, would it change the way you play? I realized immediately the increase in freedom I could feel knowing that my performance would not lead to defeat. Jesus came to bring us freedom and fullness of life so what does that look like on the field? It means I get to do my best and trust the results to the Lord. He already won the victory and I get to operate FROM victory instead of trying to strive towards it. Do I trust the Lord's purpose in a win OR a loss? There is freedom to passionately pursue winning AND to surrender control and trust that the purpose of the Lord exists even when I lose. I can surrender the outcome even before I step onto the field and focus on pouring out everything I have as an act of worship. Do I believe that the Lord has a plan for my good and His Glory? You were created to operate in freedom not in fear, not in anxiety, and not under the weight of expectations.

Are you playing in fear or in freedom?

Kristin Eggert
Wheaton College
2004-2007

October 4

"Finally, brothers, whatever is true, whatever is honorable, whatever is just, whatever is pure, whatever is lovely, whatever is commendable, if there is any excellence, if there is anything worthy of praise, think about these things. What you have learned and received and heard and seen in me—practice these things, and the God of peace will be with you." -Philippians 4:7-9 ESV

How many times have you been told that it's all about your mindset? As an athlete this concept frustrated me, because keeping a steady mindset through life's complications often seemed harder than any physical skill I could nail down. Eventually, the process of striving to align my mindset with success fed me the lie that this was the ultimate end goal, and it was on me to figure it out.

This verse is great because it acknowledges the agency we have in our thought life, and it provides guidance on how to manage that agency. However, it's important that we don't stop there, because the true value of this verse is really in the last 8 words: "the God of peace will be with you." He promises us Himself. This means that His peace and His presence are our reward and the ultimate end goal, not the perfect mindset. Walking with, surrendering to, and experiencing HIM is what we need to find peace through life's trials.

My challenge for you is to put this verse somewhere you'll see it daily. Let it remind you of the power you have in Christ over your thoughts, but most of all, let it remind you of the peace we're promised in our Savior's presence.

Jenna (Tunnell) McPherson
Pepperdine Women's Indoor and Beach Volleyball
2015-2019

October 5

"Therefore, since we are surrounded by so great a cloud of witnesses, let us also lay aside every weight, and sin which clings so closely, and let us run with endurance the race that is set before us, looking to Jesus, the founder and perfecter of our faith, who for the joy that was set before him endured the cross, despising the shame, and is seated at the right hand of the throne of God."

- *Hebrews 12:1-2*

God has gifted athletes with such a unique mission field. As a volleyball player, I got to connect with people from all different walks of life and we bonded instantly because we had the same goals we all wanted to sacrifice for. Sports are a powerful tool to unite and mobilize people. But we waste our time in it if we let it pass us by without an eternal perspective. We give all we have in workouts and games to sacrifice for our teammates, not for pride, but to point them to Jesus. And this isn't just valuable while you are an athlete.

God created us to be moved by goals, to be passionate about things bigger than ourselves. Not to win championships, but to live our whole lives as disciples of Jesus. All Christians of all different walks of life should be quickly united because we all have a common mission that's bigger than ourselves. A mission we're willing to sacrifice for: making more disciples for Jesus.

Take advantage of building relationships based on shared sacrifice. Love your teammates well by giving it your all and pointing them to Jesus. Live the rest of your life running the race toward the mission with your Christian teammates.

Daniela Tesch
Rice University Volleyball
2011-2014

October 6

"For this reason I kneel before the Father, from whom every family[a] in heaven and on earth derives its name. I pray that out of his glorious riches he may strengthen you with power through his Spirit in your inner being, so that Christ may dwell in your hearts through faith. And I pray that you, being rooted and established in love, may have power, together with all the Lord's holy people, to grasp how wide and long and high and deep is the love of Christ, and to know this love that surpasses knowledge—that you may be filled to the measure of all the fullness of God."
– Ephesians 3: 14-19 NIV

For what are our worldly successes if we do not first have life from God? "For this reason, I kneel before the Father" is such a powerful verse to me. In sports, our success becomes our identity, and people start to idolize who we are because we can do something that some can't, which may start to give us a "high and mighty" complex. However, as Christians, we know that nothing happens without Christ giving us that opportunity. We find our strength, our peace, and our talents through Him through a humble heart and servant mind.

My prayer is for all of us to exemplify Christ's love through how we use our talents and interact with those who do look up to us.

Call on the Lord to give you His strength daily, regardless of the on field/court success and praise Him through all times, good or trialing.

Chandler Hall
Philadelphia Phillies/Louisiana Tech University Baseball
2014-2017

October 7

"Whatever you do, work at it with all your heart, as working for the Lord, not for human masters." - Colossians 3:23

What is it to be a Christian athlete?

A Christian athlete does not embrace the world and all it tells us to be. Rather, we as Christian athletes walk in the grace we undeservingly receive through Jesus. Being willing to pick up our cross daily knowing that we aren't carrying it alone. We forsake the easy acceptance that comes with fitting in and embrace that we are a misfit just like Jesus. Focusing on growing through Jesus so He can grow in and through us. When we step on the field, we use our abilities to share the good news through all that we do and the way we go about our business- no matter the outcome. We are called to use it ALL for his Glory!

What does it mean to be a Christian athlete to you? Find some teammates, write down what you all believe it means, and hold each other accountable to live out those words.

Michael "Fort" McKenry
Colorado Rockies / Pittsburgh Pirates / St. Louis Cardinals
2010-2016

October 8

"And if I have prophetic powers, and understand all mysteries and all knowledge, and if I have all faith, so as to remove mountains, but have not love, I am nothing." 1 Corinthians 13:2 ESV

After reflecting on my collegiate career, I realized that I had not developed as many solid relationships with my teammates as I would have liked to. Aside from us playing the same sport for the same university, some of my teammates knew very little about me and I knew very little about them. I loved them all, and I deeply desired for them all to taste and see that the Lord is good, but that often was not evident because I was using my time and talents in a selfish way instead of using them to serve others and ultimately glorify God.

There is no other time in your life where you will be placed in a group of people like you are now. You have a special opportunity to get to know your teammates well, but they do not care about how much "Bible stuff" you know, until they know you care. So, proclaim the good news not just how you live but by how you love. Jesus' life is the best example of how to live a life of love because He is love. Jesus dined with sinners and tax collectors, and served others in a selfless way unlike any other human. That is what set Him apart from the religious leaders of that time. People were drawn towards Him because they felt seen, cared for, and loved.

What teammate(s) can you seek to know and love better? Ask God to speak in and through you whenever you spend time with your teammates.

Mari (Gillespie) Garner
Stephen F. Austin State University Women's Soccer
2016-2019

October 9

"Patient endurance is what you need now, so that you will continue to do God's will. Then you will receive all that he has promised" -Hebrews 10:36 NLT

I moved to Japan to pursue my, relatively, new professional softball career. I did not know how to speak or read Japanese, and I did not know who my teammates or coaches were until I arrived. However, I knew the Lord was calling me to such a foreign country for a purpose. The only thing that was keeping me hopeful was my relationship with Jesus, and that I knew how to play softball. However, after breaking my wrist senior year of college and missing out on most of my last opportunities to play, I questioned if I was still capable of playing softball the same. God never left my side though. He inserted me into a completely new environment with little to no comfort when I was at the softball field or even in the privacy of my own apartment. Many nights I questioned what the purpose was for me to be in such a foreign country away from my family. However, one evening I heard a voice say one word to me, and that word was "patience". I immediately knew how I needed to endure each day: with patient endurance. I began to hear and see the word 'patience' almost everywhere I went. God used subtle ways to remind me of His presence. It may not always be obvious right away, but with patient endurance in God's plan and purpose over your life, peace and perseverance will follow.

I challenge you to present your trials (big or small) to Jesus and ask for patient endurance through the adversity.

Madilyn "Bubba" Nickles
Toyota Red Terriers
2022-Present

284

October 10

"No testing has overtaken you that is not common to everyone. God is faithful, and he will not let you be tested beyond your strength, but with the testing he will also provide the way out so that you may be able to endure it." - 1 Corinthians 10:13 NRSV

Improvement and progress are paramount for the competitive athlete. To achieve this, we need to evaluate our strengths and weaknesses with objectivity. However, athletes are often their own worst critics, and can easily fall prey to negativity. Often, I was the teammate who lifted others up while secretly allowing negative self-talk to wreak havoc on my own psyche. I would persecute myself for every mistake which gave an odd sense of instant gratification but destroyed my self-confidence.

Paul tells us that God allows temptation, but that He also gives us strength to endure if we choose. When my teammates were struggling, I always came to them with a positive message. I committed to give that same grace to myself for my own mistakes, often speaking words of encouragement out loud. Perhaps it was silly from the outside, but reinforcing myself with positivity completely changed my game - I started performing better and rediscovered the love I had for the game that first inspired me to pursue soccer. God made you in His image - treat yourself as He would.

Do you fall to the temptation of negative self-talk or doubt? Try saying something uplifting to yourself after making a mistake and see how it changes your game- see how it can even change the next play.

Timmy Mueller
Oregon State University Men's Soccer
2014-2018

October 11

"For I know the plans I have for you," declares the Lord,
"plans to prosper you and not to harm you, plans to give you hope
and a future." - Jeremiah 29:11

Born in South Sudan, and growing up in a refugee camp, most of my days were spent running around playing soccer. Looking back, if anybody had told me then that I would be playing Division 1 soccer in East Tennessee I would have probably laughed in their face and ran off to chase the ball. Miraculously ten years later, here I was playing soccer at East Tennessee State University. Surely, I thought, this is God's purpose for me - why else would He pull me from a war-torn country, out of a refugee camp and bestow upon me this talent if this is not what He meant for me?

Eight-year-old me in a refugee camp didn't think I had much of a future beyond the camps, yet God proved me wrong. Eighteen-year-old me thought God's plan for me was to be a soccer player and once again, He proved me wrong. He had a plan all along and I just needed to get to a point where I say, "I am yours Lord, do with me as you please." That's when He opened my eyes to His plans for me. His future for me. Through His grace I am now the Executive Director of a Skilled Nursing Facility.

You don't have to have it figured out, but trust in Him (Yahweh) who has it figured out for you. His plans and purpose for you are far greater than anything your finite mind could ever imagine!

Emmanuel Wilson
East Tennessee State University Men's Soccer
2011-2015

October 12

"Let us then approach God's throne of grace with confidence, so that we may receive mercy and find grace to help us in our time of need." – Hebrews 4:16 NIV

As a player, I struggled with confidence. My coaches were telling me that I needed to "demand the ball." Not ask for it, not tell my setter that I wanted it, but to actually say "give me the ball". That always felt unnatural and selfish to me. It felt performative. That type of statement showed a confidence that I didn't have.

In team-sports, we've all had that moment when we look around and ask who can I rely on? Who is going to produce? I see that look from volleyball setters often. As time went on, whenever I demanded the ball from my setters, I could sense that I took a small burden off them. They now had someone who was willing to take the pressure. I began to realize that "demanding the ball" wasn't about me – it was for my team. Maybe I was faking my confidence at the time, but my team saw someone who was willing to take on the responsibility in tight situations, which gave them confidence.

God is not faking it. He is demanding the ball from us. He wants to turn our gifts into something productive that will bring us joy and purpose. How cool that we have a God that is swinging at 100%?! He does not make mistakes. We can hand over our burdens with confidence that He will guide us to where we need to be.

Give God the ball.

Meredith Hardy
East Tennessee State University Volleyball
2011-2015

October 13

And he said to all, "If anyone would come after me, let him deny himself and take up his cross daily and follow me. For whoever would save his life will lose it, but whoever loses his life for my sake will save it. For what does it profit a man if he gains the whole world and loses of forfeits himself?" -Luke 9:23-25 ESV

When I got to college, I denied myself nothing; I sought pleasure, comfort, and satisfaction in partying and being liked by those around me. I did whatever I wanted to do. During the summer after my freshman year, I lost my scholarship. God used this to clearly show that my life of self-indulgence would never fulfill or satisfy me, and I saw my desperate need for a Savior. I could never make up for my sins, but there was forgiveness and life in the gospel of Christ.

After becoming a Christian, I found it really hard to deny myself. We are all naturally selfish. But as I spent time in God's Word and in prayer, God grew my heart to delight in following Him.

Self-denial consists of being willing to follow His commands, to serve those around you, and to put aside your own desires. Being on a sports team brings amazing opportunities to lay down your life and reflect the selflessness of Jesus, in hopes that others would come to know Him.

What does it mean to deny yourself, take up your cross, and follow Jesus? Is your life marked by a willingness to obey Him and to lay your life down for those around you? Pray that God would grow your desire to lose your life for the sake of others.

Brody Cummins
Texas Christian University Men's Lacrosse
2017-2021

October 14

"For you created my inmost being; you knit me together in my mother's womb. I praise you because I am fearfully and wonderfully made; your works are wonderful, I know that full well."
-Psalm 139:13-14 NIV

Growing up, I never thought about my body much and only saw it as a means to play the sport I loved. In college that changed. I was surrounded by teammates intensely focused on their eating habits and bodies, which led me to hyperfocus on my appearance. I got into a cycle of binge eating to gain muscle after being teased for my lack of it, and later dieting as I grew insecure about my growing size. Instagram and social media fueled the fire and added to the long list of things I would've changed about myself if I could have.

This didn't change until I started to see myself and others through the lens of our Creator. While the world might reduce us to the sum of our parts, God sees us as His children. We are intentionally crafted and shaped by Him with incredible attention to detail as David describes in Psalm 139. Not only are we created intentionally, but we are also created in God's image. We look like God... what a privilege! Every stretch mark, wrinkle, roll, and scar is a brushstroke left by God Himself. God demonstrates His artistry by creating us with different shapes, sizes, and abilities. How boring would it be if we all looked the same? We are so much more than muscles, a number on a scale, or our body fat percentage. We are children of the one true King!

Read Psalm 139 aloud to yourself. Pray that God would grant you the ability to see yourself and others through His eyes.

Riley van Raaphorst
University of North Carolina Women's Lacrosse
2016-2020

October 15

*"Let no one despise you for your youth, but set the believers
an example in speech, in conduct, in love, in faith, in purity."*
-1 Timothy 4:12 ESV

Freshman year of college, I was a strong believer, but I was apprehensive when it came to sharing my faith with others. A mentor of mine shared this verse with me and encouraged me to take small steps outside of my comfort zone.

We are called to share the Gospel with others. You may be like I was as a freshman - a mature Christian who was timid. Or you may be new to your faith wondering what steps to take next. While this verse was written to Timothy from Paul, we can still take applications and encouragement from it.

Others are always noticing the small things you do. The five ways Paul instructs Timothy to live as an example are speech, conduct, love, faith, and purity. The words you say and the values you display all have an impact. We are called to live our lives in a radically transformed way that leverages them for the sake of the Gospel. Through taking small steps in each of these areas, I have grown in my love for the Lord and desire and ability to share Him with others. Others can see the good news of Jesus Christ through the way I play my sport, study, and live with the joy of the Gospel.

Until you cherish the Gospel deeply, you will never communicate the Gospel broadly. Take time to grow in your appreciation of the Gospel. After doing this, how can you be an example to others in each of the five categories?

Skyler Prillaman
High Point University Women's Soccer
2018-2023

October 16

"In the same way, let your light shine before others, that they may see your good deeds and glorify your father in heaven."
-Matthew 5:16 NIV

As an athlete, you are given a platform. A platform that can be utilized for significant impact that sets an example for others to follow.

From peewee football to Friday-night lights, to a shot at the next level and the dream of going pro, these are all seasons in which an athlete can have enormous influence. The ability to set an example is a gift that should not be taken lightly. When you put your uniform on, think about how you are letting your light shine before others. Whether it's someone who watches from afar or is standing next to you on the field.

Whether you are a 4th string long snapper on a football team or a big-time starter, we all have some level of opportunity to let our light shine.

Ask God to help you utilize the gift He has given you to glorify His kingdom. How can you let your light shine before others? What does that look like in the realm of your sport?

Randen Plattner
Kansas State University Football
2018-Present

291

October 17

"Who has ever given to God, that God should repay them?"
For from him and through him and for him are all things. To him be
the glory forever! Amen." - Romans 11:35-36 NIV

You never mean to get lost. I remember the pride I fought to hide after receiving an award before my senior year began. I thought back to all the mental and physical preparation that I went through and couldn't help but point back to everything *I did* that led to the success I was experiencing. I tried to convince myself that this award didn't mean all that much to me, but that was a lie.

After a senior year filled with personal injury and very little success as a team, I got to reflect on what started off looking like an incredible year, but then ended so miserably.

My physical and mental discipline prepared me to play the game and succeed on the field, but my lack of spiritual discipline is what caused me to believe I did it all on my own. To have viewed my success, the year before, as a product of my own strength was an attitude that was not in line with Who I said I believed God to be. I trust that God honors hard work, but we must also know that He honors the sincere and consistent acknowledgement of our opportunities and successes as blessings from above.

He honors the consistent acknowledgement of our opportunities as blessings from above. What is one way you can consistently point the glory of success back to God?

Haddon Adams
Lipscomb University Baseball
2018-2021

292

October 18

"For we are God's masterpiece. He has created us anew in Christ Jesus, so we can do the good things he planned for us long ago." -Ephesians 2:10 NLT

It is not a good feeling to miss the mark. In track and field, there are multiple measuring sticks: Two of them are: 1) How am I faring against the competition in the field? And 2) How am I faring against the competition with myself? Throughout my college career, I struggled with the feeling of not being good enough. Strangely, that feeling led to pride.

Pride can be very tricky. Some struggle with pride due to achieving enormous success. Others battle with pride as a result of insecurity. I fell into the latter group. Throughout my career, I constantly compared myself to the competition on my team, in our conference, and even against some of my times from earlier years. Why was I constantly missing the mark after putting in so much effort, both on the track and in my personal life? That question led to an extensive battle with suicide.

Eventually, I learned to accept the truth that God calls me His masterpiece, and His love for me goes further than I can imagine. The realization of who I am in Christ helped me understand that whether I succeed or miss the mark in my competition, there is no need to be prideful, because the foundation of my life lies in who I am in Christ.

Whether I succeed or miss the mark in my competition, there is no need to be prideful, because the foundation of my life lies in who I am in Christ.

Paul A. Henderson
Virginia Commonwealth University Men's Track & Field
2003-2007

October 19

"For I know the plans I have for you," declares the Lord,
"plans to prosper you and not to harm you, plans to give you hope
and a future." - Jeremiah 29:11

As kids, we have so many plans and dreams for our lives. Student athletes face extraordinary circumstances and realize very quickly that their plan has flaws. The highs and lows of day-to-day life can be overwhelming. It can certainly make you question your faith and your future.

I experienced multiple knee injuries in college. In each situation, I found myself asking "why me". At the time, I felt God had forsaken me. Navigating adversity while believing that God's plan is to prosper you and not to harm you is a challenge within itself. It is easy to lose hope when the Savior Himself doesn't immediately rescue you from your pain or suffering.

There is joy to be found in every outcome. God's plan for you is for eternity. I had forgotten that God's plan is to prosper me, so that one day I can spend eternity in his presence. No matter the outcome, praise God, for He will keep this promise. He will redeem you for your glory so that you can be in his presence for eternity.

Embrace the challenges of today, for God has a plan! Have faith that those plans are to prosper you, not to harm you. Be grateful to have been given opportunities to face extraordinary circumstances that will prepare you for His future.

Bay Daniel
University of South Carolina Women's Soccer
2012-2017

Dedicated to Matthew Whaley - August 31, 1999 - January 12, 2022

294

October 20

"Rejoice always, pray continually, give thanks in all circumstances; for this God's will for you in Christ Jesus."
- 1 Thessalonians 5:16-18 NIV

In athletics, we are conditioned to celebrate only when we have experienced success, to seek counsel only when we are in need and to give thanks only when things have gone well. We put so much weight on success as athletes that when we fall short, we can feel a lack of worth. Even when victorious, we are filled with fleeting pride and left with the feeling that there is always something more.

Through obeying the commands God calls us to in this verse, it can bring a consistency that sports lack. Rejoice ALWAYS - choosing to keep your mind set on things above; finding joy in who He is and what He's done regardless of circumstances. Pray CONTINUALLY - reminding yourself of your dependence on God in good times and bad. Give thanks in ALL THINGS - showing gratitude for the blessings and refining in each of life's seasons. We have been told that our actions should be responses to our circumstances, when, in reality, they should be daily choices in acknowledgement of God in our circumstances. This choice then moves us from allowing our lives and emotions to be dictated by sport, to being dictated by God. Find steadiness in Him through the highs and lows of life and sport. I have learned life is so much sweeter and rewarding when we choose to live it focused on Him.

What circumstances of life have you let overpower your dependence and gratitude to God?

Kealsie Robles
USA Women's Field Hockey Team
2018-Present

295

October 21

"I will instruct you and teach you in the way you should go; I will counsel you with my loving eye on you." - Psalm 32:8 NIV

Throughout my collegiate and professional career, I was constantly planning for the next step. What do I need to do to win the starting role? What do I need to do to get drafted? What affiliate team will I break with? Who's ahead of me in the level above? Every step of the way I made sure I had a plan.

In my last season of pro ball, my whole life changed. I unexpectedly lost my dad to cancer, and in a blink of an eye, baseball became the least of my priorities. After taking some time with my family, I shifted my perspective and reflected on the past 7 years of collegiate and professional baseball. The things I thought mattered the most, making the next team, starting, hitting .300, suddenly didn't matter at all. I spent so much time trying to do it on my own rather than believing that the Lord had a plan all along, and all I needed to do was trust in Him and enjoy the ride. Being an athlete is a gift, a gift we are given to glorify God. I am thankful for that title, and thankful for a God who charts our steps for us. All we need to do is trust Him.

Be where your feet are. Stop and look around, where are your feet right now? Why do you think the Lord has you in this place?

Justin Harrer
Pittsburgh Pirates
2018-2021

October 22

"I am the vine, you are the branches; the one who remains in Me, and I in him bears much fruit, for apart from Me you can do nothing." -John 15:5 NASB

Athletes love to win. The recipe for our success is simple: Attitude and Effort…the two things you can always control. Simple, but not easy. It requires sacrifice and perseverance.

As believers in Christ, we've already won! Jesus paid it all on the cross! But Ephesians 2:10 says "we are His workmanship, created in Christ Jesus for good works"! What does that mean? A fruitful life honors God. John 15 talks a lot about bearing fruit for Christ. How? Jesus says, "the one who remains in Me, and I in him bears much fruit". Stay close to God. Seek Him. Spend time with Him. It might require sacrifice and perseverance, but you're used to that, right? Only difference is, the reward on this playing field is far greater.

Jesus was telling this to the Apostles the night before He went to the cross. "Abide in Me, and I in you". Simple, yes, but not easy. It required sacrifice and a daily testing of their faith. They trusted Jesus' promises. By the power of the Holy Spirit, they spread the Gospel to many nations, preaching repentance and salvation by grace through faith in Christ. They glorified God, and led fruitful lives, by remaining in Christ. They were willing to do whatever it took, and ultimately gave it all for Jesus. They were winners.

Is your life fruitful? Seek after God's will. Spend time in the Word and pray that He will give you opportunities to glorify Him.

Kyle Dahlberg
Baltimore Orioles
2005-2007

297

October 23

"We can rejoice, too, when we run into problems and trials, for we know that they help us develop endurance. And endurance develops strength of character, and character strengthens our confident hope of salvation. And this hope will not lead to disappointment. For we know how dearly God loves us, because he has given us the Holy Spirit to fill our hearts with his love."
-Romans 5: 3-5 NLT

The words "rejoice" and "trial" don't seem to go together. In 2020, an injury shattered my dream of qualifying for the CrossFit Games. I was angry, upset, and felt like I had no purpose. During this time, God revealed to me that I was devastated because my joy was put in something other than Him. I had two options: sulk in the pain or trust in the plans that the Lord had for me.

Rejoicing in trials doesn't mean I have to ignore the pain and pretend it doesn't hurt. Instead, it means rejoice in the truth that our worth and identity goes beyond any achievement or accomplishment. Rejoice that the battle has already been won and that we serve a God that is always good- one that loves us so much that He sent His only Son to die for our sins so that we may have eternal life with Him.

Trials allow us to dig even deeper into our faith, produce endurance for the trials to come and build character that shines the light of Christ. I rejoice that my identity is not found in any success or failure that may occur and that I can rest in the peace knowing that God "works all things good for those who love him." (Rom 8:28)

When you endure a trial, what is one truth that you can find hope in?

Baylee Rayl
Professional CrossFit Athletes
2017-Present

October 24

"Therefore, I urge you, brothers and sisters, in view of God's mercy, to offer your bodies as a living sacrifice, holy and pleasing to God—this is your true and proper worship. Do not conform to the pattern of this world, but be transformed by the renewing of your mind. Then you will be able to test and approve what God's will is— his good, pleasing and perfect will." -Romans 12:1-2

Growing up I always saw worship as an act of spirituality. This is not at all how the Bible describes worship. We as human beings, created by God, were designed to be worshippers. This means worship is first our identity before it becomes an activity. The reason God designed us in such a manner was for us to innately draw to our Father, but because of the sinful world we live in, our minds, bodies, and souls shift elsewhere. You are either worshipping the Creator or His creation.

As athletes, we spend so much of our lives dedicated to a game it becomes so easy to worship our sports. We spend so many hours a day training and preparing that it becomes "who we are". Once I got to college and became a college athlete, I gave everything I had to be the best volleyball player I could be. I put so many hours into my game that it consumed me and still left me feeling unfulfilled season after season. Dedicating that time to our sport is not a bad thing, it is where our mind and heart is lined up that causes it to become an idol.

How are your words, your actions, and your choices shaped by your worship?

Sarah Hayes Farley
Samford University Volleyball
2019-2022

299

October 25

*"I have been crucified with Christ. It is no longer I who live,
but Christ who lives in me. And the life I now live in the flesh I live by
faith in the Son of God, who loved me and gave himself for me."*
-Galatians 2:20 ESV

About halfway through my sophomore year in college, God spoke to me about something I had struggled with for a while. He had opened my eyes to the fact that we are not on this earth to live this life for ourselves. Rather, He is living in us so that we can live this life for Him and put on display what His Son sacrificed on the cross for us.

Realizing that baseball is simply the blink of an eye in this lifetime took an insane amount of stress off my shoulders. Going about each day with joy and enthusiasm, knowing that I get to live this life to glorify my Creator, is the most incredible feeling ever. Whether it was a good or bad day on the field, everything became good, as well as a chance to spread the Gospel to my teammates.

No matter if you see it or not, there is good in everything and a chance to live like Christ and to display that love to other people. Breaking free from the chains of our sport and not letting it consume us is something I wish I would have learned a lot sooner in life.

When we let our sport consume us, we are taking away from what we are called to do, which is to live like Christ and to make His Word known to all.

Carson Ohl
Grand Canyon University Baseball
2020-2023

October 26

"Give your entire attention to what God is doing right now, and don't get worked up about what may or may not happen tomorrow. God will help you deal with whatever hard things come up when the time comes." -Matthew 6:34 MSG

Often as athletes, we don't like to ask for help. We are strong, capable, and full of grit. We bounce back from challenges- even to the point of extreme injuries. My sophomore year at UCLA, I was on top of the world. I walked-on for the rowing team, earned a scholarship, and a seat in the top varsity boat after one year. I was excelling as a biology major, and I had won a triathlon. However, just a few months later, I would find myself on an oxygen tank fighting for my life! I found out I had a benign football-sized tumor slowly crushing my lungs, which had been there most of my life undiscovered!

From my strongest to my weakest, God taught me to truly rely on Him alone. I realized that all my accolades were not worth much on my death bed. I prayed for God to make me an inspiration whether I lived or died. It was the most peaceful moment of my life. I truly put my whole life in the hands of God. I'm here today to tell you that I have 2 lungs, I've been a pro volleyball athlete for the past 10 years, and I have been able to inspire thousands with my story. The difference is I tell it pointing towards God, not myself. God has epic plans for your life, but they can only be accomplished with His help!

God really is the best Storyteller, trust Him to write yours.

Jessica McGuire
University of California Los Angeles Women's Rowing
2009-2013

301

October 27

"The man who had received five bags of gold went at once and put his money to work and gained five bags more. So also, the one with two bags of gold gained two more. But the man who had received one bag went off, dug a hole in the ground and hid his master's money." - Matthew 25:16-18 NIV

I am in no way, shape, or form qualified to give financial advice; in the words of Khalid, I am "young, dumb, and broke". However, I believe this parable goes far beyond money. Just like the master entrusted his wealth with the servants (*v. 14-15*), God has given each one of us gifts, talents, and opportunities and He expects us to put them to work; to create disciples (*Matt. 28:18-20)*. One thing worth mentioning is that the three servants were all given different amounts of gold. In 2022, it's almost second nature to look at the person next to us and see what they have or what we don't have. It sounds weird, but I want to be like the servant who was given two bags of gold. He wasn't satisfied by the fact that he was given more than the servant with one bag, nor was he discouraged by the other servant getting five bags. He took what was entrusted to him, put it to work, and made the most of his opportunity.

When God returns – just like the master – I want to be able to say I made the most of everything He gave me and hear Him say "Well done, good and faithful servant".

Think about what God has entrusted you with and reflect on how you are using them to bring glory and honor to His kingdom.

Parker Hazen
Lipscomb University Men's Basketball
2019-2022

October 28

"Jesus Christ is the same yesterday and today and forever."
- Hebrews 13:8 ESV

No matter where you are in your athletic career - whether it's high school, college, professional, or beyond - you will eventually let that journey end and start a new one. That's the difficult thing about being an athlete; you train your life away, pushing through sweat and tears, just for it to end at some point and be a part of your past. This is what I struggled with the most. For 17+ years I viewed myself as a swimmer. I never saw myself as anything other than that. My sport, my medals, and my achievements defined who I was. When I wrapped up my senior year of college, I struggled. I didn't know who I was outside of athletics, and I had no idea how God viewed me or the path He had for me. Then I remembered, that although my life changes, God is constant, and I am a child of God.

Our lives are constantly changing, bringing many ups and downs. Through it all, God remains unchanged and constant. Our identities are not based upon our achievements or what is going on around us, it is based on God. We are always changing but God's love for us is never changing. We are a child of God no matter where we are in life. I can have peace in my life beyond sports knowing I am loved and seen as more than an athlete by God.

In your next phase of life, learn how to adapt and lean on God. Trust in Him to write the story of your life and show you meaning through all of it.

Paige Riekhof
University of Kansas Swimming
2018-2022

303

October 29

"The Lord makes firm the steps of the one who delights in him; though he may stumble, he will not fall, for the Lord upholds him with his hand." - Psalm 37:23-24 NIV

Sometimes we know what God is telling us today, but because it doesn't go along with the plan or idea we had for our lives, we let our judgment get in the way of God's blessings.

Football was all my life consisted of. Getting my big pay day and trying to reach the goal of playing for 10 plus years was what I thought would have to bring me the joy I was looking for. Until I had the feeling God was telling me my time playing was over. But because that didn't go along with my idea for my life, I kept forcing the issue. Injury after injury and tricking myself into thinking I still enjoyed playing the game. Now that I've gotten on board with God's plan for me to retire from football, I have had so much joy and growth in so many areas of my life that I neglected. We can deny God all we want, but the only way to truly find ourselves is to turn to God.

When you hear God talking to you, put aside your own understanding and then LISTEN and PRAY.

Tyrell Williams
San Diego Chargers / Oakland Raiders / Detroit Lions
2015-2021

October 30

"Everyone then who hears these words of mine and does them will be like a wise man who built his house on the rock. And the rain fell, and the floods came, and the winds blew and beat on that house, but it did not fall, because it had been founded on the rock."
- Matthew 7:24-25

Being an athlete gives you the opportunity to build your house upon a lot of different foundations. Whether that be your performance, accolades, status, benefits, what others think of you, etc. All those things are as fickle and fleeting as a foundation built on the sand.

For me, I had built my identity in my performance on the court, in my status as an athlete, how others viewed me, and the perks I got from being an athlete. To be honest, for a season of my life these things satisfied and felt firm. But like the foundation on the sand, these things will feel firm until the rain falls. There came a time for me where I became exhausted trying to hold up the house I had built. Trying to maintain the perfect performance, status, accolades, etc. But in my need to achieve, I saw my humanness, my imperfection, and the inability of these things to hold me up.

The Lord showed me through my imperfections and through the fleeting foundations, that the gospel sustains and is firm. That putting my identity in anything else is like building my house on the sand. But in Christ is my firm foundation. For He is the only one who can satisfy, in whom your identity is found, and who won't be shaken.

What things in your life have you made or added to your foundation apart from the Lord?

Jordan Fate
University of Mississippi Volleyball
2016-2019

305

October 31

"For the sake of Christ, I am content with weaknesses, insults, hardships, persecutions, and calamities. For when I am weak, then I am strong." – 2 Corinthians 12:10 ESV

When I arrived on campus my freshman summer, I was prepared to win. It was time for recognition and praise to flood my life for all the sacrifice and effort I put into my sport. To my dismay, it quickly became clear that I was not strong enough, skilled enough, tough enough, fast enough, or smart enough to dominate college athletics like I had imagined. In fact, I struggled to get on the court.

And truthfully, hallelujah for it! Because this painful failure brought me low, where Christ meets us. He freed me of my pride and cleared my vision so that I could see the real story at play - His glory made known to all.

My role on the team was minor - minutes here and there, emotional support. My role in this part of God's story was also minor, but much more meaningful - my weakness on display so that my teammates, coaches, and surrounding staff got to witness the fruits of the Spirit through Christ's work in me, touching and feeling the hope and love of God. My position was ministry, and my wins were that my teammates would know and worship Jesus Christ our Lord.

When your sport inevitably humbles you, rejoice that weakness and hardship are a window for the world to see Christ in you.

Kendall (Ellig) Graham
Rice University Women's Basketball
2016-2020

"For he whom God has sent utters the words of God, for he gives the Spirit without measure." - John 3:34 ESV

On a random day during Spring Training, I found myself thinking about a former teammate. We weren't particularly close, but his baseball journey always stood out to me. In 2019, when we played together, he enjoyed an incredible season. One that earned himself a promotion to the major leagues! An amazing accomplishment, right? What made it more amazing was the fact that he hadn't played in the big leagues for three long years. He had to fight and persevere his way back. People don't realize how hard that is to do. There's a constantly revolving door of players at the major league level. He defied the odds.

A few days later, the team I was on signed him. Coincidence, right? No. I was particularly excited because I wanted to ask him what kept him going while he was in the minors. I'll never forget our conversation. When I asked him, I fully expected to hear about some major swing adjustment or how he never stopped believing in himself. Instead, he told me that he found Jesus. For over an hour, we talked about his walk with the Lord.

I remember feeling incredibly thankful for that interaction. I could see God so clearly that day and for many reasons in my own life, I needed that more than I realized.

Do you ever think about the people that God puts in our lives? Keep an eye out for those divine appointments. Be bold and unashamed.

Aramis Garcia
San Francisco Giants / Oakland Athletics / Cincinnati Reds
2018-2022

November 2

*"His eyes were like a fiery flame, and many crowns were on
His head. He had a name written that no one knows except Himself.
He wore a robe stained with blood, and His name is the Word of God.
The armies that were in heaven followed Him on white horses,
wearing pure white linen... And He has a name written on His robe
and on His thigh: KING OF KINGS AND LORD OF LORDS."
– Revelation 19:12-14 & 16 HCSB*

Challenges leave us weak and vulnerable. This can be as
small as losing a rep on the field or as big as a career-ending injury.
Early in my senior season in college I had two injuries that needed
surgical repair. I knew this was likely the end of football for me. I was
crushed and defeated. In that moment I needed the power of God to
lift me out of self-pity.

There is literally nothing more powerful than God. The
thought that God, the way He is described in the verses above, is
walking with us daily gives me enormous confidence. While He is
molding my life and coaching me through constant challenges, He is
also acting as my champion and protecting me. Taking this fortitude
onto the field or through the transition into our non-athletic life will
relieve anxieties and help us focus on the purpose He has set for us.

**As Christ-followers we can find courage in knowing that God is a
warrior. In moments of turmoil, reflect on how almighty God is
and that He remains with us through everything.**

Keith Orcutt
Baylor University Football
2013-2016

November 3

"O taste and see that the Lord is good; How blessed is the man who takes refuge in Him! O fear the Lord, you His saints; For those who fear Him there is no want. The young lions do lack and suffer hunger; But they who seek the Lord shall not be in want of any good thing." - Psalm 34:8-10

Do you ever feel like it's hard to see the goodness of the Lord? Throughout my playing career there were so many trials, frustrations, and disappointments that left me feeling as though I was struggling to see the Lord's goodness.

When I read through the Psalms, I see these writers felt the same way. Yet, over and over again, we see them proclaim God as a rock, a refuge, and shield for those who would take refuge in Him. Here, we're told refuge is found for those who fear Him; in other words, for those who recognize God's great sovereignty over all things as the Creator and Sustainer of the earth. Those who see the Lord as supremely valuable, as their portion and inheritance (Psalm 16). In the Scriptures, we see over and over this God be faithful in this promise. The same God who was faithful then is faithful now and provides everything He requires through His son Jesus.

So let us lean in and learn how to place our hope and our trust in the person of Jesus who longs to lead us in abundance of life and fullness of joy, and makes that possible in His life, death, and resurrection.

What are ways that you struggle to trust the Lord's goodness? How can you actively choose to put your trust in the Lord?

Sally Higgins
West Texas A&M University Women's Basketball
2010-2014

309

November 4

"Come to me, all you who are weary and burdened, and I will give you rest. Take my yoke upon you and learn from me, for I am gentle and humble in heart, and you will find rest for your souls. For my yoke is easy and my burden is light." - Matthew 11:28-30

As an athlete it is difficult to find rest. In today's sports culture we hit burnout and exhaustion often. It becomes nearly impossible to disassociate our identity with our sport. When we are asked, "tell me about yourself" we typically respond with our athletic identity. This is not sustainable. We will never find the rest Jesus promises in Matthew if our identity is wrapped into what we do.

How do we reorient our identity? Look to the spiritual disciplines. Specifically, the one most neglected by Americans (and myself), Sabbath. God is calling a new generation of athletes who will lead gently and humbly from a position of holy rest. Not just any rest but Sabbath rest. Pastor Rich Villodas says "Sabbath is not a reward for hard work. Sabbath is a gift that precedes work and enables us to work [hard]." Sabbath reminds us that we are not what we do. It reminds us that God has our health, the depth chart, relationships with your teammates and coaches covered.

Allow Sabbath to give you the holy rest Jesus promises in Matthew 11. Allow God to remind you where your identity lies and have faith that He is your biggest fan. He cares about the details of your athletic career, but you must take hold of His yoke.

This week, take hold of His yoke. Ask yourself, what do I need to do to plan? Find holy rest in the practice of taking Sabbath.

Kyle Lawrence
Ohio State University Men's Volleyball
2009-2013

310

November 5

"And whatever you do, whether in word or deed, do it all in the name of the Lord Jesus, giving thanks to God the Father through him." - Colossians 3:17 NIV

For a long time I put God in a box. I thought of Him as a sort of "sin scoreboard." I felt like He was keeping track of what I did wrong and right in life but didn't concern himself too much with my day to day. Since the Bible doesn't mention anything about punting a football, I definitely did not think He would concern himself with my sport.

What I've since learned is that God desires a personal relationship with us. This means He wants to be intimately involved in our day to day. As Christian athletes, the way we work hard in practice and games, treat our teammates and coaches, and handle adversity are all opportunities to worship. With a heavenly focus every day, we can be a light for Christ on our teams and bring glory to our Creator while playing a game we love.

When you turn on the television you see a lot of athletes bringing glory to themselves through their sport. How can you be different today and play your sport in the name of Jesus?

AJ Cole
Las Vegas Raiders
2019-Present

311

November 6

"Very early in the morning, while it was still dark, Jesus got up, left the house and went off to a solitary place, where he prayed."
– Mark 1:35 NIV

With the schedule of athletics and life, you are running between practice, workouts, school/work, sleep, etc. We are taught to be wise and intentional with our time to allow us to perform our best. There is so much to consider when trying to plan your day. We have set early alarms for practice, workouts, or an 8am tee time, but have you ever set your alarm to pray? I have made the "I'm too busy" excuse too many times. My mentor told me that two things can reveal your heart: your planner and your bank account. We make time for our top priorities, and we become busy with what we seek. Are we seeking to glorify Him through our sport and our daily schedule?

This verse exemplifies one of many times that Jesus went off to have personal time to connect with His Father. Connecting with Him is where He clothes us with our armor, strength, and endurance to run the race He has called us to each day. In time of solitude, He has humbled my prideful heart and reminded me of His great power of Mighty Counselor to Prince of Peace. He calls us to walk closely and starting your day with Him can set your heart in a place to serve for His will to be done.

Go find your quiet space. A place for you and Him. Spend 15 minutes meditating on a verse or praising, listening, and conversing with Him.

Sam Paulak
Drake University Women's Golf
2017-2022

312

November 7

"The one who enters by the gate is the shepherd of the sheep. The gatekeeper opens the gate for him, and the sheep listen to his voice. He calls his own sheep by name and leads them out. When he has brought out all his own, he goes ahead of them, and his sheep follow him because they know his voice. But they will never follow a stranger; in fact, they will run away from him because they do not recognize a stranger's voice"… "I am the good shepherd. The good shepherd lays down his life for the sheep." - John 10:2-5,11 NIV

Youth soccer tournaments can be loud. I have fond memories growing up playing in this environment. Despite all the noise and chaos, I could always distinguish when my coach was calling me. I knew his yell from any distance. This is what happens when you are coached by the same person for 5 years! When I was brand new to this team, those tournaments were overwhelming because I didn't know which voice to listen to. Over time, it became more and more clear.

This is the same with our relationship with Jesus! In the Gospel of John, Jesus refers to Himself as the Good Shepherd. He explains how sheep are so familiar with their shepherd's voice, they won't even recognize when a stranger is speaking to them. Do you know the voice of Jesus in this way? Life can be so loud: chatter, opinions, voices luring you one way or another. Yet it is possible to listen to only Jesus' voice. We must take the time to get to know His voice and learn the kinds of things He says and how He says them.

My challenge to you is this: Read all of John 10. Can you distinguish the voice of God amidst all the noise?

Natalie Lawrence
Point Loma Nazarene University Women's Soccer
2012-2015

November 8

"And he is before all things and in him all things hold together." - Colossians 1:17 ESV

As athletes, we have plans, goals, dreams, and vision to go wherever we would like to go and do whatever we would like to do. In college, I believed my strength, savvy, skill, and talents were enough to get me the accolades and put me in the best possible position to coach after I played. I thought it would be by my own strength. It was a shortsighted perspective of how I was able to play college baseball and immediately transition into the coaching world. Thankfully, surrendering my life to Christ my senior year of college in November 2003 changed my perspective.

Since then, my faith and confidence has transferred from my own strength and skill to the one that deserves all the praise, honor, and glory. The closer I walk with God, the more apparent it is that He breathes life into my lungs every morning. He sustains me. He gives me the skill, the characteristics, the motivation, and a desire to coach and minister to athletes. Without Him it is all in vain and I am nothing. He has been God for a long time, He holds it all together, and is the One that sustains it all. May we recognize the Source that gives us the ability to compete and play the sports we love.

When we put our trust in our own strength and skills, we miss the source. Christ is the one that ultimately holds all things together and appropriately deserves the praise. Where have you trusted more in your own plans and strength than in the One who supplies them?

Josh Milner
Wayland Baptist University Baseball
2002-2003

314

November 9

"So that all the peoples of the earth may know that the LORD is God; there is no other." - 1 Kings 8:60 NASB

Two weeks after being married, my wife and I chased the American Dream to Tennessee to pursue a career in the NFL. It wasn't anywhere close to what I had expected, but God was using me to bring Him glory in that locker room and in the community around us.

After a 4 year stint with the Titans, I started my career as a Football Coach at a local Christian School. I thought that I would retire from there after a long career as a mentor to young men that came through the football program I was leading.

Life was good. The football team was growing and seeing some on-field success. I felt like I was living out God's purpose in my life. Then, in January of 2022, God slammed a door shut that I never would have closed to send me and my family into full time missions work in Africa.

Looking back, playing and coaching football wasn't bad. In fact, it was God's perfect plan for my life. But now, His plan is for me and my family to do something different.

Through this journey, God has reminded me that this life that I am living is not my own. He has pressed onto my heart that I am not an owner of anything, just a steward of things that He has temporarily put in my charge. My talents and abilities are not mine, they are His. My job is to trust that His will is more perfect than mine.

Soli Deo Gloria. To God Alone be the Glory, for His name's sake.

Rusty Smith
Tennessee Titans
2010-2013

315

November 10

"But he said to me, "My grace is sufficient for you, for my power is made perfect in weakness." Therefore, I will boast all the more gladly of my weaknesses, so that the power of Christ may rest upon me." - 2 Corinthians 12:9 ESV

As athletes, it's very hard for us to accept our weaknesses. We want to feel strong. We want to be the best. We don't want to admit that we have flaws or experience failure. My entire life leading up to college, I felt so strong in my sport and didn't really have to struggle with any of these hardships. However, my first week of being on campus as a freshman and starting workouts, I tore my ACL. I felt weak and useless because I couldn't do the one thing I had been good at my entire life. I didn't know what my purpose was anymore.

It was through this experience that I realized that God not only welcomes our weaknesses, but His grace is also fully capable of providing us everything we need to endure them. God provided me with other things that gave me purpose. I realized that soccer was what I had been finding my identity in my entire life, when I needed to be finding my identity in the One who created me. Although these moments of suffering can seem as though there is no light at the tunnel, we need to experience moments of weakness to remind ourselves of God's perfect grace and to also point us towards Him.

I will gladly boast in my weaknesses because our God is a gracious God whose grace is sufficient for us. What weaknesses in your life are you hiding from? Take some time to give these weaknesses to God.

Tyler Tucker
Stephen F. Austin State University Women's Soccer
2015-2019

November 11

"Though the mountains be shaken and the hills be removed, yet my unfailing love for you will not be shaken nor my covenant of peace be removed," says the Lord, who has compassion on you."
-Isaiah 54:10

Have you felt like winning or displaying your talent on the highest level was the only way you could bring God glory through your sport? During my time as a sprinter and jumper at in college, I constantly felt that I had to get to a certain accomplishment or audience for God's glory to be made known in my life. I quickly learned that I was really looking for man's approval when I already had the Lord's.

As athletes we compete for medals, conference titles, individual records and more. All of which are amazing, however, our value in Christ is not based upon our accomplishments through the gifts He has blessed us with. Win, lose, injured, healthy or retired; God's love, acceptance, and happiness will never change. Take comfort in knowing even on your worst or best day, your Heavenly Father takes joy in seeing you use your sport as an act of worship for a greater glory we may not see or understand in this moment.

Take an index card and write, "I, _____, am free from the pressures of performance because no game, match, competition or trophy can change God's love for me". Keep this in your gym bag as a reminder.

Shayna Yon
Louisiana State University Women's Track & Field
2015-2019

November 12

"The heavens declare the glory of God; the skies proclaim the work of His hands." – Psalms 19:1 NIV

I am sorry to admit that most of my athletic career was misused as an attempt to elevate myself rather than to glorify God. Because of this, soccer began to feel more like a job than a joy. I was missing out on the richness of God's best for me! As an integral part of God's creation, believers are called to shine the light of Jesus through the gifts He has given us. Psalms 19:1 tells us that even the skies exalt our Creator!

Our value is not rooted in our ability to perform on the field because our value is found in Jesus. The gift of athleticism and the opportunity to play sports at a high level is often used to fill a void that can only be filled by God. The ultimate goal is to know Him and to share His love with the world.

Spend time in prayer before you step onto the field to align your heart with your true purpose: to declare the glory of God in all that you do.

Baylee Carkuff
Lipscomb University Women's Soccer
2011-2015

November 13

"In the early morning, while it was still dark, Jesus got up, left the house, and went away to a secluded place, and was praying there." – Mark 1:35

In rowing, the best time on the water is in the morning when the water is calm. In the same way, I also like to pray in the morning, because I feel like my heart is most at peace and able to better reflect the love from above. Even Jesus went away to spend time with His Heavenly Father to be in relationship with God the Father before going out. Prayer allows us to receive the love of God, allowing us to be reminded we are always enough.

Sometimes the way we perform isn't enough and so more is asked of us - more of our time, energy, and performance. We need to execute a play, get the grades, get extra reps, hit our goals, and be a leader. Where in your life can you go, to just be, not to be anything to anyone, but to just sit and be?

Jesus is inviting you to that place. He doesn't need you to perform and He doesn't demand anything of you. He just invites us deeper into relationship with Him. The Creator of the Universe wants to be in relationship with you. He wants you and your whole heart the way you are right now. He wants to love you and be loved by you. Prayer is our relationship with God. The love we receive in prayer fills our hearts, allowing us to share this love with our teammates and the people around us.

When is your heart the most calm and at peace? Do we turn to prayer when we feel "not enough"?

Mikaela Janes
Drake University Women's Rowing Team
2015-2019

319

November 14

"Do not be anxious about anything, but in every situation, by prayer and petition, with thanksgiving, present your requests to God. And the peace of God, which transcends all understanding, will guard your hearts and your minds in Christ Jesus." -Philippians 4:6-7 NIV

The bottom of the ninth, the two-minute drill, the final possession. Athletes and coaches are faced with some incredibly intense and stressful situations! We are asked to successfully compete at the highest levels, and no one wants to hear excuses. This can cause immense pressure and anxiety for athletes and coaches. And let's face it, sports imitate life. Each of us struggle with our anxieties in different ways: some of us wrestle with the fear of failure and are concerned with disappointing others. Often, we struggle with self-doubt and place unrealistic expectations on ourselves. Many of us fear uncertainty as we look ahead towards the future. However, in the midst of our anxiety and fear, God calls us to embrace His peace. Now this doesn't mean that we won't face difficulties in life. We should expect them. It does mean that the God of peace will be with us by His Holy Spirit and will stand guard to protect our hearts and minds from anxieties and fears. Only He can make us complete, whole, satisfied and secure in the midst of uncertainty.

Have you experienced the joy of casting your anxieties on Christ by trusting and resting in Him for wisdom, satisfaction and provision? You won't achieve peace on your own. True peace is something only God can give, and we receive it through the work of the Holy Spirit.

Matt Trent
St Louis Cardinals / Colorado Rockies
2005-2008

320

November 15

"Above all, you must live as citizens of heaven, conducting yourselves in a manner worthy of the Good News about Christ. Then, whether I come and see you again or only hear about you, I will know that you are standing together with one spirit and one purpose, fighting together for the faith, which is the Good News."
-Philippians 1:27 NLT

As followers of Christ, our job is to live as Jesus did and spread the news of the Gospel. This seems to be a daunting task for many Christians in our current environment. Thoughts such as losing friends or becoming isolated are all valid emotions.

As an athlete, I have felt these emotions many times. But we are called to a greater purpose. In my experience, I have found that the best way to approach spreading the "Good News" is through example. Philippians 1:27 says, "Above all, you must live as citizens of heaven, conducting yourselves in a manner worthy of the Good News about Christ". Many times in my life I have struggled, but this concept keeps me in check daily.

Later in the passage, we read "I will know that you are standing together with one spirit and one purpose, fighting together for the faith, which is the Good News." Our goal as Christians is to become more like Jesus and help other to come to know Jesus. By living an exemplary life after Jesus, we will slowly begin to grow the kingdom of God one changed life at a time.

My challenge for each of you is to make one small change in your daily life to become an example of Jesus.

Jake Adams
University of Kansas Baseball
2018-2022

321

November 16

"Pardon me, my Lord," Gideon replied, "but how can I save Israel? My clan is the weakest in Manasseh, and I am the least in my family." The Lord answered, "I will be with you..."
– Judges 6:15-16 NIV

"You won't be dressing out for postseason." It's the sentence no one wants to hear from their coach. Due to underperformance on the mound, my jersey was taken away, and with it, hope of making a difference for my team. Growing up, I dreamed of hitting a walk-off homerun, glorifying God in the postgame interview… not watching the game from the bench. Despite not playing an inning of the postseason, the Lord still used me. It was in a very different (and better) way than I had dreamed, though, like bringing together all four teams for a Bible study during regionals. During the Women's College World Series, not playing enabled many opportunities to share the Good News of Jesus, like staying up late on game nights with my dad making cross bracelets for the other teams. While my team warmed up, I interacted with fans from the fence and gave them cross bracelets too, each accompanied with a little paper that had Scripture and #8teams1King. By a miracle, we went on to win the WCWS that year, though the championship ring isn't what I wear and cherish; it's that bracelet—a reminder that God often uses the least expected things and people for His glory.

The reason you think the Lord won't use you may be the very way He does. How can you be a faithful steward of the gifts He's given you, even if they don't originally appear to be gifts?

Tessa (Daniels) Calhoun
Florida State University Softball
2015-2018

November 17

"However, I consider my life worth nothing to me, if only I may finish the race and complete the task that the Lord has given me- the task of testifying to the gospel of God's grace." - Acts 20:24 NIV

What is your life worth? Paul considers his worth nothing in comparison to the mission that God has called him to. Before he followed Christ, he studied law under an honorable rabbi of the first century. Paul sought after Christians to throw them in jail and persecute them. Then the Lord appeared to him and gave him a mission. You see before Christ comes into our life; we live in a way that we think is right. Before I surrendered my life to Christ, I wasn't throwing people in jail, but I was turning to the things of this world to fulfill me. I would lock myself in my room and indulged in sin. No one knew so I thought it was okay. Every time, I was living life in full, but I never felt so empty and alone. That's when I came to end of myself. I surrendered my life to Christ in June of 2020 and let Him take control of my decisions and heart. My purpose has changed. I may do great things or kick some decent field goals in big games, but all of it is nothing in comparison to the task that the Lord has given me. He is a loving Father who rescued me and you when what we deserved was eternity away from Him. Yet, He rescued you and me, not at the cost, but at the price of His perfect Son. Praise God for our new purpose.

Seth Small
Texas A&M University Football
2018-2021

November 18

" Two are better than one, because they have a good reward for their toil. For if they fall, one will lift up his fellow. But woe to him who is alone when he falls and has not another to lift him up!"
– Ecclesiastes 4:9-10 ESV

Coming into my freshman year of college I was one of twelve commits for my class. I did not know any of the girls, and my coach doubted my ability saying I was too small and too short. I did not play a single minute my first season. When I got to my end of season meeting with my coach she asked if I loved the game and my teammates- to be frank, I felt like I did not even know my teammates. I knew if I wanted to play the game I loved, I needed to get to know my team. Getting comfortable with the uncomfortable was exactly what I needed to do. It took me almost a year to do it, but none-the-less I did, and it completely changed the way I played and perceived the game.

Similarly in our relationship with God, we cannot do it on our own. The Lord built us for community, He designed us not only for a relationship with the Holy Spirit within us but also those around us. Community gives us a newfound faith in our own faith. The ability to congregate with others on a common passion renews that desire daily to chase after the Lord and spread the Gospel. Just as we needed a team on the field, we need a team in the Lord.

When we neglect community, we neglect an opportunity to grow. Think of areas in your life where you can connect to a community and grow with others in the word of Christ.

Kyler Zampiello
James Madison University Field Hockey
2015-2019

324

November 19

"So be truly glad. There is wonderful joy ahead, even though you must endure many trials for a little while. These trials will show that your faith is genuine. It is being tested as fire tests and purifies gold—though your faith is far more precious than mere gold. So when your faith remains strong through many trials, it will bring you much praise and glory and honor on the day when Jesus Christ is revealed to the whole world." - 1 Peter 1:6-7 NLT

My junior season was the best season of my career. I broke our school's all-time scoring record, broke our school's all-time assist record, went on a seven-game scoring streak, scored my first college hat trick, was the conference's Offensive Player of the Year, and made first team all-region. It was a good season for both me and our team. I remember waking up the day after we won conference tournament, and one of my teammates said, "I am so satisfied that we won conference." I remember thinking, "I don't feel satisfied." It was just like any of the other soccer games I had played in my life. I remember setting my sights to the NCAA tournament game thinking, "If we win that, then I will be satisfied." I got injured before that game, didn't play, and we didn't win. But even if I had played, and if we had won, I don't think the game would have satisfied me the way I wanted it to. Our sports are not here to satisfy us, only a relationship with God outlasts everything and can truly satisfy us. Ultimately, it is our faith that lasts and matters, not the accolades.

Take time to reflect on what you're pursuing through your sport and if it aligns with the Word of God.

Lauren 'Lo' Rivas
Rice University Women's Soccer
2012-2016

325

November 20

"For our appeal does not spring from error or impurity or any attempt to deceive, but just as we have been approved by God to be entrusted with the gospel, so we speak, not to please man, but to please God who tests our hearts. For we never came with words of flattery, as you know, nor with a pretext for greed- God is witness. Nor did we seek glory from people, whether from you or from others, though we could have made demands as apostles of Christ."
-1 Thessalonians 2:3-6 ESV

Often athletes are seen pointing to the sky after scoring a touchdown or kneeling to pray before a game. Before games in my college and professional career, I often take a knee on the sideline prior to games to pray. However, it was not until recently that I started to take note of the motives behind my public acts of worship. Was I trying to just look like a good Christian or was I doing it to be in communion with the Lord prior to competing?

God does not need performative acts of worship to glorify Himself. He will achieve His aims with or without us pointing to the sky after we score a goal for our team. However, if God grants you an audience, you should use that platform to point others to Him. In the text above, Paul is making the Gospel attractive, but notice he never compromised on its core focus and never tried to sell it in a cheap way. Paul demonstrated that God cares more about our hearts than a few kind actions in public or the perception others have of us.

Pray that the Holy Spirit would reveal your true heart posture towards worshipping Him.

Cade van Raaphorst
Atlas Lacrosse Club / Boston Cannons
2019-Present

November 21

"...And the rain fell, and the floods came, and the winds blew
and beat on that house, but it did not fall, because it has been founded
on the rock. And everyone who hears these words of mine and does
not do them will be like a foolish man who built his house on the sand.
And the rain fell, and the floods came, and the winds blew and beat
against that house, and it fell, and great was the fall of it."
— Matthew 7:24-27 ESV

Being an athlete for 15+ years, it became so easy to build my life and identity around soccer. I became consumed by my performance — whether that was on the field, in the weight room, in the classroom, or even in my relationships. It's who I was, and if I failed, it felt like my world came crumbling down. My house was built on the sand as the Scriptures say. However, our false identity as an athlete is not steady or sure — we lose games, we perform poorly, we get cut from a team, or we don't see the playing time we work so hard for. But God... He is our rock, and a solid foundation that we can build our lives upon. When we realize that our identity is not in what we do, but in who God says we are, we are able to rest securely in our identity in Him. When we face the storms and failures of our lives (which we surely will), they won't break us and we won't fall, because our foundation is built upon the rock — Jesus!

What are you building the foundation of your life upon?

Megan Proudfoot
Stjarnan FC (Iceland Professional Women's Soccer)
2015-2018

November 22

"Not only that, but we rejoice in our sufferings, knowing that suffering produces endurance, and endurance produces character, and character produces hope, and hope does not put us to shame, because God's love has been poured into our hearts through the Holy Spirit who has been given to us." - Romans 3:3-5 ESV

It was my senior year of college and my last championship swim meet. The amount of pressure I had on myself to perform was weighing on me. It was time for my first race. My pre-race routine: warm-up, stretch and say a prayer. Every prayer began with "Please give me the energy…". First race: added time. Second race: added time. Third race: added time. I was angry and confused. This was not how I was supposed to end my swimming career. It took me a long time to see what God had in store for me.

Perseverance is how we grow in faith. Life is filled with trials and tribulations. God wants us to rely on Him through all the obstacles we face in life. As Christians, we have two options in life. We can turn away from God or seek His guidance and know that He is preparing us for something even greater if we persevere. God has not stopped showing that my faithfulness to Him will bring me peace throughout the magnitude of struggles I face. As the verse above states, we are the ones that are full of hope and joy. We have the faith and endurance to overcome the challenges that come our way. We are thankful for God's love that has been shed for us.

I challenge you to take five minutes a day and reflect on the ways God has shown you peace through your challenges.

Kelsey Holmgaard
James Madison University Women's Swimming & Diving
2010-2014

November 23

"Everyone who hears these words of mine and does them will be like a wise man who built his house on rock." - Matthew 7:24

Early morning workouts, late night practices, praise, recognition- as athletes, from a young age, this can become our life and the more we succeed, this can become our identity. But what about when it's over? When we no longer get to spend our days on the field, or court and we are no longer recognized for our abilities as an athlete. Do you know who you are? This is a reality every athlete will one day be forced to face.

After a series of injuries, I had to stop playing the sport to which I had devoted my life. Having to stop playing football shook my world, but God allowed this storm to reveal how my identity was wrongly rooted in something that it was never meant to be built upon. Through His grace, He used this time to show me who He created me to be beyond just the game and allowed me to firmly root my identity in Him.

Thankfully, as humans uniquely created and shaped by our Creator, He invites us to accept his son Jesus as our Savior and our identity becomes firmly rooted in Him. Having our identity in Jesus is the only foundation that will truly stand, and the only thing that is strong enough to uphold us when the storms of life come.

Take some time to reflect on ways you may be allowing your sport, or what you do define who you are. Pray and commit to firmly rooting your identity in Christ, and what He did.

Austin Brown
Robert Morris University Football
2014-2015

329

November 24

"And we know that in all things God works for the good of those who love Him, who have been called according to His purpose."
– Romans 8:28 NIV

We serve a God that walks with us, strengthens us, and sustains us through whatever trials we walk through in this life. He asks us to trust Him and to rejoice in Him always.

I entered my senior season expectant and full of excitement, however, after suffering an injury that would keep me off the field for at least 9 months, those feelings were quickly replaced with feelings of anguish, confusion, and heartbreak. But I knew my God was sovereign, faithful, and loving. I was reminded that *His grace is sufficient for me* and that *His power is perfected in weakness*. My strength was found in Christ and my weakness was a reminder of my need for Him. I rejoiced in the truth *that in **all** things God works for the good of those who love Him.* God uses difficult, painful, and challenging times to build faith, character, and hope.

My unexpected hardship was an opportunity for me to become more rooted in Him and His Word. As a Christian everything you endure has a purpose, be careful not to miss the blessings hidden in the difficulty and remember to give God all the glory. As difficult as it seems, I encourage you to trust in the Lord with all your heart and delight in hardships you face because the *testing of your faith produces perseverance.*

Ask Him to use the challenging times for His purposes and to help you not to overlook the blessings hidden in the difficulty.

Natalie (Robles) Tallent
Virginia Commonwealth University Women's Soccer
2012-2017

330

November 25

"Since, then, you have been raised with Christ, set your hearts on things above, where Christ is, seated at the right hand of God. Set your minds on things above, not on earthly things. For you died, and your life is now hidden with Christ in God."
-Colossians 3:1-3

It is so easy to find your identity in the things you are skilled at. As athletes, we are creatures of habit and consumed by our routines. Weights, skill work, practice, eat, recover, sleep, repeat. Where does Jesus fall into your routine? I've had to ask myself this question so many times throughout my athletic career. I will be going through the motions of the year: preseason, in-season, off-season, and I'll find myself feeling so lonely and I know something is missing.

Your sport can be taken from you at any time, whether it be an injury, coaching situation, or a medical issue. When you are forced to step away from the things you are most comfortable with, life can seem clouded and confusing. Jesus is ready, waiting there to walk with you through the fog to show you that you are more than your sport. If your identity is rooted in athletic performance, and your ability to compete is stripped from you, it will leave you feeling isolated and lost. When you anchor your identity in Christ and you go through trials, you won't have to stand on your own. Jesus desires to walk through life alongside us

If you remain close to The Father, He will remain in you. Take time to find a place in your busy routine for Christ.

Hank Hutcheson
Trevecca Nazarene University / Lipscomb University Basketball
2020-2024

331

November 26

*"And Jesus answered and said to her, "Martha, Martha, you are worried and troubled about **many things**. But **ONE THING** is needed, and Mary has chosen that good part, which will not be taken from her." - Luke 10:41-42 NKJV*

So often, like Martha, I have become distracted with many things. Many times, I would get caught up in the pursuit of success and the need to perform. I would fall into that place Martha was in and I would do and work for God but neglect the relationship He wanted us to have. I had become an expert at performing for God but remained a novice at loving Him. This led me down many frustrating, discouraging, and overwhelming paths pushing me to breaking points of wanting to walk away and quit.

God, in His goodness and grace, would seem to meet me with a "Bradley, Bradley" moment. I would feel the Lord tugging on my heart for me to lay down my efforts and striving in order to simply BE with Him. The Lord would convict me of many things while calling me back to the ONLY THING of loving Him.

Jesus, I ask that you cleanse me from all the "many things" so that I can find the "ONLY thing." Help me to see You rightly and to live my life captivated by You. Holy Spirit, empower me to live everyday with the "***ONE THING***," and that is loving You. I want to live every day of my life deeply in love with You.

I encourage you to slow down and lay down all your activities to simply love Him. I pray that your life would flow from intimacy with Christ.

Bradley Adkins
Texas Tech University Track & U.S. Olympic High Jumper
2012-2016

November 27

"The thief comes only to steal and kill and destroy. I came that they may have life and have it abundantly." -John 10:10

I first read this verse in my mid 20's after years of trying to find that abundant life my own way. I was so moved by this verse, and all of John 10 because it revealed that Jesus wanted me to have an abundant life even more than I did.

I was fortunate enough to be able to pursue my dream of college baseball. I wanted that *full* college experience, so I poured myself into baseball and leaned into things like drunkenness, porn, and sex as I was convinced that those things were part of that full experience. What I found was momentary excitement that was quickly replaced by profound emptiness in my soul. The opposite of *fullness*. I did some Christian "things" like praying and going to FCA events. I had prayed a prayer as a kid asking Jesus into my heart. But the reality for me (and maybe for you too?) was that I was lost. John 10:10 is one of my favorite verses because it teaches that the abundant, full life we all seek, is found in trusting Jesus like sheep trust their shepherd. It's the very reason He came and died on the cross. Jesus *is* abundance. To know him, to receive his forgiveness and grace, and to therefore live your life in willing, joyful submission to him as your Shepherd and your treasure is the way to abundant life! (Eph. 3:14-21).

I challenge you to read John 10:1-21 and consider the analogy of the sheep and the Good Shepherd... Do you trust that Jesus is the way to abundance? Or do you believe you can find "pasture" your own way?

Matt Warren
University of Central Arkansas baseball
2004-2007

November 28

"But the Lord said to him, "Go! For this man is my chosen instrument to carry My name before the Gentiles, kings, and sons of Israel. I will certainly show him how much he must suffer for My name!" So Ananias left and entered the house. Then he placed his hands on him and said, "Brother Saul, the Lord Jesus, who appeared to you on the road you were traveling, has sent me so you may regain your sight and be filled with the Holy Spirit." – Acts 9:15-17

Leave it to God Almighty to assemble a team with a bunch of characters that don't fit the mold of what we picture to be "Christ-like". Saul was known for his persecutions of Christians throughout the region and was feared. Yet, he was chosen to play a role nobody could have dreamed of, becoming the Apostle Paul. The scriptures are filled with these misfits the Lord chose to be on His team to further His message. What's the message? The message is His redemptive grace that has no discrimination. If He can choose an enemy of God's people and transform him for His glory, we should take comfort in knowing His grace extends to any of us who are willing to receive it.

As athletes, we help ourselves out to have a short memory. To forget that last at bat or that interception. We all fail and fall short of the people we should be, whether big or small.

Don't let your past failures define you, let God's grace define you and allow Him to use you today!

Nate Thomas
Texas Christian University Baseball
2001-2004

334

November 29

"The fear of the Lord is the beginning of wisdom, and knowledge of the Holy One is understanding." – Proverbs 9:10

Humility is the key to growth: we cannot learn until we acknowledge that we do not already have all the answers. As believers in Christ, we know where to find the answers. Awe and fear of the Lord are the beginning of wisdom; knowledge of God is the key to understanding. Christians embrace God's authority over our lives. As athletes, we acknowledge the authority of coaches, teachers, teammates, and others whose mission is to help us grow into men and women of character (Rom 13:1). When we are faced with correction or coaching, we should accept it as a form of love. Our pastors, coaches, and others care enough to guide us away from our sins and mistakes. They help us "put off our old self and put on the new" (Ephesians 4:22-24).

As Christians, and athletes, we do not choose a path of complacency. In this, we get to "taste and see that the Lord is good" and the experience the "peace that surpasses all understanding" (Psalms 34:8). But the true adventure of our lives, as Christians and athletes, is to share the light and peace of God with others. The first step on that path is having the strength to accept where we are weak, and the humility to recognize where we must grow.

Find a friend or mentor to "coach" you in where they see you needing to grow in your walk with the Lord. Pray and ask the Lord to give you wisdom in these areas.

Dominic Cruciani
University of Texas Football
2012-2015

November 30

"God created man in His own image, in the image of God He created him; male and female He created them. God blessed them; and God said to them, "Be fruitful and multiply, and fill the earth, and subdue it; and rule over the fish of the sea and over the birds of the sky and over every living thing that moves on the earth."
- Genesis 1:27-29

Summer of 2021, the Supreme Court ruled that athletes can make personal profit for their own image. We now have an ever-growing generation of young athlete-influencers desperately seeking to make purpose out of their lives by using their own skills and image. In college, I earned the right to play on special teams. At the time, I thought my purpose was to accumulate stats, 'likes' on social media, and gain popularity with friends just by my association with a storied program. It wasn't until my senior season, after I medically retired following a knee injury, that God showed me that my purpose far exceeded playing time or popularity on a football team.

In Scripture we see that our general purpose of life is to: a) to Glorify God and b) Enjoy God- Psalm 16:11. God has uniquely created man in the image of God. Apart from all other creations, He chose us to put the beauty of Jesus Christ on display to the world. When we choose to serve others, we reflect the image of God's selflessness. When we choose to stay committed to our coaches and team, we reflect the image of God's faithfulness.

If you want to find your purpose, don't go looking for your purpose. Look for the Purpose Giver.

Chris Terry
University of Texas Football
2011-2014

December 1

"For just as each of us has one body with many members, and these members do not all have the same function, so in Christ we, though many, form one body, and each member belongs to all the others." – Romans 12:4-5 NIV

I want you to take a second to imagine you are in the Roman age and you are a Roman soldier. You are getting to go out for battle. You are training, fighting, and bleeding together as one unit. You prepare to fight like your life depends on it. You do not care about the differences you have with the soldier standing next to you; you only care that soldier has your back.

Now think about your teammates. Do you have their backs? You train with them, you fight with them, you bleed with them. You are preparing to help your team fight until the end of the game.

I played football in college, and we had an old Roman battle cry we would chant together as a team before each game. It didn't matter what teammate was standing next to me, whether I got along with them or not, I was going to go on that field and fight for them.

Think of Jesus and what He did for us. He fought for us, He bled for us, He was beaten and hung on the cross for us. Why? He died on the cross so that everyone, regardless of race, gender, social status, or age, could receive eternal life. Every single person has the opportunity to put their trust in Him.

Be intentional with your teammates, even the ones you might not get along with as much and share God's love with them.

Fletcher McKee
East Mississippi Community College Football
2012-2013

December 2

"You will keep him in perfect peace, whose mind is stayed on You, Because he trusts in You." - Isaiah 26:3 NKJV

In sports there is a lot you can control, but the result is not always in your hands. You may pitch the best game of your life but lose on a bloop single and an error. You may be hot at the plate but have an off game when it matters most, get a bad call from the umpire, or have a season altering injury. You must perform every time out while also relying on others. Meanwhile sports reporters, parents, coaches, and teammates are constantly poking holes in your game.

Teamwork may cause tension and distrust. The lack of control may cause anxiety, obsession, or fear and the outside responses may cause self-doubt and identity issues.

We are shaped in sport and life with how we respond to things. Do we lean on our own strength until we crumble or rely on the One who has infinite strength He desires to give?

When is a time you had Peace in a difficult situation? How can you keep your mind on the giver of Peace?

Brian Miller
Vanderbilt University Baseball
2012-2014

December 3

"Trust in the Lord with all your heart and lean not on your own understanding; in all your ways submit to him, and he will make your paths straight." - Proverbs 3:5-6 NIV

God places growth on the other side of adversity. After my first semester playing baseball in college, I was cut from the roster. It was hard for me to come to terms with my situation as being an athlete has been part of my identity since I was 3 years old. I knew I still wanted a group or a team that I could be a part of on campus. I had a passion for football growing up and decided I would try-out for the football team. I worked out all winter to prepare for the tryouts and ended up earning a spot on the team the following spring.

When God closes one door, another one usually opens. I was devastated after being cut from the baseball team but ended up having the best college athletic experience on the football team I could have asked for. God asks for us to trust Him even when we can't see the other side, because He can, and there's no better path to be on. You'll face adversity, grow, and best of all, you'll become closer with God.

See adversity as an opportunity to grow stronger in your faith. Can you think of a time in your life that God has closed a door for you, only to open up a better opportunity later on?

Jack Sroba
James Madison University Football
2018-2021

December 4

"If I give all I possess to the poor and give over my body to hardship that I may boast, but do not have love, I gain nothing. Love is patient, love is kind. It does not envy, it does not boast, it is not proud. It does not dishonor others, it is not self-seeking, it is not easily angered, it keeps no record of wrongs. Love does not delight in evil but rejoices with the truth. It always protects, always trusts, always hopes, always perseveres. Love never fails."
-1 Corinthians 13:3-8 NIV

God reveals to us through Jesus' Resurrection that His love for us is not competitive. We are loved as we are because Christ died for us all. I have always been hard on myself (as most athletes are) and would respond to adversity with hatred, negative self-talk, and punishment for myself. However, God revealed to me that every time I speak or act with hatred toward myself that I am also speaking and acting that way toward Him.

Loving ourselves can be hard but we are made in His image and the way we treat ourselves and others is the way we are treating our Lord. Track and field is temporary but the love I have for my Father is not. If we use our sport to love others, ourselves and to glorify our Father then we will be successful to Him. God's love never fails, so Lord, teach us to love.

What do you value or prioritize in your life? Are they centered around God or around something else such as success? What if God's love was the foundation of them all?

Landon Kemp
University of South Dakota Track & Field
2017-2023

December 5

"For me, living is Christ and dying is gain."
-Philippians 1:21 HCSB

I have spent a lot of my life living with an earthly mindset. I have been consumed with ways to fill me up and give me purpose. Football, among many other things, has been something that has become an idol in my life at times. How easy it has been for me to dedicate my time and energy and give everything I have for me to be the best I can be on the field. So, why do I play football? Is it really for the Lord, or is it for me? I could say it's for the Lord and His glory, but if you would look at my heart and deep into my desires, why am I really doing it?

In Philippians 1:21, Paul basically tells us the purpose of his life. He says for him to live, is to be Christ to everyone he encounters, and if he dies, great, because he will be with the Lord for eternity. This verse has always struck me deep and made me think, how does he live like this? Paul lives with an eternal mindset, an eternal perspective that everything he does filters through. His greatest desire is to be with Christ, so whether he is living, or if he dies, he wants to be with Christ! This is how I want to strive to live.

When we go through life with an eternal perspective, our priorities shift, and our desires start to align with God's. Take time daily to ask Jesus to align your desires with His. For God wants nothing more than to be in relationship with you, now and forever.

Jake Wieneke
Montreal Alouettes / Saskatchewan Roughriders
2019-Present

December 6

"Whoever sows to please their flesh, from the flesh will reap destruction; whoever sows to please the Spirit, from the Spirit will reap eternal life." - Galatians 6:8 NIV

I am not a farmer, but this passage of Scripture has always spoken to my heart. God's word reminds us that there are two particular fields in which we all farm. And God even gives warning and tells us what happens when we farm into those fields. The first field is the field of flesh. Your flesh is out to get as much territory as it can! It outgrows its borders and seeks control at about any cost. Our flesh is our sinful nature that will cause mass destruction in our lives if not kept in check. The second field is the Spirit. The spot in your heart that is made for God. Farming this field has great reward. When we farm well, God promises us fruit; He also promises us eternal life.

When I think of athletes nowadays, I think of platform. Imagine a world in which the athlete uses their platform for Christ and sows into the field of the Spirit. Think about how much fruit would reap from using your platform well! It can be the little things- how we handle adversity, how we talk about our coaches, how we treat our teammates. God wants to use us as athletes to bring others closer to him. My prayer is that you would sow the right field.

Sowing into the wrong field can reap hard things in our lives, and ultimately ruin our platform for Jesus. Be a game changer and sow into the Spirit and see how the Lord uses you.

Jared Hall
Bethel University Football
2003-2007

December 7

A voice says, "Cry!" And I said, "What shall I cry?" All flesh is grass, and all its beauty is like the flower of the field. The grass withers, the flower fades, when the breath of the Lord blows upon it; surely the people is grass. The grass withers, the flower fades; but the word of our God will stand forever." – Isaiah 40:6-8 NRSVCE

Our society idolizes youth, beauty, fitness. The "cult of the body" is real. But growing old is an inescapable fact of life - those who fight it are fighting a losing battle. Christians should have a different perspective. St. Paul tells us that "Though our outer man is wasting away, our inner man is being renewed every day" (2 Corinthians 4:16). Christian athletes have a unique opportunity to witness to this. Within a culture that prizes physical fitness and athletic excellence, we must emphasize moral fitness and spiritual excellence. We must show by our lives that the "perishable wreaths" that we strive for as athletes pale in comparison to the imperishable wreath of eternal life that we ultimately seek.

It is also necessary for us to come to terms with our mortality - with feebleness and aging. The strength and vigor of youth is not forever. "All flesh is grass," as Isaiah says, and we shall all wither and fade. It is God's word and God's promises that stand forever, and it is to this that we should cling.

Ask yourself: Do I work with God on sculpting my soul as much as I work on sculpting my body? If not, why not?

Jon Wisnieski
University of Iowa Football
2013-2017

December 8

"Jesus said to the man, "Stretch out your hand." And he stretched it out, and his hand was restored as whole as the other one was." -Mark 3:5 NKJV

I think God is constantly asking us to stretch out our hands to Him, to relinquish the false sense of control we think we have over our lives. He showed me this as a competitive runner in high school and college. In such an individual-focused sport, I quickly became consumed with pushing my body, my personal goals, and anything I could do to become the best on the team. I put restrictions and forced control on all aspects of my life, from counting every calorie to doing additional runs and workouts outside of practice. This eventually led to an eating disorder and breaking point, where my body was withering away and was told by a dietician that I had to restrict my running until I gained a certain amount of weight. I was devastated, but realized God was pointing me to something bigger…Himself. Turns out, I was actually out of control when I thought I was in control.

God never wavered and He continues to unfurl my hands on this false sense of control, even past my years of competitive running. He wants to ungrasp our fingers one by one, take our hand and walk alongside us. When we try to run the show, we distance ourselves, when really God just wants to draw near to us, His Beloved. Praise God He is in control instead of us.

Where might God be asking you to 'stretch out your hand' to open up space for Him in your daily life?

Elle Brewer Ternes
College of Charleston Cross-Country / Track & Field
2010-2014

344

December 9

"In the same way, let your light shine before others, that they may see your good deeds and glorify your father in heaven."
– *Matthew 5:16 NIV*

Are you "On Fire" for God? Every morning I have a burning desire to be my best for God. I strive to use my talents and strengths to honor Him in all aspects of my life. I encourage you to get "On Fire" for God and shine your unique light for Him each day.

F. First

Do you put God first in your life? Do you make time for Him each day? Is He a priority in your life? Every morning I wake up and spend my first 30-45 minutes reading my devotion and praying. Make Him First! Be Second!

I. Inspire

We are all called to be role models in some way. We may the only Bible someone will ever read. What are you doing to inspire and make a difference on your team?

R. Relentless

Be relentless in spreading His word. Be relentless in showing others that what you have with God is far better than what they have without Him. Be a difference maker!

E. Enthusiasm

Enthusiasm catches people attention. Be so enthusiastic that others may see something different in you. Be uncommon!

Are you "On Fire" for God? SHINE YOUR LIGHT!

Allison Clark
Tennessee Tech Women's Basketball
1998-2002

345

December 10

"For God alone, O my soul. Wait in silence." - Psalm 62:5

In a silent world, how can one hear the voice of God? I was born profoundly Deaf. My language is visual and signed, TV and movies are subtitled, phone calls don't happen for me and drive-thrus are a nightmare.

To play college football, I relied on hand signals to know the play, I asked teammates to take out their mouthpiece to read lips and was dependent on body language and gestures. All was done in silence.

To overcome, I relied on the voice of God. To hear His voice meant to be attentive to the encouraging, peaceful, and patient inner voice inside me and to notice the selfish, self-reliant, anxious voice that was not from God. To find Him, I entered into my silence. Instead of being overwhelmed by not hearing a whistle, I prayed for patience. Instead of being anxious by not hearing the QB say "hike", I prayed for focus. In the silence of my sport, I found God and He found me.

Our lives as athletes are filled with so much busyness and distraction that it can be difficult to find which voice to listen to, if any at all. To find God's voice, find the time and space for silence. Learn to listen to God and you may find He is waiting to share a conversation with you and wants to be with you. Silence is God's first language. In the silence of your heart, God speaks.

Are you listening? Who are you listening to?

Todd Honas
University of Nebraska Football
2016-2020

December 11

"Only let each person lead the life that the Lord has assigned to him, and to which God has called him… This is my rule in all the churches." - 1 Corinthians 7:17, 24

Have you ever wondered what God's plan for you is or what you should be working towards? Have you ever been frustrated working towards a goal for a long time, yet nothing seems to happen? Maybe you're struggling to find motivation? Or maybe you have already accomplished more than you thought possible and don't know what to do with your success? If you're anything like me you've found yourself in one of these places.

Now what? Well, chances are you've heard a coach tell you to focus on the process, not the results, and success will come. This is exactly what the passage in 1 Corinthians is talking about. Every day, when you wake up you, have an assignment for that day. We may not know what God's plan for us is next week, month, or year, but we know what to do for today. We know what kind of teammate we're called to be, that we're to respect our coaches, give everything we have as if done unto the Lord, and, most importantly, repent of our sins and walk in dependence on Jesus in all things. God cares so much more that you *know* Him, rather than that you know His plan for your life. Resting in His sovereignty every day is the only place peace is found.

What is your assignment today? Start by thanking God for today's gifts, and then asking Him to help you live the life assigned for today and trust Him with the rest.

Elliott Farris
Texas A&M University Track & Field
2013-2017

347

December 12

"For I know the plans I have for you," declares the Lord, "plans to prosper you and not to harm you, plans to give you hope and a future." - Jeremiah 29:11 NIV

There's going to come a time where everything we try to do by our own strength won't be enough. My freshman year of college had been the most mentally difficult part of my life. I was eight hours away from where I grew up, away from family and friends, in a long-distance relationship, and experiencing the most failure I've ever had in baseball. A combination of that, the high expectations of coaches, and the navigation of being a new guy on a new team, sent my identity and who I thought I was into absolute chaos. My identity had been fragile, and I questioned how I could be blessed with so much in life, but still be at the lowest point I'd ever been at. As a result, I isolated myself, but through this isolation I began to realize that my circumstances and the outlook I had turned me into something I was not.

Being present in your circumstance is essential to remaining true to who God created us to be. True peace comes from trusting that God has nothing but His best intentions for our life. We can then rejoice in knowing that we're a work in progress; using our struggles and hardships, molding us into who He created us to be.

True peace comes from trusting that God has nothing but His best intentions for our life.

Tyler Malone
San Diego Padres
2016-2023

December 13

"As water reflects the face, so one's life reflects the heart."
– Proverbs 27:19 ESV

As athletes, what we do, or chose not to do, impacts our performance. What we choose to eat; the workouts we choose to do; who we choose to spend time with. Our choices influence our athletic performances. Like water can reflect the physical features of our faces, our performances are often reflective of the choices we've made.

Our souls can be thought of similarly—that they are fed by our daily choices. These choices are either growing a soul that produces fruits of the Spirit—love, joy, peace, patience, kindness, goodness, faithfulness, gentleness, and self-control—or a soul that is becoming *of* the world (instead of *in* the world). Our daily actions—how we live our lives—reflect the desires and posture of our hearts.

What is your life reflecting? What are you known for? Do others see the fruits of the Spirit in how you live your life?

Phillip Laux
University of Iowa Men's Wrestling
2013-2018

349

December 14

"The heart of man plans his way, but the Lord establishes his steps." – Proverbs 16:9 ESV

I spent 22 years of my life playing baseball. From 4 to 26 years old. Growing up I loved the game and always played it hard. I was fortunate that it took me many places. My life goal was to make it to the major leagues. I worked my way through high school ball, college ball, and then had the opportunity to play professionally. Inching closer and closer to a childhood dream.

It was in my first season as a professional where my body began to take on injuries. Some were big enough to have to go through surgery; twice. I began to have doubts on my future as a player. What I had always loved seemed like it could be gone tomorrow. I found the Lord my 3rd year in pro ball, in the midst of all this pain. As I learned the character of God and what purpose He has called us to live by, I realized that my childhood dream may not be what the Sovereign Lord has in store for me. My hope of playing in the Big Leagues was starting to fade. However, my trust in the Lord began to grow. Doing what you love is a great way to live out the Lord's will and to use your platform for His name. In some cases, He may take us from something that we love, but I thank God for the change in my plans. He has led me to seek out what is most important in this world. Bringing Glory to Him and living out His will that He has for me.

If what you loved was stripped from you today how would that change your view on God?

Brock Hartson
Cleveland Indians
2015-2020

December 15

"Therefore, since we are surrounded by so great a cloud of witnesses, let us also lay aside every weight, and sin which clings so closely, and let us run with endurance the race that is set before us, looking to Jesus, the founder and perfecter of our faith..."
- Hebrews 12:1-2 ESV

As Christians, we all have our own races that we must run and endure. We are called to 'lay aside every weight and sin which clings so closely' to us. This weight is a burden or hindrance that is slowing us down from running towards Jesus. Despite the sin of this world, we are called exiles and strangers because we are to walk with authority, fixing our eyes on the everlasting.

From an athletes' perspective, one might visualize being the final leg of your team's 4x400 meter relay. You lean into your last 100 meters and begin to see the finish line. The crowd begins to stand to their feet, screaming and cheering you on to finish the race that you started. The pain throughout your body is agonizing, maybe even numbing, but you endure.

This endurance that we are challenged to run with is not in our own strength, but in the 'great crowd of witnesses' that have run before us. It is in our Lord and Savior enduring the cross so that we may live abundantly with Him. Let us fix our eyes on Jesus and run towards Him.

What weight do you need to lay aside in your life that is slowing you down from running towards Jesus? What sin is easily distracting you from seeing this finish line?

Bryce Torneden
Pittsburgh Maulers
2022-Present

351

December 16

"I am the vine: you are the branches. If you remain in me and me in you. You will bear much fruit: apart from me you can do nothing." - John 15:5 NIV

In the summer of senior year, I had the privilege of working with refugee families in the city of Nashville. During that summer I was reading John 15:5 and for some reason the word "remain" could not get out my head. I was being reminded to remain in all I do, but most importantly remain in His love. With these thoughts being engraved into my heart over the summer and into the beginning of fall, I had no greater feeling than remaining in the Lord while playing the sport I love, softball. My goal for the year was to remain in each situation and continue to bear the fruits of the Spirit no matter what the game brought that day. Spending alone time with Jesus daily gave me the self-instinct to turn to Him automatically in every situation no matter what. At the end of day when the sport is over, you will have forever memories but experiencing those memories while having the heart and service of Jesus, there is no greater thing.

When times are good, it's easy to be joyful, but when the days get hard, do you remain in Jesus and His faithfulness? Take some time and silence the noise of your life and spend time with your precious Creator, Jesus Christ.

Jessie Brown
Lipscomb University Women's Softball
2019-2022

December 17

"And let us consider how we may spur one another on toward love and good deeds, not giving up meeting together, as some are in the habit of doing, but encouraging one another—and all the more as you see the Day approaching." – Hebrews 10:24-25 NIV

No athlete enjoys a loss, but there is a lesson to be learned in losing. When my soccer career ended in a defeat, the heartbreak was not easy for me to get over. I felt angry, lost, and resentful towards God for ending my career in this way. Why wasn't it on a high? Why couldn't my last game be a win? Then, God revealed to me that playing was not about winning the most games or about being better than everyone. It was about togetherness and sharing His heart in community with those who are different from me.

When we play and train together, we are building community. When we travel and eat together, we are building community. Christ's presence in fellowship gives us the opportunity to discover His grace and identify the talents He gives us while encouraging others to do the same. God wants us to build each other up, to shape a team of believers to do good because He didn't design us to live the gift of life alone. We are made to be together.

God is present in a win or a loss. Make it a habit to encourage and love those with whom you share your time.

Becky Huddleston
Waubonsee Community College /
Trevecca Nazarene University Women's Soccer
2010-2014

353

December 18

"Do nothing out of selfish ambition of vain conceit. Rather, in humility values others above yourselves, not looking to your own interests but each of you to the interests of the others."
– Philippians 2: 3-4 NIV

As every athlete transitions into the next level of their sport, there is an anticipation of the physical, emotional, and spiritual challenges that are to come. Upon entering college, I knew that if I desired to play consistently, I would have to compete for my position. What I did not expect was that my competition for this starting spot would be against a teammate who became one of my best friends and sister in Christ. Through this season, the Lord challenged me to surrender my own selfish desire and vanity of being on the court and put my focus into playing my best, giving all the glory to Him.

There were countless times in which I envied her starting position she earned. My prideful flesh lacked dignity which led to me wishing that she would mess up so that I could have my "shining moment of success" to see external validation I so desperately desired. Comparison only opened the door to steal the joy from what God had for me in that moment, trusting that the present assignment God had for me in on the bench was equally purposeful. Celebration is greater than comparison. The Lord has opened my heart into humility, honoring my teammates' accomplishments in rejoicing and encouraging them as God is honored in what they do.

What is one tangible way you can intentionally elevate a teammate today and speak God's truth into their purpose?

Hannah Eskes
Grand Canyon University Women's Volleyball
2019-2023

354

December 19

"She had a sister called Mary, who sat at the Lord's feet listening to what he said. But Martha was distracted by all the preparations that had to be made. She came to him and asked, "Lord, don't you care that my sister has left me to do the work by myself? Tell her to help me!" "Martha, Martha," the Lord answered, "you are worried and upset about many things, but only one thing is needed. Mary has chosen what is better, and it will not be taken away from her." - Luke 10:39-42 NIV

Athletes are busy. My schedule was slammed with lifts, traveling, practices, and competitions. The go-go-go pace of life only seemed to accelerate. Moments of rest seemed few and far between. How do we find space to sit at the feet of Jesus slow down if the pace of life does not seem to be letting up any time soon?

Two challenges: (1) It is okay to slow down. Rest is important. Rest is good. Jesus wants us to physically and literally slow down, to sit at His feet and enjoy His presence. (2) We have the invitation to cultivate a heart posture of rest AS we are amid the busyness of athletics. Martha often gets a bad rap in this story. I think that Jesus might have been more concerned with her heart posture rather than the fact that she was busy. Work is good. Training is good. As we work and as we train, we are invited to adopt a heart posture that resembles sitting at the feet of Jesus in the midst of the busy.

First, slow down. Just be. Then, allow the invitation to sit at His feet to direct the posture of your heart amid the busyness today.

Kristen Seibert
Wofford College / Messiah University Volleyball
2017-2021

December 20

"Therefore, as you received Christ Jesus the Lord, so walk in him, rooted and built up in him and established in the faith, just as you were taught, abounding in thanksgiving."
- Colossians 2:6-7 ESV

As athletes, there are many things we know how to do within our sport because we have been taught and practiced them for so long. When things may or may not be going the way we planned or thought, we fall back on our teaching. As we are taught and put things into practice, we have a newfound confidence in our play because we have done it countless times. Not only in our sport, but in life, there will be situations that arise where we fall back on what we've been taught.

Paul's call to the church of Colossae was to remember their original teachings when they first became Christians. He's calling them to remember their original "training" so that they may walk in obedience to Christ (1:10). We 'walk in obedience' by living in a Godly manner, continuing to grow spiritually, and through Christian understanding. We are continually "practicing" these habits daily as we go throughout our lives. As believers, if we have accepted Jesus as our Lord and Savior and given him dominion over our lives, walking with Him and being rooted in a firm foundation is key. Our experience of first coming to Christ ought to mirror how we walk in Him all the days of our lives.

We all have areas where we can continue to grow. Ask the Lord to reveal to you what areas can you grow spiritually in your own walk.

Hayden Wall
Abilene Christian University Football
2013-2016

December 21

"Truly I tell you, anyone who will not receive the kingdom of God like a little child will never enter it." -Luke 18:17 NIV

Teaching children the game of golf requires simplifying the swing. Without a coach, they struggle to aim in the correct direction, hold the club properly, and hit the ball. This is why I, as an instructor, help set their feet and model how to swing. Once children hit the ball, they joyfully jump up and down. When they miss, I don't scold them or allow them to feel ashamed; rather, I encourage another attempt, reassuring that I am there to help. These junior golfers have taught me a lot about both simplifying the swing when I am experiencing struggles on the course and simplifying faith in everyday life.

As God's children, we are fully dependent on Him for every need. Trying to do things in our own strength and human knowledge will only get us so far. We must approach Him in childlike faith, trusting that He will guide us in every situation we face on and off the playing field. The greatest Teacher, Jesus, is our perfect example for living a godly life. He calls us to humbly submit to God's authority, obey His grace-filled commands, and find joy in the simplest of moments with which He has gifted us. And when we feel as if we have failed at these tasks, our attention must be turned back to God, who has never stopped singing over us in love and holding us in the palm of His hand.

What are ways you can uncomplicate faith and instead live it out in a childlike manner?

Danica Badura
University of South Dakota Women's Golf
2020-2024

December 22

"That is, in Christ God was reconciling the world to himself,
not counting their trespasses against them, and entrusting to us the
message of reconciliation. Therefore, we are ambassadors for Christ,
God making his appeal through us. We implore you on behalf of
Christ, be reconciled to God." - 2 Corinthians 5:19-20

In sports, it can be easy to develop tunnel vision – to focus on only your personal goals. I put so much of my worth into how many goals I had or where I ranked on the depth chart. Yes, the drive to win and succeed is crucial to becoming a successful athlete, but it is not everything.

As Christian athletes our call is higher than anything we could imagine. Yes, our call is to work at our sport with all our heart. But by wearing the name of Christ, it is even more important to be His ambassador. As an ambassador, knowing this is not our home, our charge is to glorify the Father through our lives and make the name of Christ known. Looking back at my collegiate lacrosse career, it was a unique opportunity. We are given this rare mission field for a limited time. Teammates, coaches, and trainers that we GET to show the love of Christ to each day. Whether you see it or not, every one of your teammates is searching. Today, you can allow God to work within and through you. Though we may not see the fruit of our work, every seed we plant in the life of another has value.

Today I challenge you to think beyond your own desires and pray for the teammates God has put in your life. Ask God to show you how He can be glorified today.

Julia Golden
Christopher Newport University Women's Lacrosse
2015-2019

358

December 23

"Because God wanted to make the unchanging nature of his purpose very clear to the heirs of what was promised, he confirmed it with an oath. God did this so that, by two unchangeable things in which it is impossible for God to lie, we who have fled to take hold of the hope set before us may be greatly encouraged. We have this hope as an anchor for the soul, firm and secure."
-Hebrews 6:17-19 NIV

What is the most important thing in your life? What would bring you great distress if you lost connection to it? Take 60 seconds to think about what you would lay on the line to protect it. Then consider the distance Jesus went for us: from heaven to earth, from life to death, from the presence of his Holy Father to taking on the darkness of the entirety of sin. In His harrowing journey from His ministry to His death and resurrection, Jesus confirms the promises of God to us to be unchanging, unshakable, and undeniable. If we think we would go so far to save that which we hold most dear, how much greater should our hope be in Christ since He has *already* liberated us! This is the intimate and infinite love that God has for us, of which we only know shades and glimmers and echoes. And this was not something that we deserved, nor is it something we can repay – it is because of grace and grace alone that we are saved by Jesus' blood.

Even through the storms that rage above our heads or the rapidly shifting currents around us in life and our sports, let's live with a hope that overflows because we know that God's love for us, as proven by the work of Jesus, is steadfast.

Alex Dunlap
Washington Nationals
2017-2021

December 24

"For it is by grace you have been saved, through faith – and this is not from yourselves, it is a gift of God—not by works, so that no one can boast" -Ephesians 2:8-9 ESV

When I first went to college, my mindset was that if I outworked everyone, there would be no excuse not to find success. I ran harder and practiced longer only to be physically and spiritually depleted. My accomplishments were easily quantified by wins, losses and broken records. In a vicious cycle of perfectionism, I was weary, finding significance only in temporary victories. As I desperately drew closer to Jesus, He unveiled truth that left me shattered. My efforts became meaningless when I relinquished control to Him. I realized that as God pursued me, I felt empty in the pursuits that once defined my identity. Little did I know that the rest my spirit longed for was found in my surrender. Personal success only brought empty promises, but surrender brought hope and cultivated significance.

In surrendering to Christ, significance is redefined. A significant life is nurtured by rejecting the temporal culture and living intentionally to glorify God. God helps us see beyond our narrow vision, allowing us to embrace significance as more valuable than success. We can't work for our salvation, but we can work from it. We are made to know and serve Him. He created us with unique abilities and He invites us to glorify Him through our athletic talents.

Where is your significance? Who are you honoring through your talents? Step into your uniqueness and invite God to transform the way you think.

Shelby Craft
Lipscomb University Women's Soccer
2021-2023

360

December 25

"I am not saying this because I am in need, for I have learned to be content whatever the circumstances." - Philippians 4:11 NIV

As an athlete I am ambitious. I saw success in sports didn't magically occur, I needed to work to attain my goals. So, I worked hard. I attained many goals, yet I fell short of many also. When I won, I felt complete and everything in life made sense. When I lost, I felt broken, empty, confused. Sports and life accompany us with many mountain-top moments as well as valley lows.

It wasn't until the Lord spoke to me on the concept of "contentment in Christ" that results in sports no longer having a deep, drastic toll on my life. I learned Christ is enough! Christ is the all-powerful God, and He loves me. Christ being all-powerful means He's in control of everything going on in my life. Knowing Christ loves me helps me know and believe that everything in my life is working together for my good. Now if I win, my mindset is thank you and praise God. And this one sounds odd, but when I lose it's also thank you and praise God. Why? Because I know that God can use that loss for my good. You never lose if you grow from it. So what lessons, character development, protection, and more have come from sports/life's losses that we didn't even see? I find my life contentment in Christ now, and it has brought more freedom than I could've imagined.

Sit in the Bible. Find how powerful God is and how much He loves us. Then pray for this contentment in Christ.

Trey Culver
Texas Tech University Track & Field
2014-2018

December 26

"Therefore, everyone who hears these words of mine and puts them into practice is like a wise man who built his house on the rock. The rain came down, the streams rose, and the winds blew and beat against that house; yet it did not fall, because it had its foundation on the rock. But everyone who hears these words of mine and does not put them into practice is like a foolish man who built his house on sand. The rain came down, the streams rose, and the winds blew and beat against that house, and it fell with a great crash."
-Matthew 7:24-27

Jesus provides a clear and comprehensive vision for how a follower of Jesus is to live in the Sermon on the Mount (Matthew 5-7). His final instruction is simple, HEAR and DO. In other words, LISTEN. In High School, I was a Shot Put and Discus thrower which is what I was recruited to compete in at UC Irvine. By the time I arrived I was asked to compete in the Hammer Throw (look it up), a sport I had never done before because it is not allowed in most high schools. I learned pretty quickly that the only way I would become the kind of athlete that my coach envisioned me to be was to LISTEN to his words and put them into practice. To truly listen to my coach required me to pay attention to his instruction, trust his character and plan for me, and obey him.

Jesus is inviting us to pay attention to His words, to trust His goodness and grace, and to do what He says to become the kind of people He made us to be.

Trevor W. Lawrence
University of California Irvine Track & Field
2011-2013

December 27

"Then he said to me, "This is the word of the Lord to
Zerubbabel: Not by might, nor by power, but by my Spirit, says the
Lord of hosts." – Zechariah 4:6

Spring ball of 2013 was a tough time. I was a freshman walk-on running back and I had fumbled a handoff a few practices prior to the spring game. I was told I would never get a carry in practice again if it happened another time. In the spring game I was given a second chance and managed to work my way into the endzone for a touchdown. As an athlete we spend countless hours training, practicing, and preparing our bodies to perform better. Hard work on the field can correct mistakes, improve technique, and make us more competitive. I always welcomed challenging responsibilities because I knew I could muster up the strength to push through. Over time, the rigorous practice schedule, challenging coursework, and concerns of what direction my life would take after college produced anxious thoughts I couldn't muscle through. I needed my ultimate source of peace. It's easy to trust in yourself and your own strength when things are going well but life's trials prove time and time again that we cannot do this on our own.

In Christ, we are offered a peace that transcends understanding; we have restoration of the joy of our salvation, and we are offered forgiveness of sins that makes us whiter than snow.

When Christ is not our ultimate source of peace, anxiety can rule over us. Ask God to search your heart and show you where you are trusting in yourself and need to give Him control.

Gastón Davis
University of Texas Football
2012-2016

363

December 28

"We know that in everything God works for the good of those who love him. These are the people God chose because that was his plan." - Romans 8:28 ERV

The season of waiting. A season that is not usually talked about yet is often experienced by every athlete at some point in their career. This was very well the case for me during my freshman year of college; where I endured a season of waiting when it came to playing time, as many college freshmen do. However, through this new season, I came to the realization that even in the waiting, He is working. The Lord provided me with a huge shift in my perspective of the situation and the overall idea of "waiting". Despite what felt like a never-ending cycle of putting in extra work with no opportunity to display it, the Lord emphasized to me that there was not only purpose and preparation behind the waiting, but also an understanding that He is in control and has a plan at the end of this season.

As believers, we are bound to encounter difficulty and even a "season of waiting" as we seek to live faithfully for Christ. But when we choose to surrender to the waiting, when we strive to believe this moment is part of a larger story and when we embrace the ache of the longing, the wait is never wasted.

God invites us to trust His goodness today and His faithfulness tomorrow. Take some time to fully surrender and accept the invitation to the season of waiting the Lord may have you in.

Landry Williams
University of Missouri, Kansas City
Oklahoma State University Women's Basketball
2021-2025

December 29

"If anyone would come after me, let him deny himself, and take up his cross daily." - Luke 9:23

Much of humanity chases pleasures of the world, whether that's food, sex, material goods, and worldly achievements. Being a Christian does not mean that we are promised a good and pleasurable life. Being a Christian means that we must be willing to suffer, willing to accept God's will, and willing to deny our own will and passions. Many of the ancient Christians and saints have lived a very tough and scrupulous life. Many of the greatest Christians have willingly lived a life of poverty and pain; however, they lived in immense joy and peace. Neither poverty nor misfortunes can keep a rightly ordered person from the ultimate goal: the salvation of soul, eternal life. Your salvation is solely dependent on your interior life and your spiritual love for our Lord. No matter what life brings, it is important to keep first what matters most, eternal life of your soul.

If you call yourself a Christian, make sure you constantly strive to live up to that. God may not use dirty tools to shine his light, make sure your tool is clean!

Blake Trahan
Cincinnati Reds
2015-2020

365

December 30

"Delight yourself in the Lord and He will give you the desires of your heart. Commit your way to the Lord; trust in Him, and He will act." - Psalm 34:7-8

As athletes we face the pressures to perform, succeed, and meet the expectations of others as well as our own. Our entire lives revolve around sports and achieving athletic success, though it will never give us ultimate satisfaction. This was true of me as well before I found true delight and satisfaction in Christ. My identity is in Christ and no longer just in my sport. Since coming to Christ, my goal and perspective on who I am and who I am competing for has changed, allowing me to find peace and true joy in playing for something greater than myself. As Christian athletes, we commit our sports to the Lord and trust Him in failure and success. In this, God transforms the desires of our heart from success and notoriety to knowing Him and making Him known on our respective teams. The gospel is a privilege that God not only wants to give to us but to work through us in our sport. The opportunity to play sports is a unique gift of God that we are to steward and should not be taken lightly. This unique platform as athletes makes it important to not only be hearers of the word, but doers also. As we delight ourselves in the Lord, God promises to act not only in our lives, but also the lives of those around us.

Lord, thank you for the opportunity to serve you as an athlete. I pray that you'd help me to truly delight myself in You and that my words and actions would lead to those around me having a personal relationship with You. Amen.

Anderson Kopp
University of Missouri Kansas City Men's Basketball
2019-Present

December 31

*³ And when the people came to the camp, the elders of Israel
said, "Why has the Lord defeated us today before the Philistines? Let
us bring the ark of the covenant of the Lord here from Shiloh, that
it may come among us and save us from the power of our enemies."*
- 1 Samuel 4:3

The Israelites thought they had the ultimate omnipotent tool
with the ark on their side. A "genie in a bottle" which granted them
the ability to summon the power of the Lord whenever needed.
Despite their outward displays of confidence, their spiritual devotion
was lacking, and their hearts were far from God. The ark was captured
and the Israelites were defeated and put in bondage.

God may not always answer our prayers the way we want but
our call is to trust Him and seek Him with all our heart. There have
been times in my basketball career where I have tried to make God
more of an accomplice than a King. I have wanted a trophy to parade
around and do my bidding but God is not a trophy. God has a purpose
and plan for my life and my call as a Christian is to simply follow
Him and trust Him.

Thankfully, God does not answer our every whim. Above all,
He wants our heart. He wants us to trust Him and to seek Him through
the ups and downs of life. He is a loving Father and will surely give us
what we need but ultimately, we have Jesus. We can rest in knowing
that trusting in Christ gives us eternal life and a deep abiding peace.

**Let us not be those who honor God with our lips but have hearts
that are far from Him. Take time today to offer Him your heart
through prayer and repentance.**

Casey Shaw
University of Toledo Men's Basketball
1994-1998

367

Acknowledgements

This project could not have been completed without the prayer and support of a countless number of family and friends. First, I would like to thank my beautiful wife, Molly, for never ceasing to pray for the completion of this project. Thank you for continually encouraging me to keep pressing on through every roadblock, and for reminding me that the Lord will provide for the book and lead me through every step of this process. Thank you to my parents, Mark, and Ro, for your constant support of this project. Every time I talked with you both about this project, I left feeling more encouraged. Thank you to my brothers and sisters, Amy, Daniel, Matthew, and Marygrace, for your help in recruiting an incredible group of athletes for this book. I could not have done this without you. Thank you to my sister-in-law, Emarie, for taking on the near impossible task of having to edit a book written by 365 athletes. Lord knows the time and attention to detail it took to correct all of our grammar errors. You might have had the toughest job of all! Thank you to several of my mentors and friends, Steve Cherrico, Bobby Austin, Vince Walsh, and Jared White, for your constant prayers, guidance, and encouragement through this process. A special thank you to Bryce Wheeler for coming in at the last minute and bringing this book cover to life. To the other 364 athletes who partook in this journey alongside me in both writing, promotion, and prayer, I can never say thank you enough. I have loved getting to know and form friendships with each one of you. I pray this journey has been as much of a blessing to you as it has been to me.

Finally, thank you, Lord, for your faithfulness and guidance throughout this entire process. I pray this book draws athletes from all over the world nearer to you. Thank you for the work you have done in each of our lives. May the words of this book bring glory and honor to Your Name.

Made in the USA
Las Vegas, NV
23 December 2023

83473021R00203